实用外贸英语

主　编　马　俊　郑汉金

副主编　杨云勺　周艳丽

清华大学出版社
北京

内 容 简 介

本书以"好用、务实、有特色"为宗旨,在遵循外贸业务准确清晰、英语地道纯正原则的基础上,力求不仅灌输知识,还可提升能力。将国际贸易中最广泛、频繁使用的语言英语与国际贸易业务充分地融合,让学习者能实实在在地运用英语和外贸业务技巧解决些问题,使外贸谈判顺利、经营顺畅。全书分 11 个单元,内容涉及外贸业务流程的各环节,包括建立业务联系、询盘和答复、报价、还盘、接受、订货、签约、支付、备货、包装、检验、装运、保险、异议、索赔、仲裁等。

本书既可作为大专院校外经贸专业的外贸英语教材使用,也可供外经贸从业者和广大英语爱好者自学使用。

图书在版编目(CIP)数据

实用外贸英语/马俊等主编. --北京:清华大学出版社,2015(2025.1重印)
(高等学校应用型特色规划教材 经管系列)
ISBN 978-7-302-41462-9

Ⅰ.①实… Ⅱ.①马… Ⅲ.①对外贸易—英语—高等学校—教材 Ⅳ.①H31

中国版本图书馆 CIP 数据核字(2015)第 209394 号

责任编辑:温 洁
版式设计:杨玉兰
责任校对:周剑云
责任印制:杨 艳
出版发行:清华大学出版社
    网　　址:https://www.tup.com.cn,https://www.wqxuetang.com
    地　　址:北京清华大学学研大厦 A 座　　邮　　编:100084
    社 总 机:010–83470000　　邮　　购:010-62786544
    投稿与读者服务:010-62776969,c-service@tup.tsinghua.edu.cn
    质量反馈:010-62772015,zhiliang@tup.tsinghua.edu.cn
    课件下载:https://www.tup.com.cn,010-62791865
印 装 者:三河市铭诚印务有限公司
经　　销:全国新华书店
开　　本:185mm×230mm　　印　张:19.25　　字　数:420 千字
版　　次:2015 年 9 月第 1 版　　印　次:2025 年 1 月第 10 次印刷
定　　价:49.00 元

产品编号:064389-03

出版说明

应用型人才是指能够将专业知识和技能应用于所从事的专业岗位的一种专门人才。应用型人才的本质特征是具有专业基本知识和基本技能，即具有明确的职业性、实用性、实践性和高层次性。应用型人才的培养，是"十二五"时期教育部关于进一步深化本科教学改革，全面提高教学质量的目标之一，也是协调高等教育规模速度与市场人才需求关系的重要途径。

教育部要求"十二五"期间有相当数量的高校致力于培养应用型人才，以满足市场对应用型人才的巨大需求。为了培养高素质应用型人才，必须建立完善的教学计划和高水平的课程体系。在教育部有关精神的指导下，我们组织全国高校的专家教授，努力探求更为合理有效的应用型人才培养方案，并结合我国当前的实际情况，编写了这套《高等学校应用型特色规划教材　经管系列》丛书。

为使教材的编写真正切合应用型人才的培养目标，我社编辑在全国范围内走访了大量高等学校，拜访了众多院校主管教学的领导以及教学一线的系主任和教师，掌握了各地区各学校所设专业的培养目标和办学特色，推进了优质教育资源进课堂，并广泛、深入地与用人单位进行交流，明确了用人单位的真正需求。这些工作为本套丛书的准确定位、合理选材、突出特色奠定了坚实的基础，同时逐步形成了反映时代特点、与时俱进的教材体系。

✧ 教材定位

➤ 以就业为导向。在应用型人才培养过程中，充分考虑市场需求，因此本套丛书充分体现"就业导向"的基本思路。

➤ 符合本学科的课程设置要求。以高等教育的培养目标为依据，注重教材的科学性、实用性和通用性，融入实践教学环节。

➤ 定位明确。准确定位教材在人才培养过程中的地位和作用，紧密结合学科专业发展和教育教学改革，正确处理教材的读者层次关系，面向就业，突出应用。

➤ 合理选材、编排得当。妥善处理传统内容与现代内容的关系，大力补充新知识、新技术、新工艺和新成果。根据本学科的教学基本要求和教学大纲的要求，制定编写大纲(编写原则、编写特色、编写内容、编写体例等)，突出重点、难点。

➤ 建设"立体化"的精品教材体系。提倡教材与电子教案、学习指导、习题解答、课程设计、毕业设计等辅助教学资料配套出版。

✧ 丛书特色

➢ 围绕应用讲理论，突出实践教学环节及特点，包含丰富的案例，并对案例作详细解析，强调实用性和可操作性。

➢ 涉及最新的理论成果和实务案例，充分反映岗位要求，真正体现以就业为导向的培养目标。

➢ 国际化与中国特色相结合，符合高等教育日趋国际化的发展趋势，部分教材采用双语形式。

➢ 在结构的布局、内容重点的选取、案例习题的设计等方面符合教改目标和教学大纲的要求，把教师的备课、授课、辅导答疑等教学环节有机地结合起来。

✧ 读者定位

本系列教材主要面向普通高等院校和高等职业技术院校，以满足培养应用型人才的高等院校的教学需要。

✧ 关于作者

丛书编委特聘请执教多年且有较高学术造诣和实践经验的教授参与各册教材的编写，其中有相当一部分的教材主要执笔者是各专业精品课程的负责人，本丛书凝聚了他们多年的教学经验和心血。

✧ 互动交流

本丛书的编写及出版过程，贯穿了清华大学出版社一贯严谨、务实、科学的作风。伴随我国教育教学改革的不断深入，要编写出满足新形势下教学需求的教材，还需要我们不断地努力、探索和实践。我们真诚希望使用本丛书的教师、学生和其他读者提出宝贵的意见和建议，使之更臻成熟。

清华大学出版社

前　言

　　考虑到市面上已有的《外贸英语函电与会话》、《外贸函电》、《外贸英语口语》等书侧重英语语言知识的讲解，而《国际贸易实务(双语)》和其汉语版的重点在国际贸易、进出口业务知识，我们编写这本《实用外贸英语》，不是上述两类教材的简单重复，力争有所突破，以"好用、务实、有特色"为宗旨，在遵循外贸业务准确清晰、英语地道纯正原则的基础上，力求不只灌输知识，尽可能提升能力，将国际贸易中最广泛使用的语言——英语与国际贸易业务充分融合，让学习者能实实在在地运用英语和外贸业务技巧解决些问题，使外贸谈判顺利、经营顺畅，为国际经贸复合型人才的培养作点儿努力。为此，编者结合自身长期的外贸从业经验和外贸英语教学经验，并参考大量专家学者的著作，对编写方案、结构和内容，作了一些特别的安排。本书中"外贸"和"英语"，不再互为所谓"定语"与"主语"，每一单元中专门著有一节纯英文的 Solution to Problem(解决之道)。

　　全书分 11 个单元(Unit)，内容涉及外贸业务流程的各环节，包括建立业务联系、询盘和答复、报价、还盘、接受、订货、签约、支付、备货、包装、检验、装运、保险、异议、索赔、仲裁等，每单元基本上分 5 节(section)，第 1 节介绍(Section 1 Introduction)，中英双语介绍国际贸易、进出口业务相关知识，由杨云匀负责；第 2 节函电(Section 2 Correspondence)，外贸业务英文函电配注释(notes to text)以及实用外贸函电英语表达方式包括好词、短语及句型(useful expressions including words, phrases and sentence patterns)，由郑汉金负责；第 3 节对话(Section 3 Dialogs)，外贸业务英语对话配注释(notes)，由马俊负责；第 4 节练习(Section 4 Exercises)，外贸函电、对话各种句型的英汉互译及场景会话(Role Play)练习，由周艳丽负责，第 5 节解决之道(Section 5 Solution to Problem)，运用英语解决外贸谈判、经营问题，由马俊负责。马俊负责本书的编写构思、方案、框架和校对工作，郑汉金还负责附录 1~4(Appendix 1-4)的编写，周艳丽还负责附录 5(Appendix 5)的编写。

　　本书可作为大专院校外经贸专业的外贸英语教材使用，也可供外经贸从业者和广大英语爱好者自学使用。

　　编写过程中参考了有关专家、学者的著作，外籍专家 John Knox 和 Sarah Miller 为本书的对话和函电精心录音，2013 年全国商科院校专业技能大赛国际贸易专业竞赛总决赛一等奖获得者杨兵等同学参与了资料的收集，在此，一并表示诚挚的感谢！

　　由于编者的业务和外语水平有限，难免存在不尽人意和疏漏之处，敬请广大业界、学界专家同仁和读者批评指正。

编　者

目　录

Part 1　Negotiation of Business

Part 2　Fulfillment of Contract

Part 1　Negotiation of Business

Unit 1

Establishing Trading Relations

Section 1 Introduction

1. Origin of Establishing Business relations(建立业务关系的原因)

To establish business relations with prospective dealers is one of the vitally important measures either for a newly established firm or an old one that wishes to enlarge its business scope and turnover. As it is well known, customers are the basis of business development and expansion. No customers, no business, and no orders, no the company.

对于一个新成立的公司或一家希望扩大其业务范围和营业额的老公司来说，与潜在的交易商建立业务关系是极其重要的经营举措之一。众所周知，客户是企业发展和扩张的基础。没有客户，就没有生意，没有订单，没有公司。

2. Channels of Establishing Business Relations(建立业务关系的渠道)

Usually information about the merchants in foreign countries can be obtained through the following sources:

(1) The exhibitions and trade fairs;

(2) Banks;

(3) Chambers of commerce both at home and abroad (e.g. CCPIT);

(4) Commercial counselor's office subordinate to the Embassy of a certain country;

(5) The media of the newspapers, magazines and television;

(6) Introduction by friends in business circles;

(7) A branch office or representative abroad;

(8) The internet;

(9) Trade dictionary;

(10) Market research.

通常国外贸易商的信息可以从以下来源获得：①展览会与交易会；②银行；③国内外的商会(如：中国国际贸易促进委员会)；④各国大使馆下属的商务参赞处；⑤报纸、杂志和电视媒体；⑥商界朋友介绍；⑦国外分公司或代表；⑧互联网；⑨工商行名录；⑩市场调查。

Section 2　Correspondence

1. Writing Skills

This type of letter is generally made up of 4 parts as follows:

(1)　Show the source of information (how you learned of his company).

(2)　Briefly introduce your own company (the scope of your business, little "advertising" on your products or service).

(3)　Express the intention of writing the letter(what kind of business you want to do with them, e.g. to purchase their products, to sell your own products, to enter into a joint venture with them, etc).

(4)　Express the wish of cooperation and early reply.

2. Sample Letters

Letter 1 (Exporter to Importer)

China Foodstuff Import & Export Co.

32 Xisanhuan Rd., Beijing, China

January 1, 2014

New Asia Inc.

Room No. 40, Maruchi Building

Tokyo, Japan

Dear Sirs,

Learning from the Commercial Counselor's Office[1] of our Embassy in your country that you are one of the leading importers of canned[2] foodstuffs. We have the pleasure of introducing ourselves to you as a state corporation[3] specializing in[4] the export business of canned goods, and express our desire to enter into[5] business relation with you.

In order to give you a general idea of[6] our canned goods, we are sending you by separate airmail a copy of our latest catalogue[7]. Quotations[8] and samples[9] will be sent to you upon receipt of[10] your specific inquiry[11].

We are looking forward with interest to hearing from you soon.

Yours faithfully,

Zhou Yanming

Zhou Yanming

Manager

Export Department

Letter 2 (Importer to Exporter)

Dear Sirs,

Through the introduction of the United States Chamber of Commerce[12] in Beijing, we were advised of your company and your ability to export hardware[13]. We are writing to you with a view to establishing business relations with you and introducing your special lines[14] into our market.

There is a considerable[15] demand for hardware on our local markets. Our company is dedicated to[16] the trading of hardware for over ten years, and is one of the leading dealers in this line in China.

We shall always be very happy to hear from you and will carefully consider any proposals likely to lead to business between us.

Yours truly,

3. Notes to Text

(1)　the Commercial Counselor's Office　商务处；商务参赞处

(2)　canned (American English) 罐装的= (British English) tinned

(3)　state corporation, state-owned corporation　国有公司

(4)　specialize in …专营

This travel firm specializes in charter flights. 这家旅游公司专营包机业务。

Our company specializes in importing arts and crafts for many years.

本公司专门从事工艺美术商品进口多年。

(5)　enter into…开始(某种事业、谈判、关系等)；缔结(契约等)

We hope to enter into business relations with your company for the supply of electronic shavers. 我方愿意与贵公司建立商务关系，以便取得电动剃须刀的供货。

(6)　to give you a general idea of … 为了使您了解……

To give you a general idea of the scope of our business activities, we enclose herewith a complete set of catalogues that we are dealing in. 为使您全面了解本公司的业务范围，特别随

函附上一套我们经营产品的目录。

(7) catalogue 产品目录=(美)catalog

(8) quotation 报价，行情

quotation table (list) 价目表

exchange rate quotation 外汇行情

discount quotation 贴现行情

market quotation 市场行情

quote 开价，报价

The seller quoted the shirt at ten dollars.

(9) sample 产品样本，样品

sample card (衣料等)样品卡

sample discount 样品折扣(一般样品均系免费寄送，但应买方要求寄送较高价值的样品时，卖方通常给予折扣，酌收样品费)

sample export 样品出口(输出)(指小量货物以样品名义出口，虽仍收取货款，但可免办出口手续)

sample fair 样品展览会; trade fair 大型工商展览会，如法兰克福书展、伦敦古董展销会等

sample order=trial order 试订

sample shipment 试销

(10) upon/ on receipt of 收到……后

On receipt of your instructions we will send the goods. 一收到你方通知，我方即可发货。

(11) inquiry (American English) =enquiry (British English)询问，询价；

(12) the Chamber of Commerce 商会

(13) hardware 硬件

(14) line: one's trade of occupation, or the things he deals in

What's his line?

We have completed many successful transactions with Oriental Horizons Inc. in this line of business.

(15) considerable 客观的；大量的

The losses are considerable. 损失颇大。

(16) be dedicated to or dedicate to 致力于

Enterprises with outstanding quality, reasonable price will be dedicated to customer service. 企业以优异的质量，合理的价格将竭诚为客户服务。

China will continue to be dedicated to international cooperation in this area. 中国将继续致力于加强在该领域的国际合作。

4. Useful expressions

(1) 各种信息来源的表达方式。

① 从中国驻贵国大使馆商务参赞处获悉。

Having had your name and address from the Commercial Counselor's Office of the Embassy of the People's Republic of China in your country, we now write to you and see if we can establish business relations.

② 从贵国商务办事处获悉。

Through the recommendation of your commercial office here, we got your name and have known you specialize in chemical products for years.

③ 通过中国国际贸易促进委员会了解。

We have learned from China Council for the Promotion of International Trade that you are in the market for Electric Appliances.

④ 通过贵国最近来访的贸易代表团了解。

Through your trade delegation that recently paid a visit to Shanghai, we learned that you are well-established importers of electronic components.

⑤ 承老客户介绍。

Mr. Alex Black of MGD Co., Ltd., our mutual friend, gave us your name and recommend that you are an experienced importer of the Jewelry products in the UK.

⑥ 承银行介绍。

The HSBC Bank in your city has been kind enough to inform us that you are one of the leading importers of sports goods.

⑦ 从报刊上获悉。

We are glad to know from CPU magazine that you are interested in the silicon rubber pads, and enclose our relevant catalogs for your initial reference.

⑧ 从互联网上获悉。

From alibaba.com, we understand that you are a potential buyer of Chinese textiles, which just fall within our business scope.

⑨ 在展览会上结识。

We would like to thank you for your visit our booth and your interest in our products at the CeBIT Fair held in Hanover last month. As required, we are now glad to send you our catalogue of cooling fans for your evaluation.

CeBIT 是办公及信息技术中心(德语：Centrum der Büro-und Informations Technik)的缩写，又称"CeBIT 信息及通信技术博览会"，是一个国际性的以信息技术(IT 业)和信息工程(IE 业)为主的大型展览会，1986 年起的每年春季在德国汉诺威举行。展览会的组织者是德意志展览股份公司(Deutsche Messe AG，DMAG)。CeBIT 是全球最大的信息和通信工程类展览会。(http://zh.wikipedia.org/wiki/CeBIT)

(2) 致函目的示例。

① 希望是互利关系的前奏。

We are glad to send you this introductory letter, hoping that it will be the prelude to mutually beneficial relations between us.

② 盼望能有机会合作，扩展业务。

We have the pleasure to introduce ourselves to you and hope we may have a cooperation opportunity with you in your business extension.

③ 期待与贵公司建立业务关系。

We are writing to you with a view to building up business relations with your firm.

④ 愿与贵方进行交易。

Specializing in the export of Chinese arts and crafts, we express our desire to trade with you in this line.

⑤ 盼能建立业务关系，以满足贵方需求。

We take pleasure in contacting you in the hope of establishing business relations and rendering you assistance in a wide range of your requirements.

⑥ 希望建立互利的业务关系。

We wish to introduce ourselves in the hope of setting up mutually beneficial business relations between our two corporations.

⑦ 探求发展贸易的可能性。

The purpose of this letter is to explore the possibilities of developing trade with you.

⑧ 在平等互利、互通有无的基础上与你公司建立业务关系。

We are willing to enter into business relations with your firm on the basis of equality, mutual benefit and exchanging what one has for what one needs.

⑨ 建立友好业务关系，互惠互利。

We wish to establish friendly business relations with you to enjoy a share of mutually profitable business.

⑩ 将贵公司专营品引入本地市场。

We wish to enter into direct negotiation with you with a view to introducing your special lines into our market.

(3) 出口商介绍公司优势示例。

① 本着优良品质、创新产品及诚信交易的原则，我们在世界市场已赢得良好声誉。

Persisting the principles of superiority in quality, innovation in products and integrity in business, we have won a very good reputation in the world market.

② 本着"品质优秀、价格合理、服务卓越"的原则，我方在所有的客户中，包括美国德州仪器公司、荷兰飞利浦公司等，享有很高声誉。

By keeping the principle of "Excellent Quality, Competitive Price, Superior Service", we have enjoyed high integrity among all of our customers including Texas Instruments in USA and Philips in Netherlands.

③ 我方具备十多年的经验，是中国专业的玩具出口商。由于良好的管理制度和出色的售后服务，我们已在国际市场建立了良好的声誉。

We are a professional exporter of toys in China with more than 10 years' experience and have already set up a long-lasting good reputation in the world market, due to our good management system and excellent after-sales service.

④ 我方商品均由本国一流厂商提供，因此，我方有条件向贵方提供质量最可靠的商品。

Our products are all supplied by the first-class manufacturers of this country, and so we are in a good position to serve your customers with the most reliable quality of the line we suggest.

⑤ 我们是中国最有专业经验的家具制造商，享有很好的声誉。

We would like to show you that we are the most experienced and most professional manufacturer of furniture in China, with an excellent reputation.

⑥ 每天5000件的产量确保我方能顺利执行买主的订单，而且我们的研发部门已拥有了设计前瞻款式的能力。

Certified production of 5,000 pieces a day will ensure smooth execution of buyer's orders, and our R&D department has made it possible to create tomorrow's styles today.

⑦ 我方与本地大厂商有多年的持续业务往来，所以自信能以最低的价格来执行贵方的订单。

Having many years of constant dealings with the leading makers here, we are confident that we can execute your order at the lowest possible price.

⑧ 我公司贸易经验丰富，熟悉国际市场情况，相信这能使我们有资格得到贵方的信任。

We trust that our rich experience in foreign trade and intimate knowledge of international market conditions will entitle us to your confidence.

⑨ 凭借突出的出口量及完美的售后服务，最近我公司被政府评为绩优出口商。

Recently, we have received our government's recognition as a well-performed exporter due to our outstanding export turnover and flawless after-sales service.

⑩ 我公司管理良好，销售人员经验丰富，对贵方市场的偏好和需求十分了解。

We are a well-organized exporter with experienced salesmen who have comprehensive knowledge of the requirements and preferences of your market.

(4) 出口商介绍产品优势示例。

① 我们都知道中国拖鞋因价廉物美而畅销于你方市场。

We all understand that Chinese slippers are very popular on your market on account of their superior quality and competitive price.

② 从随附的目录和价目表可以看出，我方总以货真价实来维护买家的利益。

From the brochure and price-list enclosed, you will find we always try our best to protect buyer's interest by offering value-for-money prices.

③ 虽然我方所报价格非常低，但品质却非常优良。

Although the prices we offered are exceptionally low, the quality is still very good.

④ 贵方尽可放心，我们所有产品均可以各种款式供应，足以满足像贵方这样的时尚行业的需求。

You may rest assured that all of our items can be supplied in a wide range of designs to meet the requirements of a fashion trade such as yours.

⑤ 我们能以具有竞争力的价格和出色的品质提供广泛多样的电子产品。

We can offer a comprehensive range of electronic products with sensible prices and high quality.

⑥ 我们的产品受到各地消费者的欢迎，我们的经销商也从未反映有任何销售困难。

Our products are indeed welcomed by consumers everywhere; no sales difficulties have ever been reported from our customers.

⑦ 我方产品工艺精致，受到世界各地人们的欢迎。

Our products are welcomed by people throughout the world because of their exquisite workmanship.

⑧ 由于优秀的品质、吸引人的外观和良好的价格，二十多年来我方产品在国际市场上一直有很好的销量。

With the excellent quality, attractive appearance and good prices, our products have been winning good sales for more than 20 years on the world market.

⑨ 我们最近开发了一项新产品，此产品在美国、德国、法国等国销售得很好。

We recently developed a new product－×××, which is selling very well in many countries such as U.S., Germany, France, etc.

⑩ 请贵方注意，我方新型材料在今年的国际商展上引起了很大的震撼。

We would like to have your attention to our new material which created a great sensation at this year's International Trade Fair.

(5) 进口商介绍公司情况示例。

① 我们是中国化工产品的主要进口商之一。

We are one of the leading importers in the field of chemical products in China.

② 基于十多年经营农产品的经验，我们不仅在各地区拥有很多分销商，而且也有很好的直接销售渠道。

With more than 10 years' experience in handing agricultural products, we not only have many distributors in each area but also have very good direct sales channel.

③ 我方与本地经销商有很好的关系，因为它们靠我公司从世界各地进口他们所需要的各种产品。因此，我方确信，如果贵方的价格富有竞争性，我方定能从我方客户那里得到大订单。

We have close relations with local dealers and distributors, who depend on our services to import all various products they need from all over the world. For this reason, we are confident that we can obtain large orders from our customers, if your prices are competitive enough.

④ 我方是经验丰富而且专业的进口商，在中国各地区都有经销商，有很强的销售渠道和很好的商业关系，能很快很好地推广贵公司的产品。

We are a well-experienced and professional importer. With many distributors spreading in China, we also have strong sales channels, and good business relations. We are able to promote your products quickly and well.

(6) 进口商介绍市场需求示例。

① 本地市场对此类产品需求很大。

There is a considerable demand for these articles on our local markets.

② 中国对高品质的鞋子和手套有稳定的需求。

There is a steady demand for high quality shoes and gloves in China.

③ 我国国内市场对贵方的水果需求很大。

Your fruits are in great demand on our domestic market.

④ 市场上对进口时尚用品的需求变得十分巨大。

Our market demand for imported fashion products has become very heavy.

⑤ 这两年我方对于贵方皮具的需求将会大大增长。

Our requirement for your leather products will increase greatly in the current years.

⑥ 我们每年对于金属工具的需求量是很客观的，并且这种需求呈稳定上升趋势。

Our annual requirements for metal tools are considerable, and will increase steadily.

⑦ 中国对这种产品的优势品种有稳定的需求，销售量虽不会很大，但流行款式能卖很好的价格。

There is a steady demand in China for high-quality goods of this kind. Sales are not high, but a very good price can be ensured for fashionable designs.

实用外贸英语

Section 3　Dialogues

Dialogue 1

Where shall we start?

Ms. Zhou is showing Mr. Knox round the showroom.

Zhou: Would you like to have a look at our showroom, Mr. Knox?

Knox: Yes, that would be a good idea.

Zhou: This way, please.

Knox: Thank you. (Entering the room) Quite a selection!

Zhou: Where shall we start?

Knox: It would take hours if I really look at everything.

Zhou: You may be interested in only some of the items. Let's look at those.

Knox: Good idea! I can just have a glance at the rest.

Zhou: Have you been in textiles business a long time?

Knox: Yes, I've been in textiles for more than 20 years, but the company has been in business since 1935.

Zhou: No wonder you're so experienced.

Knox: The textile business has become more difficult since the competition grew.

Zhou: That's true.

Knox: Do you have a catalog or something that tells me about your company?

Zhou: Yes, I'll get you some later.

Knox: Thanks. When can we discuss some details?

Zhou: Would tomorrow be convenient?

Knox: Yes, that'll be fine.

Dialogue 2

It makes negotiations easier if we meet each other in person.

Zhang is sent by Kunming Electronics Import & Export Company to meet Thomas at the airport.

Zhang: Excuse me, aren't you Thomas from New Jersey?

Thomas: Yes. And you are …?

Zhang: I'm Zhang Ling from Kunming Import and Export Company.

Thomas: How do you do, Mr. Zhang? Thanks a lot.

Zhang: You're welcome. I'm very pleased to meet you.

Thomas: Do you know where the baggage claim area is?

Zhang: Yes, it's over there. How many pieces of luggage do you have?

Thomas: Only one suitcase.

Zhang: Let's go to pick up your luggage.

Thomas: OK.

(At the baggage claim area)

Zhang: How was your flight?

Thomas: Just wonderful! Good food and good service.

Zhang: Is this your first visit to Kunming?

Thomas: Yes.

Zhang: We are glad you come to meet us in person.

Thomas: Thank you for meeting my plane.

Zhang: It is the least we can do, since you have traveled so far to see us.

Thomas: It makes negotiations easier if we meet each other in person.

Zhang: How's business these days?

Thomas: Not bad. But sales are down a bit due to the revaluation.

Zhang: Do you think it's a general trend?

Thomas: Oh, I hope not. I think it's just a slump. Things will improve soon.

Zhang: I hope so.

Thomas: The blue canvas one is my suitcase.

Zhang: Our car is out in the parking lot. We'll take you to the Gold Dragon Hotel.

Thomas: Very good.

Dialogue 3

We'll be glad to show you what's available.

Xu and Brown are at the fair.

Brown: Excuse me, could you tell me where I could see some electrical appliances?

Xu: This area. We'll be glad to show you what's available. Here's my card.

Brown: Thanks. Mr. Excu ...

Xu: Xu is my last name.

Brown: Sorry, I'm not good at Pinyin. Here's my card. I'm Amy Brown from ABC Trading Co., Ltd. We import electronics and transistors.

Xu: Please have a look at our samples.

Brown: Your development of electronic products has been remarkable.

Xu: Yes, our research has had good results.

Brown: Do you produce video tape recorders?

Xu: Yes.

Brown: What's that? Is it a television set?

Xu: No, that's a television phone. It's still experimental.

Brown: What's the problem?

Xu: We have to solve the problem of using ultrahigh frequency waves at around one thousand hertz.

Brown: I see.

Xu: I've forgotten to ask you that what products you're interested in.

Brown: I think I've already seen some items we might like to order, although I'd still like to study them a bit further.

Xu: OK, go ahead.

Brown: I'll probably be able to let you know tomorrow.

Xu: I'll be expecting you tomorrow morning, say, at nine.

Brown: Tomorrow at nine. Good. I'll see you then.

Notes

To show sb. round the showroom 领某人参观样品间(陈列室)

Would you like ...? 征求对方意见的婉转说法

You may be interested in only of the items. 你可能对某些产品感兴趣

When can we discuss some details? 什么时候我们能谈点具体的(业务)？

Excuse me, aren't you ...? 对不起，(请问)你是……？

The baggage claim area 行李认领处

Sales are down a bit due to the revaluation. 由于货币升值销售稍有下降

Ultrahigh frequency 超高频

Hertz 赫兹(频率单位；周/秒)

Section 4　Exercises

1. Translate the following sentences into English:

(1)　经由中国国际贸易促进委员会推荐，我们得知贵公司的名称和地址。

(2) 我方很高兴向您自荐，以期与贵方建立贸易关系。

(3) 随函附上一份产品目录供参考。

(4) 我想推荐您一些适合欧盟市场的新产品。

(5) 我们已经专营化工产品出口 20 多年了。

(6) 有任何问题，请随时向我方询问。

2. Translate the following sentences into Chinese:

(1)　We have more than 20 years' experience in manufacturing and have exported various kinds of products to European and U.S. markets.

(2)　The offer sheet in detail will be sent to you in another separate mail.

(3)　We are interested in the leather products demonstrated by your company at the recent Canton Fair.

(4)　We not only provide the most competitive prices with best quality, but also have the ability to help the customers to solve their problems.

(5)　We sincerely invite you to visit our website: www.AAA.com.cn to see if any item interests you.

(6)　We are looking forward to hearing your comments or inquiry soon.

3. Translate the following letter into English:

敬启者：

承蒙中国轻工业品进出口公司告知，我方获知贵公司名称和地址。我们很高兴地获悉贵公司欲购买中国产的自行车。

我公司成立于 1990 年，现已发展成为中国领先的自行车生产和出口企业。由于我公司的产品质量上乘，价格合理，所以在客户中享有很好的信誉。

我们冒昧地写信给您是想和贵公司建立业务往来，并随信寄送我们的产品图解目录以供参考。如果有你们感兴趣的产品，请告知我们。

期待您早日回复。

...... 谨上

4. Translate the following letter into Chinese:

Dear Sirs,

We learn your name and contact information from the Chamber of Commerce of London.

We wish to buy fully automatic coffee machines with superior quality. If you can supply the above mentioned goods, please kindly airmail us your price list and illustrated catalog with detailed specification.

We look forward to your early reply.

Sincerely,

5. Compose a dialogue based on the following situation:

Mr. Smith, a businessman from London, is visiting Canton Fair with the intention to purchase TV sets. Mr. Li, an exhibitor from TCL Co., is trying to promote their TV sets. They meet at Canton Fair and begin a business talk.

Section 5   Solution to Problem

What are major channels of seeking and finding an importer or vice versa? What channels are less useful? and how to utilize them?

The great master of Management, Peter F. Drucker has ever said: "The purpose of enterprise is to create a customer", it is commonly understood no customer no business, the development and expansion of a business depends on customers. In international trade, the importer is usually in one country and the exporter in another, they are separated sometimes by thousands of miles, to seek prospective customers and establish business relations with them is the first step, we could also say, it is one of the most important step in international trade for not only a newly established enterprise but also an old one that wishes to expand its market and enlarge its business scope and turnover, because transaction could only be made after the business connections have been set up.

According to descriptions in most text books, usually a firm may approach its new business counterparts abroad or obtain necessary information through the following channels:

(1) Banks

(2) Chambers of Commerce or industry associations or council for trade promotion

(3) Commercial counselor's offices in embassies in various countries

(4) Advertisements in newspapers and magazines

(5) Trade directories or yellow pages

(6) Attendance at trade fairs, shows and exhibitions

(7) Recommendations from friends in business circle

(8) Mutual visits by trade groups and delegations

(9) Internet

Let's analyze what are major channels, what are less useful, and how to utilize them.

(1) Regarding Banks

We are afraid we are unable to count on banks to provide us with enough names and other information of prospective customers, because it is not banks' major business, we may refer to the website of Bank of China (BOC), we could only find under the title of Integrated Business Solution (IBS), there is a service named Business Information Survey, BOC could be commissioned by it's customer to survey customer's target business count part's legal existence, registration information, operation status, management background, business scale, bad records, ability to pay and so on to help it's customer to control commercial risks while exploring and enlarging market. In fact, banks aren't always ready to supply names and addresses of importers or exporters, what banks such as BOC could do is mainly credit survey rather than plenty names of prospective buyers or sellers that we want eagerly. So banks are less useful in seeking and finding business counter part.

While, China Export & Credit Insurance Corporation, a nonbanking financial institution in China, is helpful in acquiring prospective customers' information. It has not only the same credit survey and rating service as that of BOC but also service of providing overseas customers' names, addresses and other information. That service is called "Credit Rating service\International Market Developing Program".

(2) Regarding chambers of Commerce or industry associations or council for trade promotion

① China Council for the Promotion for International Trade (CCPIT) is the most important organization in promotion for international trade, it has another name China Chamber of International Commerce (CCOIC), it is also The National Committee of International Chamber of Commerce in China in brief ICC China. How do we utilize CCPIT in seeking and finding customers? At least, we are able to do through following 2 ways, a.To be embodied in it's publication "Directory of China's Foreign Trade", in this way we are likely sought and found by overseas customers. b. Attendance at trade fairs organized by CCPIT.

② China Chamber of Commerce for Import and Export of Textiles and Apparel, China Chamber of Commerce for Import and Export of Light Industrial Products and Arts-Crafts, China Chamber of Commerce for Import and Export of Metals, Minerals and Chemicals, China Chamber of Commerce for Import and Export of Foodstuffs and Native Produce, China Chamber of Commerce for Import and Export of Machinery and Electronic Products, China Chamber of Commerce for Import and Export of Medicines and Health Products and China International Contractors Association are 7 biggest industry association affiliated to Ministry of Commerce of China, to be member of one of them, participate in events organized by it such as trade fairs, we are able to get customers' information.

We may also avail ourselves of World Importers Net of above mentioned Ministry of Commerce of China to obtain plenty of buyers' names and etc.

(3)　Regarding Commercial counselor's offices in embassies in various countries

We could link sub-websites of Ministry of Commerce of China or Ministry of Foreign Affairs of China to connect Commercial counselor's offices in China's embassies in various foreign countries and foreign chambers of commerce to seek and find prospective customers.

(4)　Regarding advertisements in newspapers and magazines

This is a way to make foreign customers find us in their local newspapers and magazines.

(5)　Regarding trade directories or yellow pages

Finding trade directories or yellow pages published or given online by specific foreign institution are effective for us to get most customers' information. "Kompass", "Dialog" and "Thomas Global Register" are in a position to sell trade directories.

(6)　Regarding attendance at trade fairs, shows and exhibitions

This is the most traditional and common way of face to face to seek and find customers. We may make good use of Canton fair and other fairs held in China and other overseas trade fairs.

(7)　Regarding recommendations from friends in business circle

This way is direct and fast for us to contact new customers, anyway numbers of customers are likely limited.

(8)　Regarding mutual visits by trade groups and delegations

In most cases, it is a way of contacting regular and old customers, not new customers.

(9)　Regarding internet

Introduction to some useful methods of e-business

①　Construction of one's own website

②　Search engine: Google, Yahoo and etc.

③　The 3rd party B to B trade platform: alibaba.com, globalsources.com and etc.

④　Directory sites: Yahoo.com, DOMZ.org and etc.

⑤　Suppliers of Buyers' directory: kompass.com, dialog.com, tgrnet.com (i.e. above mentioned in article 5 Thomas Global Register) and etc.

Unit 2

Inquiries and Replies

Section 1   Introduction

1. Definition of An Inquiry (询盘的定义)

As a business person, if you are interested in merchants in foreign countries and their products after establishing trading relations, you will have to write many letters to ask for information, to give information and to get your business done. Among the most common in business are letters to make an inquiry and their replies.

In international trade, business negotiation usually starts with an inquiry or an offer by one party of the seller or buyer sending to another. An inquiry which is also called enquiry in British English refers to the buyer or the seller putting forward the enquiry about trading conditions to the opposite party in order to buy or sell a commodity. An inquiry is not legally binding upon both parties, which is not a necessary procedure of trade negotiation, but it is usually the starting point of a transaction.

An inquiry is usually made to seek a supply of products, service or information. The content of an inquiry can only include the price of the goods, also can ask for the specification, performance, packaging and delivery time of the goods, and the terms of payment etc. The buyer in an inquiry can also ask the opposite party for catalogues or samples.

In the international trade, a buyer/seller usually makes an inquiry to invite a quotation or offer from the seller/buyer in order to buy/sell a certain commodity or obtain/provide a kind of service. So the inquiry can be made by either the importer or the exporter. An inquiry made by the buyer is called the invitation to make an offer. An inquiry made by the seller is called the invitation to make a bid.

作为贸易商，如果你在建立业务关系后对国外客户和其产品感兴趣，你将写信给他以询问信息、提供信息和达成交易。最常见的业务就是询盘及回复函电。

在国际贸易中，交易磋商一般开始于买卖双方的一方主动向对方发出询盘或发盘。所谓询盘又称询价，是指买方或卖方为了洽购或销售某项商品，而向对方提出关于交易条件的询问。询盘对双方均无法律约束力，而且它不是交易磋商的必经的程序，但它往往是一笔交易的起点。

询盘通常是寻求供应的产品，服务或信息。询盘的内容可只包括有关货物的价格，也可兼问商品的规格、性能、包装和交货期，以及付款方式等各项交易条件。买方在贸易询盘中也可要求对方提供商品目录或样品。

在国际贸易中，为了购买/出售某种商品或获得/提供某项服务，买方/卖方通常发出询盘以邀请卖方/买方做出发价或发盘。故询盘可由进口商或出口商发出。由买方发出的询盘，习惯上叫邀请发盘。由卖方发出的询盘，习惯上叫邀请递盘。

2. The categories of inquiries (询盘的分类)

Generally speaking, inquiries fall into two categories: a general inquiry and a specific inquiry.

A general inquiry is a request to get information about the goods by asking for a catalogue, a price list, samples and so forth. Generally, a general inquiry should include the following contents: ① The source of information and a brief self-introduction; ② The intention of writing the letter (e.g. ask for a catalogue, samples or a pricelist); ③ Stating the possibility of placing an order.

A specific inquiry is a request to get specific information about the goods to be ordered, such as price, catalogue, delivery date, terms of payment, discounts, packing and specifications. Generally, a specific inquiry should include the following contents: ① The names and descriptions of the goods inquired for, including specifications, quantity, etc.; ② Asking whether there is a possibility of giving a special discount and what terms of payment and time of delivery you would expect; ③ Stating the possibility of placing an order.

通常询盘可分为两种：一般询盘和具体询盘。

一般询盘是通过索要产品目录、价格单、样品等询问获取产品的信息。通常一般询盘应包括以下内容：①信息的来源和简短的自我介绍；②写这封信的目的(如索取目录、样品或价格表)；③提出下订单的可能性。

具体询盘是询问获取具体订购商品的有关信息，如价格、目录、交货日期、付款条件、折扣、包装及规格。通常具体询盘应包括以下内容：①询价货物的名称和描述，包括规格、数量等。②询问是否有给予特别折扣的可能性，以及付款条件和交货时间；③提出下订单的可能性。

Section 2　Correspondence

1. Writing Skills

An inquiry is generally made up of three parts as follows:

(1)　The beginning paragraph (the first part) is where you express what you are interested, make brief introduction of your company or state the purpose to write the inquiry.

(2)　In the following paragraph the specific information is asked in detail.

(3)　The last paragraph is for courteous close where to extend thanks and express the hope of receiving replies as soon as possible.

A reply is composed of the following three paragraphs.

(1)　The opening paragraph in reply to inquiry begins with expressing thanks and acknowledging the enquiry. The date the inquiry was written should be mentioned, and what has been requested in the inquiry should be summarized in the acknowledgement.

(2)　The second paragraph is used to answer the inquiry in detail.

(3)　The final paragraph is used to express the hope that the information which you have given will be useful, and to look forward to the reply again.

2. Sample Letters

Letter 1 (A Specific Inquiry)

Oriental Horizons Inc.

48 East Street Ramsey, NJ 07446 U.S.A.

February 2, 2014

Ningbo Textiles United Import & Export Corp.

207 Kaiming St.

Ningbo 315000, Zhejiang

P. R. China

Dear Sirs,

　This company is one of the largest textile importers in New Jersey. We sincerely hope to establish business relations with your company so as to promote trade between our two countries.

　We are enclosing an inquiry note[1] No. 303 and looking forward to receiving your quotation soon, CIF New Jersey inclusive of[2] our 5% commission[3]. While quoting, please state[4] the earliest shipment[5] and quantity available[6].

　If your quotation is competitive[7], we are ready to conclude substantial[8] business with[9] you. Your early reply will be very much appreciated[10].

Sincerely,

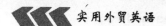

Michael S. Barnwell

Michael S. Barnwell

Manager

MSB/sh

Letter 2 (A General Inquiry)

Dear Mr. Black,

As we plan our fall[11] inventory[12], we are again in market for[13] woolens[14]. We are principally[15] interested in the traditional sweater[16] (men's and women's cardigans[17] and pullovers[18]), and would like to request a sample.

Please also send information on any other knitwear[19] that your company produces and a current price list.

If you plan to have a representative[20] at the Paris Trade Fair[21] at the end of March, please advise us of your stand[22] number so that we can contact you at that time.

Thank you for your attention.

Yours sincerely,

Letter 3 (Reply)

Dear Sirs,

We are very pleased to receive your inquiry of April 10 and thank you for your interest in our products.

We are glad to tell you that we are in a position to supply the items inquired for from stock[23]. We feel confident that the superior material and exquisite craftsmanship[24] of our silk blouses appeal to[25] the most selective buyers.

On regular purchases of over 100 dozen of individual item a discount[26] of 3% is granted. If you place your order not later than the end of this week, we would guarantee[27] prompt delivery within 20 days, and demand your payment by sight L/C.

Enclosed please find our quotation sheet and a copy of illustrated catalogue giving the details you ask for. As the market is showing an upward tendency, it is profitable for you to place an order immediately.

We look forward to your first order.

Faithfully yours,

3. Notes to Text

(1) inquiry note 询价单

(2) inclusive of = include 包括

(3) commission 佣金

(4) state 说明，提到

In your quotation, please state the delivery time. 请在你们的报价中说明交货时间。

(5) shipment 装运 make (effect) shipment

When can you make shipment? 什么时候装运？

(6) available 可以得到的，可以用的

There are no such men's shirts available for export. 没有可供出口的这样的男士衬衫。

(7) competitive 有竞争力的，即价格低的

Our price is the most competitive. 我们的价格是最低的。

(8) substantial 大量的

If your price is competitive, we can place a substantial order. 如果你放价格低的话，我们可以大量订货。

(9) conclude business with (sb.) 与某人达成交易

(10) appreciate 感谢 sb. appreciate sb.; sb. appreciate it if; sth. be appreciated

We shall appreciate it if you will send us a brochure and two sample books by air immediately. 如果你能立即航空邮寄给我们一个小册子和两个样品簿，我们将不胜感激。

Your early reply is highly appreciated. 感谢你们的早日回复。

(11) fall = autumn 秋季

(12) inventory 库存

We plan to reduce our inventory. 我们计划减少库存。

(13) (be) in the market for 想要购买

They have informed us that you are in the market for chemicals. 他们已经通知我方你们有意购买化工制品。

(14) woolens n. 毛织品，毛料织物；毛织品，羊毛织物，毛料衣服(woolen 的名词复数)

(15) principally 主要的

We handle principally textiles. 我们主要经营纺织品。

(16) sweater n. 毛衣，运动衫

(17) cardigan n. 毛衣，羊毛衫(cardigan 的名词复数)

(18) pullovers n. 套头的毛衣，套衫(pullover 的名词复数)

(19) knitwear n. 针织品

(20) representative 代表，这里指代理，意思同 agent

(21) trade fair 贸易交易会

(22) stand 摊位

(23) supply from stock 供应现货，stock 意为库存，现货

in stock 库存中，有现货　　 out of stock 缺货，无现货

If you have cotton in stock, please make a quotation for it.

We are sorry the item is out of stock now.

(24) exquisite craftsmanship 精湛的技艺

(25) appeal to 受到……的欢迎

Good products appeal to everyone.

(26) discount 折扣

(27) guarantee 保证，担保 (名词，动词)

Changhong TV is guaranteed for two years.

We guarantee the payment of the debts.

Goods in this shop are sold with money-back guarantee.

South winds in winter are a guarantee of rain in this area.

guarantor 保证人，担保人

When asking for a loan, we must have a guarantor.

4. Useful expressions

(1) 请贵公司尽快惠寄运动鞋的最新价目表和带有图片的商品目录，并给予最优惠的报价。

We will be appreciative if you could deliver us as soon as possible your latest price list of your sports shoes with the lowest quotations, together with an illustrated catalogue.

(2) 请告知中国产餐具的价格和最早的交货日期。

Please inform us of the price of Chinese dinnerware and the possibly earliest date of delivery.

(3) 我们对贵公司 2008 年 1 月 12 日来信中提到的"宏碁"计算机很感兴趣，如蒙提供具有竞争性的报价，将十分感激。

We are interested in Acer computers you stated in your letter of January 12th, 2008 and shall be obliged if you could care to offer us competitive quotations.

(4) 我们欲求购下列产品，如贵公司能寄来样品，我们将不胜感激。

We are on the look-out for the following items and should be grateful if you would send samples of the same.

(5) 贵公司刊登在《商务周刊》2008 年第 38 期上的家具广告引起了我方的兴趣，我们想了解贵公司全面详细的报价。

The advertisement of your furniture in the thirty-eighth issue of Business Weekly in 2008 appeals to us, and we would like to have full details of your offer.

(6) 应贵公司 11 月 25 日的来函询问，现寄上我方的报价和几副式样不同的与贵方要求近似的皮手套样品。

In reply to your inquiry dated November 25th, we are sending you here with our quotation, along with various samples of leather gloves closely resembling what you want.

(7) 你将发现，我们给贵公司的报价是相同产品中最低的。

You will find that we have given you the most favored quotation for the same products.

(8) 应贵方 5 月 21 日的询盘，我方将很高兴以每台 CFR 东京港 120 美元的价格供应此款传真机。

With reference to your inquiry of May 21st we shall be happy to supply fax machines at the price of USD 120 per set CFR Tokyo.

(9) 我方不能提供贵方在 2 月 2 日的来信中所要求的信息，很抱歉。

We are sorry that we are not able to offer you the information you requested in last letter of February 2nd.

(10) 非常感谢贵公司 3 月 20 日来函询问，现寄去第 14 号样品一套。

We thank you very much for your inquiry of March 20th, and glad to send you a set of samples of No. 14.

Section 3 Dialogues

Dialogue 1

I'd like to have your lowest quotations, C.I.F. Vancouver.

Mr. Clive from a company in Canada comes to a machinery plant for the prices of small hardware. Mr. Yang is meeting with him.

Clive: I'm glad to have the opportunity of visiting your corporation. I hope we can do business together.

Yang: It's a great pleasure to meet you, Mr. Clive. I believe you have seen our exhibits in the showroom. What is it in particular you're interested in?

Clive: I'm interested in your hardware. I've seen the exhibits and studied your catalogues. I think some of the items will find a ready market in Canada. Here's a list of requirements. I'd like to have your lowest quotations, C.I.F. Vancouver.

Yang: Thank you for your inquiry. Would you tell us what quantity you require so that we

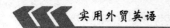

can work out the offer?

Clive: I'll do that. Meanwhile, could you give me an indication of the price?

Yang: Here are our F.O.B price. All the prices in the lists are subject to our confirmation.

Clive: What about the commission? From European suppliers I usually get a 3 to 5 percent commission for my imports. It's the general practice.

Yang: As a rule we do not allow any commission. But if the order is a sizable one, we'll consider it.

Clive: You see, I do business on a commission basis. A commission on your prices would make it easier for me to promote sales. Even 2 or 3 percent would help.

Yang: We'll discuss this when you place your order with us.

Dialogue 2

When can I get a firm offer?

Barbara Jones, a hardware dealer, is visiting the Guangzhou Trade Fair.

Sun: Hello, Ms ...

Jones: I'm Barbara Jones.

Sun: Nice to meet you, Ms. Jones. I'm Sun Lili. Please have a seat!

Jones: Thanks, Ms. Sun.

Sun: Is this your first time to the Fair?

Jones: Yes.

Sun: Have you had a look round the exhibition halls?

Jones: Yes. I took a walk around the day before yesterday. The halls are so spacious that I lost my way several times.

Sun: Really? You should follow the signs.

Jones: I did, but, you know, the exhibits are so spectacular.

Sun: I see.

Jones: And there's such a wide variety.

Sun: It's very nice of you to say so. As a matter of fact, many of our products have not yet caught up with advanced world levels.

Jones: I must say you've done a marvelous job in recent years.

Sun: Thank you.

Jones: I'd like to find out about hardware. Here's my list. I hope you'll give me your best offer.

Sun: I'll try my hardest.

Jones: Thanks. If your prices are good and if I can get the commission I want, I can place the order with you right away.

Sun: I'm sure you'll find our prices are very competitive. Hardware has gone up a lot in recent years, but our prices haven't changed much.

Jones: Glad to hear that. When can I get a firm offer?

Sun: We'll have it worked out by this evening and let you have it tomorrow morning. Would you be free to come by then?

Jones: Fine. I'll be here tomorrow morning at nine. How's that?

Sun: Perfect. See you tomorrow then.

Jones: Bye!

Notes

1. showroom 样品间

2. hardware 小五金

3. indication of price 估计价格

4. subject to 以……为准，有效

The prices are subject to our confirmation. 所有价格经我们确认后有效。

5. as a rule

As a rule, our prices are given on a C.I.F. basis. 通常我们的报价都是到岸价。

6. spacious 宽敞的

7. spectacular 场面富丽的、壮观的景象

8. commission 佣金，代理人或经纪人代委托人进行交易而收取的报酬

9. firm offer 实盘，不能撤销的发价

Section 4　Exercises

1. Translate the following sentences into English:

(1)　我方对贵公司产品目录中的 A1009 号产品感兴趣，请报该产品 CIF 上海价格。

(2)　如贵方能报给我们 FOB 洛杉矶的最优惠价格，我们将不胜感激。

(3)　请告知我们详细的产品信息，以及最早的交货时间。

(4)　感谢贵方 5 月 6 日对丝绸产品的询盘。

(5)　我们已收到贵公司 4 月 20 日关于皮革制品的询价函，很高兴你们喜欢我们的产品。

2. Translate the following sentences into Chinese:

(1)　Please provide us with quotes for the goods listed on the enclosed inquiry sheet.

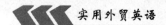

(2) In reply to your inquiry of March 4, we are sending a copy of our latest price list by air mail for your reference.

(3) Should your price be competitive and delivery time be acceptable, we shall place a large order.

(4) It would be appreciated if you can send us samples.

(5) If you can supply 50 tons of peanuts, please inform us of the price per ton and the payment term.

3. Translate the following letter into English:

×××先生：

感谢你的来信及随附的产品目录。

经过对目录的仔细研究，我们认为货号 15 的商品较适合我方市场。我们可能需要订购 50000 件，2014 年 8 月交货。如能供应，请报上述货物 CIF C3 纽约最优惠的价格，以及包装、运输、保险、支付等详细信息。

期待您早日回复。

…… 谨上

4. Translate the following letter into Chinese:

Dear Mr. …,

Thank you for your inquiry dated June 3 about our electron products.

As requested, we are sending you our price list and some samples by separate post. As to term of payment, it is our custom to trade on the basis of irrevocable L/C at sight.

If you can place your order no later than the end of this month, we would ensure prompt shipment.

We await your early reply.

Yours faithfully,

…

5. Compose a dialogue based on the following situation:

Mr. Jones, an Australian businessman, makes an inquiry for microwave ovens.

Mr. Chen, a salesman from GREE Co., China, makes an offer and tries to persuade Mr. Jones to accept the price.

Section 5 Solution to Problem

1. Buyer would better make inquiry as specific as possible, why?

The reason is very simple, inquiry is usually a request made by buyer for the information on the supply of certain goods, it is an invitation to make offer, if inquiry is not specific, accordingly offer won't be made to meet buy's real request, if buyer does not want waste time to make seller to ask what on earth you want to buy and you give answers over and again, you would better make your inquiry specific.

For example, if buyer makes inquiry like this: "Please quote your lowest price for men's shirts and state the earliest delivery date." Let's analyze buyer's request for the price of men's shirts and leave alone delivery, if you do not make seller know what materials, style, size, color and etc. you exactly want, seller is certainly going to have to ask you, it obviously wastes time, as you know, price of cotton shirts is usually different from that of polyester shirts, there is also difference between long sleeve shirts and short sleeve shirts.

2. Seller needs to make sure of what exactly buyer wants to get from you, a quotation or an offer?

Generally speaking, an offer is a proposal usually made by the seller to the buyer for the selling of the goods. It includes name of the goods, specification, price, quantity, packing, payment, delivery time and so on.

A quotation is also made by the seller to the buyer, but it is usually related to price only. In a typical quotation, there are 4 components, for example

USD	60.00	PER DOZEN	CIF NEW YORK
Type of currency	figure of unit price	unit of measurement	trade term

An offer certainly includes a quotation.

Anyway, we would better make sure of what exactly buyer wants to get a quotation or an offer, especially in oral speaking.

For example,

When buyer says: "Would you please offer me the price of that shirt?" Obviously buyer's real intention is a quotation rather than an offer. When buyer says: "Could you quote the whole terms and conditions of that shirt?" Buyer actually wants to get an offer rather than a quotation.

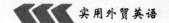
3. In "United Nations Convention on Contracts for the International Sales of Goods" there is not description of non-firm offer, while it is often used in business practice, why?

Non-firm offer is that kind of offer without engagement or without obligation, offerer can refuse to sell the goods he offers even if is accepted by offeree.

For example,

We are making you this offer subject to our final confirmation.

This offer is made subject to the goods being unsold.

Although In "United Nations Convention on Contracts for the International Sales of Goods" there is not description of non-firm offer, while it is often used in business practice, it is just because seller would probably come across unforeseen things or seller is conservative and cautious.

When we get a non-firm offer, we would better be careful too.

Unit 3

Bargaining

Section 1　Introduction

1. Quotation (报价)

(1)　Definition of A Quotation (报价的定义)

Making a quotation or an offer is a most important step in negotiating an export transaction. A quotation is a reply to an inquiry. It is an offer in simple form, which usually includes information related to the price of the goods being sold.

The quotation is also an important item in the offer. In international trade, quotation usually refers to quoting the unit price of the commodity, which consists of type of currency, price per unit, measurement unit and trade term. For example: US$100 per dozen FOB New York，or GBP150 per metric ton CIF London.

报价或发盘是出口交易谈判中最重要的一个环节。报价是对询盘的简单回复，这是一种简单形式的发盘，只包括要出售的特定商品的价格信息。

报价也是发盘中的重要内容。在国际贸易中，报价通常是指报商品的单价，是由计价货币、单位价格金额、计价数量单位和贸易术语构成。例如：每打 100 美元 FOB 纽约，或者每吨 150 英镑 CIF 伦敦。

(2)　Trade Terms (贸易术语)

① 　What Are Trade Terms? (什么是贸易术语？)

What do FOB or CIF mean in the example above? They are called trade terms, or delivery terms. Under no circumstance can a buyer get a quotation without trade term in international trade. Trade terms are short terms and abbreviations which are used to explain the price composition, to define the delivery of the goods, to indicate which party bears the freight, insurance and other relevant charges, and assume the liability in case damage or loss of the goods occurs. Trade terms ensure both exporter and importer know their own responsibilities.

在上例中的 FOB 或 CIF 是什么意思？它们被称作贸易术语，或者叫作交货条件。在国际贸易中，买方收到的报价绝对不能没有贸易术语。贸易术语是用简单的概念或外文缩写来表明价格的构成，规定所售货物的交货方法，指明由哪方负担运费、保险费和其他相关费用，由哪方承担货物损坏或灭失的责任。贸易术语使进出口双方明确各自的责任。

② International Trade Usages Relating to International Trade Terms (有关贸易术语的国际贸易惯例)

In order to avoid, or at least reduce to a considerable degree, the uncertainties of different interpretations of such terms in different countries, the International Chamber of Commerce(ICC) first published a set of international rules for the interpretation of the most commonly used trade terms in foreign trade. These rules were known as "Incoterms 1936". Amendments and additions were later made in 1953, 1967, 1976, 1980, 1990, 2000 and presently 2010 in order to bring the rules in line with current international trade practices. There are also other rules to be observed in international trade: Warsaw-Oxford Rules, 1932 and The Revised American Foreign Trade Definitions, 1941.

为了避免在不同的国家对这类术语可能产生的歧义，或者至少把产生歧义的可能性减少到最低限度，国际商会于 1936 年首次出版了一套国际通则，解释对外贸易中最常用的贸易术语，即《国际贸易术语解释通则 1936》(简称《1936 通则》)。为了使这些通则符合现实的国际惯例，后来曾于 1953 年、1967 年、1976 年、1980 年、1990 年、2000 年和最近的 2010 年对其进行了修改和补充。在国际贸易中也还有其他的规则：1932 年华沙—牛津规则和 1941 年美国对外贸易定义修订本。

③ Incoterms 2010 (国际贸易术语解释通则 2010)

Incoterms 2010 contains 11 trade terms (See Table 3-1 Incoterms 2010), now let's discuss the 11 terms one by one and have a clear understanding of them.

国际贸易术语解释通则 2010 包含 11 种贸易术语(见表 3-1 国际贸易术语解释通则 2010)，现逐一讨论这 11 种贸易术语并做清晰的理解。

Table 3-1   Incoterms 2010 (表 3-1   国际贸易术语解释通则 2010)

Categories 分类	Abbreviation 术语缩写	Full Name 术语全称	Chinese Interpretation 中文解释
Rules For Any Mode of Transport 适用于任何运输方式	EXW	Ex Works	工厂交货
	FCA	Free Carrier	货交承运人
	CPT	Carriage Paid To	运费付至
	CIP	Carriage and Insurance Paid To	运费和保险费付至
	DAT	Delivered At Terminal	运输终端交货
	DAP	Delivered At Place	目的地交货
	DDP	Delivered Duty Paid	完税后交货

续表

Categories 分类	Abbreviation 术语缩写	Full Name 术语全称	Chinese Interpretation 中文解释
Rules For Sea And Inland Waterway 适用于海运和内河运输	FAS	Free Alongside Ship	船边交货
	FOB	Free On Board	船上交货
	CFR	Cost And Freight	成本加运费
	CIF	Cost Insurance and Freight	成本、保险费加运费

A. EXW: Ex Works (… named place of delivery) (工厂交货(……指定交货地))

"Ex Works" means that the seller delivers when it places the goods at the disposal of the buyer at the seller's premises or at another named place (i.e., works, factory, warehouse, etc.). The seller does not need to load the goods on any collecting vehicle, nor does it need to clear the goods for export, where such clearance is applicable. The parties are well advised to specify as clearly as possible the point within the named place of delivery, as the costs and risks to that point are for the account of the seller. The buyer bears all costs and risks involved in taking the goods from the agreed point, if any, at the named place of delivery. EXW represents the minimum obligation for the seller.

工厂交货是指卖方在其所在地或其他指定地点(如工厂、车间或仓库等)将货物交给买方处置时，即完成交货。卖方不需将货物装上任何前来接收货物的运输工具，需要清关时，卖方也无须为货物办理出口清关手续。双方应尽可能明确地指定货物交付地点，因为此时(交货前)的费用与风险由卖方承担。买方必须承担在双方约定的地点或在指定地受领货物的全部费用和风险。EXW 术语是卖方承担责任最小的术语。

B. FCA: Free Carrier (…named place of delivery) (货交承运人(……指定交货地))

"Free Carrier" means that the seller delivers the goods to the carrier or another person nominated by the buyer at the seller's premises or another named place. The parties are well advised to specify as clearly as possible the point within the named place of delivery, as the risk passes to the buyer at that point. Delivery is completed: a) If the named place is the seller's premises, when the goods have been loaded on the means of transport provided by the buyer. b) In any other case, when the goods are placed at the disposal of the carrier or another person nominated by the buyer on the seller's means of transport ready for unloading. FCA requires the seller to clear the goods for export, where applicable. However, the seller has no obligation to clear the goods for import, pay any import duty or carry out any import customs formalities.

"货交承运人"是指卖方在其所在地或其他指定地点将货物交给买方指定的承运人或其他人即为卖方完成交货。双方应尽可能明确地指定货物交付的具体地点，因为风险在该地点转移给买方。于下列情形下即算完成交货：a) 如指定地为卖方所在地，则于货物装载于买方所安排或提供的运输工具时；b)在任何其他情形，则于将置于卖方运输工具上且可供卸载的货物交由买方指定的承运人或其他人处置时。FCA 要求卖方在需要时办理出口清关手续。但是，卖方没有办理进口清关手续的义务，也无须缴纳任何进口关税或者办理其他进口海关手续。

C. CPT: Carriage Paid To (… named place of destination) [运费付至(⋯⋯指定目的港)]

"Carriage Paid To" means that the seller delivers the goods to the carrier or another person nominated by himself at an agreed place (if any such place is agreed between the parties) and that the seller must contract for and pay the costs of carriage necessary to bring the goods to the named place of destination. The seller fulfils its obligation to deliver when it hands the goods over to the carrier and not when the goods reach the place of destination. The parties are well advised to identify as precisely as possible in the contract both the place of delivery, where the risk passes to the buyer, and the named place of destination to which the seller must contract for the carriage. If several carriers are used for the carriage to the agreed destination and the parties do not agree on a specific point of delivery, the default position is that risk passes when the goods have been delivered to the first carrier at a point entirely of the seller's choosing and over which the buyer has no control. Should the parties wish the risk to pass at a later stage (e.g., at an ocean port or airport), they need to specify this in their contract of sale. The parties are also well advised to identify as precisely as possible the point within the agreed place of destination, as the costs to that point are for the account of the seller. The seller is advised to procure contracts of carriage that match this choice precisely. If the seller incurs costs under its contract of carriage related to unloading at the named place of destination, the seller is not entitled to recover such costs from the buyer unless otherwise agreed between the parties.

CPT requires the seller to clear the goods for export, where applicable. However, the seller has no obligation to clear the goods for import, pay any import duty or carry out any import customs formalities.

"运费付至⋯⋯"指卖方将货物在约定地点(如果双方已经约定了地点)交给其指定的承运人或其他人，且卖方必须签订运输合同并支付将货物运至指定目的地所需的费用。卖方的交货义务在将货物交付承运人，而非货物到达指定目的地时，即告完全履行。双方应在合同中尽可能精确地确认交货地点，在此地点风险转移至买方，以及卖方必须订立运输合同所到达的指定目的地。如果使用多个承运人将货物运至指定目的地，且买卖双方并未对具体交货地点有所约定，则合同默认风险自货物由买方交给第一承运人时转移，卖方对这一交货地点的选取具有排除买方控制的绝对选择权。如果当事方希望风险转移推迟至稍后的地点发生(例如：某海港或机场)，那么他们需要在买卖合同中明确约定这一点。由于将货物运至指定目的地的费用由卖方承担，因而当事人应尽可能准确地确定目的地中的具体地点。且卖方须在运输合同中载明这一具体的交货地点。卖方基于其运输合同中在指定目的地卸货时，如果产生了相关费用，卖方无权向买方索要，除非双方有其他约定。

CPT 术语要求卖方办理货物出口清关手续。但是，卖方没有义务办理货物进口清关手续、支付进口关税以及办理任何进口所需的任何海关手续。

D. CIP: Carriage And Insurance Paid To (… named place of destination) [运费和保险费付至(……指定目的地)]

"Carriage and Insurance Paid to" means that the seller delivers the goods to the carrier or another person nominated by himself at an agreed place (if any such place is agreed between the parties) and that the seller must contract for and pay the costs of carriage necessary to bring the goods to the named place of destination. The seller also contracts for insurance cover against the buyer's risk of loss of or damage to the goods during the carriage. The buyer should note that under CIP the seller is required to obtain insurance only on minimum cover. Should the buyer wish to have more insurance protection, it will need either to agree as much expressly with the seller or to make its own extra insurance arrangements. The seller fulfils its obligation to deliver when it hands the goods over to the carrier and not when the goods reach the place of destination. The parties are well advised to identify as precisely as possible in the contract both the place of delivery, where the risk passes to the buyer, and the named place of destination to which the seller must contract for carriage. The detail rules about this part are as same as CPT term.

CIP requires the seller to clear the goods for export, where applicable. However, the seller has no obligation to clear the goods for import, pay any import duty or carry out any import customs formalities.

"运费和保险费付至"是指卖方将货物在约定地点(如果双方已经约定了地点)交给其指定的承运人或其他人，且卖方必须签订运输合同和支付将货物运至指定目的地所需的费用，此外，卖方还必须为买方在运输途中货物的灭失或损坏风险签订保险合同。买方应注意到 CIP 术语只要求卖方投保最低限度的保险险别。如买方需要更多的保险保障，则需要与卖方明确地达成协议，或者自行做出额外的保险安排。当卖方将货物交付与承运人时而不是货物到达目的地时，卖方已经完成其交货义务。双方应在合同中尽可能精确地确认交货地点，在此地点风险转移至买方，以及卖方必须订立运输合同所到达的指定目的地。与此相关的详细规则与 CPT 术语一致。

CIP 术语要求卖方在必要时办理货物出口清关手续。但是，卖方不承担办理货物进口清关手续，支付任何进口关税，或者履行任何进口报关手续的义务。

E. DAT: Delivered At Terminal (… named terminal at port or place of destination) [运输终端交货(……指定目的港或目的地)]

"Delivered at Terminal" means that the seller delivers when the goods, once unloaded from the arriving means of transport, are placed at the disposal of the buyer at a named terminal at the named port or place of destination. "Terminal" includes any place, whether covered or not, such as a quay, warehouse, container yard or road, rail or air cargo terminal. The seller bears all risks involved in bringing the goods to and unloading them at the terminal at the named port or place of destination. The parties are well advised to specify as clearly as possible the terminal and, if possible, a specific point within the terminal at the agreed port or place of destination, as the risks to that point are for the account of the seller. The seller is advised to procure a contract of carriage that matches this choice precisely.

DAT requires the seller to clear the goods for export, where applicable. However, the seller has no obligation to clear the goods for import, pay any import duty or carry out any import customs formalities.

"运输终端交货"是指当卖方在指定的目的港或目的地指定运输终端将货物从抵达的运输工具上卸下，交给买方处置时，即完成交货。"运输终端"意味着任何地点，无论该地点是否有遮盖，例如码头、仓库、集装箱堆场或公路、铁路、空运货站。卖方应承担将货物运至指定的目的港或目的地的指定运输终端并将其卸下期间的一切风险。双方应尽可能明确地指定运输终端，如果可能，(指定)在约定的目的港或目的地的运输终端内的一个特定地点，因为(货物)到达这一地点的风险是由卖方承担。建议卖方签订一份与这样一种选择准确契合的运输合同。

DAT 术语要求卖方办理货物出口清关手续。但是，卖方没有义务办理货物进口清关手续并支付任何进口税或办理任何进口报关手续。

F. DAP: Delivered At Place (… named place of destination) [目的地交货(……指定目的地)]

"Delivered at Place" means that the seller delivers when the goods are placed at the disposal of the buyer on the arriving means of transport ready for unloading at the named place of destination. The seller bears all risks involved in bringing the goods to the named place. The parties are well advised to specify as clearly as possible the point within the agreed place of destination, as the risks to that point are for the account of the seller. The seller is advised to procure contracts of carriage that match this choice precisely. If the seller incurs costs under its contract of carriage related to unloading at the place of destination, the seller is not entitled to recover such costs from the buyer unless otherwise agreed between the parties.

DAP requires the seller to clear the goods for export, where applicable. However, the seller has no obligation to clear the goods for import, pay any import duty or carry out any import customs formalities.

"目的地交货"是指卖方在指定的目的地将置于抵达的运输工具上且可供卸载的货物交给买方处置，即完成交货。卖方须承担货物运至指定目的地的一切风险。双方应尽可能明确地指定目的地，因为(货物)到达这一地点的风险是由卖方承担。建议卖方签订恰好匹配该种选择的运输合同。如果卖方按照运输合同承受了货物在目的地的卸货费用，那么除非双方达成一致，卖方无权向买方追讨该笔费用。

DAP 术语要求应由卖方办理货物的出口清关手续，但卖方没有义务办理货物的进口清关手续，支付任何进口税或者办理任何进口海关手续。

G. DDP: Delivered Duty Paid (… named place of destination) [完税后交货(……指定目的地]

"Delivered Duty Paid" means that the seller delivers the goods when the goods are placed at the disposal of the buyer, cleared for import on the arriving means of transport ready for unloading at the named place of destination. The seller bears all the costs and risks involved in bringing the goods to the place of destination and has an obligation to clear the goods not only for export but also for import, to pay any duty for both export and import and to carry out all customs formalities. The parties are well advised to specify as clearly as possible the point within the agreed place of destination, as the costs and risks to that point are for the account of the seller. The seller is advised to procure contracts of carriage that match this choice precisely. If the seller incurs costs under its contract of carriage related to unloading at the place of destination, the seller is not entitled to recover such costs from the buyer unless otherwise agreed between the parties. Any VAT or other taxes payable upon import are for the seller's account unless expressly agreed otherwise in the sales contract. DDP represents the maximum obligation for the seller.

"完税后交货"是指卖方在指定的目的地将仍处于抵达的运输工具上，但已完成进口清关手续，且可供卸载的货物交由买方处置时，即完成交货。卖方承担将货物运至指定的目的地的一切风险和费用，并有义务完成货物出口、进口清关，支付所有的出口和进口关税及费用，以及办理一切海关手续。双方应尽可能明确地指定目的地，因为(货物)到达这一地点的费用和风险是由卖方承担。建议卖方在签订的运输合同中也正好符合上述选择的地点。如果卖方按照运输合同承受了货物在目的地的卸货费用，那么除非双方达成一致，卖方无权向买方追讨该笔费用。任何增值税或其他进口时需要支付的税项由卖方承担，合同另有约定的除外。DDP 术语是卖方承担责任最大的术语。

H. FAS: Free Alongside Ship (… named port of shipment) [船边交货(……指定装运港)]

"Free Alongside Ship" means that the seller delivers when the goods are placed alongside the vessel (e.g., on a quay or a barge) nominated by the buyer at the named port of shipment. The risk of loss of or damage to the goods passes when the goods are alongside the ship, and the buyer bears all costs from that moment onwards. The parties are well advised to specify as clearly as possible the loading point at the named port of shipment, as the costs and risks to that point are for the account of the seller and these costs and associated handling charges may vary according to the practice of the port. The seller is required either to deliver the goods alongside the ship or to procure goods already so delivered for shipment. The reference to "procure" here caters for multiple sales down a chain ("string sales"), particularly common in the commodity trades.

FAS requires the seller to clear the goods for export, where applicable. However, the seller has no obligation to clear the goods for import, pay any import duty or carry out any import customs formalities.

"船边交货"是指当卖方在指定的装运港将货物交到买方指定的船边(例如码头上或驳船上)时，即完成交货。货物交到船边时起，货物灭失或损坏的风险转移，并且由买方承担所有费用。双方应当尽可能明确地指定在指定装运港的装货地点，因为到这一地点的费用与风险由卖方承担，且这些费用及相关的处理费用，可能因为港口作业习惯而不同。卖方须在船边交付货物或者实现货物如此的交付装运。这里所谓的"procure(实现或完成)"迎合了链式销售，在商品贸易中十分普遍。

FAS 术语要求卖方在需要时办理货物出口清关手续。但是，卖方没有任何义务办理货物进口清关、支付任何进口税或者办理任何进口海关手续。

I. FOB: Free On Board (… named port of shipment)

"Free on Board" means that the seller delivers the goods on board the vessel nominated by the buyer at the named port of shipment or procures the goods already so delivered. The risk of loss of or damage to the goods passes when the goods are on board the vessel, and the buyer bears all costs from that moment onwards. The seller is required either to deliver the goods on board the vessel or to procure goods already so delivered for shipment. FOB requires the seller to clear the goods for export, where applicable. However, the seller has no obligation to clear the goods for import, pay any import duty or carry out any import customs formalities.

"船上交货"是指卖方在指定的装运港将货物交至买方指定的船上或者实现货物的如此交付。货物装上船时起，货物灭失或损坏的风险转移，并且由买方承担所有费用。货物灭失或损坏的风险买方将承担货物灭失或损坏造成的所有风险。卖方须将货物交至船上或者实现货物如此的交付装运。FOB 术语要求卖方负责办理货物出口清关手续。但是，卖方无义务办理货物进口清关手续、缴纳进口关税或是办理任何进口报关手续。

J. CFR: Cost And Freight (… named port of destination) [成本加运费(……指定目的港)]

"Cost and Freight" means that the seller delivers the goods on board the vessel or procures the goods already so delivered. The risk of loss of or damage to the goods passes when the goods are on board the vessel. The seller must contract for and pay the costs and freight necessary to bring the goods to the named port of destination. The seller fulfils its obligation to deliver when it hands the goods over to the carrier in the manner specified in the chosen rule and not when the goods reach the place of destination.

This rule has two critical points, because risk passes and costs are transferred at different places. The parties are well advised to identify as precisely as possible the point at the agreed port of destination, as the costs to that point are for the account of the seller. The seller is advised to procure contracts of carriage that match this choice precisely. If the seller incurs costs under its contract of carriage related to unloading at the specified point at the port of destination, the seller is not entitled to recover such costs from the buyer unless otherwise agreed between the parties.

The seller is required either to deliver the goods on board the vessel or to procure goods already so delivered for shipment. In addition, the seller is required either to make a contract of carriage or to procure such a contract. CFR requires the seller to clear the goods for export, where applicable. However, the seller has no obligation to clear the goods for import, pay any import duty or carry out any import customs formalities.

"成本加运费"是指卖方将货物交至船上或者实现货物的如此交付。货物装上船时起，货物灭失或损坏的风险转移。卖方必须签订合同，并支付将货物运至指定的目的港的必要成本和运费。卖方的交货义务在将货物交付承运人，而非货物到达指定目的地时，即告完全履行。

本规则有两个关键点，因为风险转移地和运费转移地是不同的。双方应尽可能精确地确认指定目的港的特定地点，因为到达此地点的运费由卖方承担。建议卖方在签订的运输合同中也正好符合上述选择的地点。如果卖方按照运输合同承受了货物在目的港的卸货费用，那么除非双方达成一致，卖方无权向买方追讨该笔费用。如果因买方原因致使运输合同与卸货点基于目的港发生关系，那么除非双方达成一致，否则卖方无权从买方处收回这些费用。

卖方须将货物交至船上或者实现货物如此的交付装运。另外，卖方必须签订运输合同或获得这类协议。CFR 术语要求卖方办理出口清关手续。但是，卖方无义务为货物办理进口清关、支付进口关税或者完成任何进口地海关的报关手续。

K. CIF: Cost Insurance And Freight (… named port of destination) [成本、保险加运费(……指定目的港)]

"Cost, Insurance and Freight" means that the seller delivers the goods on board the vessel or procures the goods already so delivered. The risk of loss of or damage to the goods passes when the goods are on board the vessel. The seller must contract for and pay the costs and freight necessary to bring the goods to the named port of destination. The seller also contracts for insurance cover against the buyer's risk of loss of or damage to the goods during the carriage. The buyer should note that under CIF the seller is required to obtain insurance only on minimum cover. Should the buyer wish to have more insurance protection, it will need either to agree as much expressly with the seller or to make its own extra insurance arrangements. The seller fulfils its obligation to deliver when it hands the goods over to the carrier in the manner specified in the chosen rule and not when the goods reach the place of destination.

This rule has two critical points, because risk passes and costs are transferred at different places. The parties are well advised to identify as precisely as possible the point at the agreed port of destination, as the costs to that point are for the account of the seller. The seller is advised to procure contracts of carriage that match this choice precisely. If the seller incurs costs under its contract of carriage related to unloading at the specified point at the port of destination, the seller is not entitled to recover such costs from the buyer unless otherwise agreed between the parties.

The seller is required either to deliver the goods on board the vessel or to procure goods already so delivered for shipment. In addition the seller is required either to make a contract of carriage or to procure such a contract. CIF requires the seller to clear the goods for export, where applicable. However, the seller has no obligation to clear the goods for import, pay any import duty or carry out any import customs formalities.

"成本、保险费加运费"指卖方将货物装上船或者实现货物的如此交付。货物灭失或损坏的风险在货物于装运港装船时转移。卖方须自行订立运输合同，支付将货物运至指定目的港的必要成本和运费。此外，卖方还必须为买方在运输途中货物的灭失或损坏风险签订保险合同。买方应注意到 CIF 术语只要求卖方投保最低限度的保险险别。如买方需要更多的保险保障，则需要与卖方明确地达成协议，或者自行做出额外的保险安排。卖方须在向承运方移交货物之时而非在货物抵达目的地时，卖方的交货义务在将货物交付承运人，而非货物到达指定目的地时，即告完全履行。

本规则有两个关键点，因为风险转移地和运费转移地是不同的。双方应尽可能精确地确认指定目的港的特定地点，因为到达此地点的运费由卖方承担。建议卖方在签订的运输合同中也正好符合上述选择的地点。如果卖方按照运输合同承受了货物在目的港的卸货费用，那么除非双方达成一致，卖方无权向买方追讨该笔费用。如果因买方原因致使运输合同与卸货点基于目的港发生关系，那么除非双方达成一致，否则卖方无权从买方处收回这些费用。

卖方须将货物交至船上或者实现货物如此的交付装运。另外，卖方必须签订运输合同或获得这类协议。CIF 术语要求卖方办理出口清关手续。但是，卖方无义务为货物办理进口清关、支付进口关税或者完成任何进口地海关的报关手续。卖方必须将货物送至船上或者(由中间销售商)承接已经交付的货物并运送到目的地。除此之外，卖方一个运输合同或者提供这类的协议。术语要求卖方在适用的情况下办理货物出口清关手续。然而，卖方没有义务办理货物进口清关手续，缴纳任何进口关税或办理进口海关手续。

2. Offer (发盘)

(1)　Definition of An Offer (发盘的定义)

An offer refers to a proposal made by one party to another willing to enter into a contract on the terms and conditions stated, in which the seller not only quotes the terms of price but also indicates all necessary terms of sales for the buyer's consideration and acceptance, just as: The name of the goods, Quality, Quantity, Price, Time of Shipment, Terms of Payment and so on. In other words, it refers to trading terms put forward by offerers to offerees, on which the offerers are willing to conclude business with the offerees.

An offer becomes effective when it reaches the offeree. It may be withdrawn if the withdrawal reaches the offeree before or at the same time as the offer even if it is irrevocable. Until a contract is concluded an offer may be revoked if the revocation reaches the offeree before he has dispatched an acceptance. However, an offer cannot be revoked: ① if it indicates, whether stating a fixed time for acceptance or otherwise, that it is irrevocable; ② if it was reasonable for the offeree to rely on the offer as being irrevocable and the offeree has acted in reliance on the offer. An offer, even if it is irrevocable, is terminated when a rejection reaches the offerer.

发盘是指由一方向另一方提出的愿意按约定的条件和条款订立合同的建议，卖方不仅要报价格条款，也要表明一切必需的交易条件以供买方考虑和接受，就如货物的名称、品质、数量、价格、装运时间、支付条件等。换句话说，它指的是发盘人向受盘人提出的交易条件。按此条件，发盘人愿意与受盘人进行交易。

发盘于送达受盘人时生效。如果撤回通知书于发盘送达受盘人之前或同时，这项发盘即使是不可撤销的，也可以撤回。在未订立合同之前，如果撤销通知于受盘人发出接受通知之前送达受盘人，发盘可以撤销。但在下列情况下，发价不得撤销：①发价写明接受发价的期限或以其他方式表示发价是不可撤销的；②被发价人有理由信赖该项发价是不可撤销的，而且被发价人已本着对该项发价的信赖行事。一旦发盘，即使是不可撤销的，于拒绝通知送达发盘人时终止。

(2)　Types of Offers (发盘的类型)

There are two kinds of offers: one is the firm offer, the other is the non-firm offer.

A firm offer means the offerer can't withdraw or make any changes to the offer during the period of time stipulated in the offer. The key feature is that a firm offer has binding force. Once the firm offer is made, the offerer cannot refuse to sell the goods he offers if it is accepted by the offeree. Major contents of an firm-offer: ①The offer must be written clearly that the offer is firm or irrevocable; ②All necessary terms of sale; ③The offer state the time of validity. The commonly used expressions of validity time in firm offer are as follows:

-Subject to your reply reaching us by (before)…;

-Subject to your reply (acceptance) here within …days;

-This offer is firm (open, valid, good) for… days.

A non-firm offer is also called a free offer, which means a proposal made by offerer willing to sale on certain conditions with reservations. It has no binding force upon the offerer and the offeree. The major feature of non-firm offer is that the offerer is free from any obligations. In a non-firm offer the offerer need not state the complete terms of sale and the time limit clearly. An offer used the following expressions is a non-firm offer:

-Without engagement;

-Subject to prior sale;

-All quotations are subject to our final confirmation unless otherwise stated;

-Our offer is subject to approval of export license.

发盘有两种：一种是实盘；另一种是虚盘。

实盘是指一经发出，在发盘规定的期限内，发盘人不得撤销或进行随意更改发盘的内容。发盘的关键特征就是具有约束力。一旦发出实盘，如果被受盘人接受则发盘人不能拒绝按发盘中提出的条件将货物出售给受盘人。实盘的主要内容包括：①必须清楚地写明此发盘是实盘或不可撤销；②一些交易必需的条件；③发盘中写明此发盘的有效期。实盘有效期的常用表示方法如下：

——以你方在……(前)回复为准；

——在……天内以你方回复(接受)为准；

——本发盘……天有效。

虚盘也称不受约束的发盘，是指发盘人有保留地愿按照一定条件达成交易的表示。它对发盘人和受盘人均没有约束力。虚盘的主要功能是要约人不受任何义务。发盘人不必在虚盘中明确地写明交易的所有条件和时限的规定。出现下列一类词句者，皆为虚盘：

——不负任何责任；

——有权先售；

——所作报价，除特别注明外，须经我方确认后方能生效；

——出口许可证准许签证，我方报价才有效。

3. Counteroffer (还盘)

Definition of Counter-offer (还盘的定义)

A reply to an offer, which doesn't agree with any or some of the terms of an offer, is a rejection of the offer and constitutes a counter-offer. Counter-offer means that the offeree doesn't accept the offer wholly and put forward some additions, modifications, limitations, etc. as to the basic terms and conditions contained in the offer. Once a counter offer is made, the original offer made by the offerer loses its effectiveness.

"The United Nations Convention on Contracts for the International Sale of Goods" stipulates:

①   A reply which purports to be an acceptance but contains additional, limitations or other modifications is a rejection of the offer and constitutes a counter-offer.

②   However, a reply to an offer which purports to be an acceptance bit contains additional or different terms which do not materially alter the terms of the offer constitutes an acceptance, unless the offerer, without undue delay, objects orally to the discrepancy or dispatches a notice to that effect. If he doesn't, so object the terms of the offer with the modifications contained in the acceptance.

③   Additional or different terms relating among other things, to the price, payment, quality and quantity of the goods, place and time of delivery, extent of one party's liability to the other or the settlement of disputes are considered to alter the terms of the offer materially.

In the counter-offer, the offeree may show his disagreement to the certain term and conditions and state his own idea instead. Such alterations, no matter how slight they may appear to be, signify that business has to be negotiated on the renewed basis. After the offerer receives the offeree's counter-offer, he has the full right of acceptance or refusal. In the latter case, the offerer may make another counter-offer of his own. This process can go on for many a round till the business is finalized or called off.

对发盘做出回复，但不接受发盘中提出的任何或部分条件的答复，即为拒绝该项发盘并构成还盘。还盘是指受盘人不能完全接受发盘的内容，提出了一些补充、修改、限制等基本条款和条件。一经还盘，原发盘即失效。

《联合国国际货物销售合同公约》对还盘的规定如下：

①   包含了附加条件、限制和其他修改是对发盘的拒绝，构成了还盘。

②   但是，对发盘表示接受但附有添加或不同条件的答复，如所附的添加或不同条件在实质上并不变更该项发盘的条件，除发盘人在不过分迟延的期间内以口头或书面通知反对其间的差异外，仍构成接受。如果发盘人不做出这种反对，合同的条件就以该项发盘的条件以及接受通知内所附的更改为准。

③   有关货物价格、付款、货物质量和数量、交货地点和时间、一方当事人对另一方当事人的赔偿责任范围或解决争端等的添加或不同条件，均视为在实质上变更发盘的条件。

在还盘中，受盘人会表明他对某些特定条件和条款的分歧并写明自己的建议。不管这种变更看似多么微小，它都意味着交易应按新的条件磋商。发盘人收到受盘人的还盘，他也完全有权力接受或拒绝。在后一种情况下，发盘人可能会做出另一个他自己的还盘。这个过程可能要持续多轮一直交易达成或取消。

4. Acceptance (接受)

Definition of Acceptance (接受的定义)

Acceptance is a statement made by or other conduct of the offerees indicating unconditional consent to an offer. A contract is concluded once the offer is accepted. If the offer is a firm offer, a deal is concluded after acceptance. If the offer is a non-firm offer, a deal is not concluded until the acceptance is confirmed by the buyers or sellers.

In a letter for acceptance, all the necessary terms and conditions may need a further confirmation/check from both sides. To make an effective acceptance, the offeree should do all of the following: ①The acceptance should be given by the offeree; ②The acceptance should accept all of the contents of the previous offer; ③The acceptance should be given within the validity of the previous irrevocable offer; ④The acceptance should reach the offerer. An acceptance of an offer becomes effective at the moment the indication of assent reaches the offerer.

接受指的是受盘人声明或做出其他行为表示无条件同意一项发盘。受盘人声明或做出其他行为表示同意一项发盘，即是接受，缄默或不行动本身不等于接受。发盘接受以后，合同随即达成。如果发的是实盘，则在接受后合同成立。如果发的是虚盘，则直至接受经买方或卖方确认后合同才成立。

在接受所有必要的条件和条款可能还需双方进一步确认/检查。一个有效的接受应包含以下要件：①还盘必须由受盘人做出；②接受必须对发盘中的所有内容表示同意；③接受必须在发盘的有效期内做出；④接受必须送达发盘人。发盘人收到受盘人表示接受发盘的通知书时，接受开始生效。

Section 2　Correspondence

1. Writing Skills

An efficient quotation or offer includes the following parts:

(1)　An expression of thanks for the inquiry, if there is previous inquiry.

(2)　Name of goods, quality, quantity and specifications.

(3)　Details of prices, discounts and terms of payment.

(4)　Clear indication of what the prices cover, e.g. packing, transport, agents' commission, insurance.

(5)　An undertaking as to packing and date of delivery.

(6)　An expression of hope that the quotation will be accepted.

A letter of counter offer is usually structured as the following parts:

(1)　The first paragraph is to acknowledge the arrival of the offer and say thanks.

(2)　The middle part is where you state why you can not accept the offer completely and put forward your new terms and conditions.

(3)　At last, give your hope for a prompt reply and business success.

An acceptance is generally made up of three parts as follows:

(1)　To acknowledge the arrival of the offer or counter offer, and say thanks.

(2)　To inform them of the confirmation.

(3)　To express the hope.

2. Sample Letters

Letter 1 (A Non-firm Offer)

Zhejiang Cereal, Oils & Foodstuffs Imp. & Exp. Corp.

102, Fengqi Rd. Hangzhou 310006, Zhejiang

March 19, 2014

Mulsen Trading Co., Ltd.

3823 56th Avenue S. W. Seattle, Washington 98116 U.S.A

Re: GREEN BEANS

Dear Sirs,

In reply to your letter of March 10, we have pleasure in offering, subject to[1] our final confirmation, the captioned goods as follows:

Commodity: Green Beans

　　　　　　　Hangzhou Origin, 2013 Crop

Quantity:　300 metric tons

Price:　　 at US$1500-Per metric ton CIF Seattle

Packing:　 in ordinary second-hand gunny bags[2]

Shipment:　in May, 2014

Payment:　 by irrevocable L/C[3], payable by draft at sight[4]

We hope this offer will be of interest to you, and look forward to hearing from you.

Yours faithfully,

Zhou Yanming

Zhou Yanming

Manager

Export Department

Letter 2 (A Firm Offer)

Dear Sirs,

IBM CPU 80586

We confirm your letter of 10th August, asking us to make you an offer for the captioned

personal computers, FOB Xingang. Now we are making you a firm offer as follows:

Commodity: IBM Personal Computer

Specification: CPU 80586

Quantity: 200 sets

Packing: Each set is wrapped[5] in a polybag[6] and packed in a standard export cardboard carton[7] lined with[8] foam[9].

Shipment: September/October, 2014

Payment: by confirmed, irrevocable L/C payable by draft at sight to be opened 30 days before the date of shipment.

This offer is subject to your reply here on or before 5th August. Please note that we have given you our most favorable price and we trust that the above will be acceptable to you.

We highly appreciate your early reply.

Yours faithfully,

Letter 3 (A Counter Offer)

Dear Sirs,

We thank you for your quotation of February 3 for 1000 sets of Panasonic 2188 Color TV. We find your price as well as delivery date satisfactory, however we would give our suggestion of an alteration of your payment terms.

Our past purchase of other household electrical appliances[10] from you have been paid as a rule[11] by confirmed, irrevocable letter of credit sight. On this basis, it has indeed cost us a great deal. From the moment to open credit till the time our buyer pays us, the tie-up[12] of our fund lasts about four months. Under the present circumstances, this question is particularly taxing[13] owing to the tight[14] money condition and unprecedented[15] high bank interest.

In view of our long business relations and our amicable[16] cooperation prospects, we suggest that you accept either "cash against documents on arrival of goods[17]" or "drawing on us at 60 day's sight[18]".

Your first priority[19] to the consideration of the above request and an early favorable reply will be highly appreciated.

Yours faithfully,

Letter 4 (An Acceptance)

Dear Sirs,

We confirm having your email of May 17, asking us to make a 10% reduction in our price for Men's Shirts.

Much to our regret, we find it intolerable to comply with your request because ours is the best possible price if you take the quality into consideration. However, in order to develop our market in your place, we have decided to accept your counter as an exceptional case.

We hope you will send us your formal order by return, which we will execute with our best attention.

Yours very truly,

3. Notes to Text

(1) subject to 易受……的；受制于……；以……为条件

The plan is fulfilled subject to the manager's approval. 实施这项计划须得到经理的同意。

The offer is subject to our final confirmation. 此报盘以我方最后确认为准。

(2) ordinary second-hand gunny bag 普通旧麻袋

(3) irrevocable L/C 不可撤销信用证

confirmed L/C 保兑信用证

transferable and divisible L/C 可转让与可分割信用证

revolving L/C 循环信用证

back to back L/C 背对背信用证

reciprocal L/C 对开信用证

(4) draft at sight = sight draft 即期汇票

即期信用证：L/C available by draft at sight; L/C payable against draft at sight;

L/C at sight; sight L/C

远期信用证：usance L/C; time L/C; term L/C

见票 30 天议付远期信用证：L/C available by draft at 30 days after sight;

(usance/time/term) L/C at 30 days after sight;

(usance/time/term) L/C at 30 days;

30days (usance/time/term) L/C

(5) wrap 包；缠绕；用……包裹(或包扎、覆盖等)；掩护

(6) polybag 塑料袋

(7) standard export cardboard carton 标准出口纸板箱

(8) line with 以……填塞

(9) foam 泡沫；泡沫塑料；泡沫材料

(10) household electrical appliances 家用电器

(11) as a rule = usually 通常

As a rule, we give our agents 3% of commission. 通常我们给代理商 3%的佣金。

(12) tie-up of funds 资金占用

(13) taxing 难以负担的，使人感到有压力的

Such an amount is taxing for a firm of moderate means. 这样一笔数额对一个中等财力的商户来说是有压力的。

(14) tight (钱、商品等)紧的，难得到的

tight money 银根紧

(15) unprecedented 空前的

As a result of energy crisis, the price of oil is unprecedentedly high. 由于能源危机，是有价格空前高涨。

(16) amicable = friendly 有好的

(17) cash against documents on arrival of goods 货到后凭单付款，简称 CAD (Cash Against Documents)，凭单付款是从买方的角度说的，即买方付款是以卖方提供单据为条件。

(18) drawing on us at 60 day's sight 开出见票 60 天付款的汇票向我们收款

As agreed, we are drawing on you at sight against your purchase of sample lot. 按照商定，对你方所购样货我们开出即期汇票向你方索款。

(19) priority 优先

top priority，first priority 最优先考虑的事

give priority to 给……以优先权；优先考虑……

enjoy priority in 在……方面享有优先权

4. Useful expressions

(1) Voluntary Offers 主动、自愿报价

① 去年，我方荣幸地向贵方提供……，相信贵方十分满意。现函告贵方我方能提供……(现货)

Last year we had the pleasure of supplying you with…and trust that it has given you every satisfaction. We are writing to inform you that we can supply (from stock)…

② 我们了解你方市场对……需求强劲，借此良机，附上我方第……号报价单，供你方考虑。

We understand that there is a good demand for … in your market, and take this opportunity of enclosing our Quotation No. … for your consideration.

③ 我们希望扩大在你方市场的……(产品)销售量，冒昧寄上我方第……号报价单，希望贵方将它推荐给可能的买主。

We wish to extend the sale of … to your market and take the liberty of sending you herewith our Quotation No. … in the hope that you will introduce it to prospective buyers at your end.

(2) Replies to Inquires 答复询盘

① 根据要求，现我方就如下货物向贵方报价，以我方最后确认为准。

As requested, we are offering you the following subject to our final confirmation.

②　再次收到老朋友的来函，非常高兴。是的，我们仍生产著名的……(产品)。十分高兴告诉你，我们的货物质量有了提高，而且不提价。

It is always a pleasure to hear from an old friend again. Yes, we are still making our famous … and pleased to tell you that we have been able to improve their quality without any increase in price.

③　兹复你方……月……日来函，很遗憾我方不能向你方供应与样品质量相同，每吨……(价)……产品。但是，我们准备……

In reply to your letter of … we regret that it is impossible for us to supply you with … in the quality of the sample quoted, at … per ton. However, we are prepared to …

(3)　Inability to Supply　无力供应

①　我方无法提供你方现在所需货物，甚歉。

We very much regret that we are unable to supply that you require just now.

②　我方歉难供应你方所要求的小批数量。

We regret that we are unable to supply you with the small quantity you require.

③　由于制造厂商大量承约，目前无法满足你方需求，十分遗憾。一旦我方可以供货，就立即与你方联系。

Owing to the heavy commitments of our manufacturers, we regret that we are unable to meet your requirements for the time being, however, we will contact you as soon as we are in a position to offer.

(4)　Sending Samples, Catalogues and Descriptive Literature　寄送样品、目录和说明书

①　现另封邮寄一包裹，内装……相信这些样品将使你方对我产品的优异质量确信无疑。

We are sending you under separate cover a parcel containing … We trust that our samples will convince you of the fine quality of our products.

②　为了便利你方促销我方产品，现航邮寄上一件小样品，并随函附上一份有关的说明书。

To facilitate your work in pushing the sales of our products, we are sending you by airmail a small sample. A copy of the relevant descriptive leaflet is enclosed.

③　现随函寄上你方……月……日来信中所需的我方产品目录一份。

We are enclosing a copy of our catalog as requested in your letter of …

(5)　Inquiry Concerning Special Offers　询问特殊报价

①　请告贵公司能给多少特价优待。

Please inform us what special offer you can make us.

②　以……数量为基础，贵公司能给特价吗？

Can you make us a special offer based on a quantity of …?

③ 为介绍贵公司的产品进入我方市场，贵公司能否给予特别价格？

Can you make us any special offers for the purpose of introducing your products to our market?

(6) Validity of Offer 发价有效期

① 此发盘为实盘，以你方不迟与 4 日复到为准。

This offer is firm subject to your reply reaching us not later than the 14th.

② 若现行原料价格不变，我方价格是有效的。

The prices are valid only if the current prices of raw materials do not change.

③ 如 5 日内不接受，该盘撤销。

This offer must be withdrawn if not accepted within five days.

Section 3　Dialogues

Dialogue 1

To tell you the truth, we are greatly surprised at the price

After he got the offer from an European Trade Company, Mr. Linger is talking about the price with Nobat, a representative from the company.

Linger: To tell you the truth, we are greatly surprised at the prices you offer us. We had expected much lower prices.

Nobat: This year's prices are higher than last year's. But they are still lower than the quotations you can get elsewhere.

Linger: I'm afraid I can't agree with you there. I can show you other quotations that are lower than yours.

Nobat: When you compare the prices, you must take everything into consideration. Our products are of high quality, while the quotations you get from other sources are for goods of ordinary quality.

Linger: I grant that yours are of better quality. But still we don't think we can succeed in persuading our clients to buy at such high prices.

Nobat: If I were you, I wouldn't worry about that. Taking everything into consideration, I can assure you the prices we offer are very favorable. I don't think you'll have any difficulty in pushing sales.

Linger: But the market prices are changing frequently. How can I be sure that the market will not fall before the arrival of goods at our port?

Nobat: No, I don't see that you can. It's up to you to decide.

Linger: If you can promise delivery before July, 2006, I'll be able to decide. It looks as if the market won't go down until then.

Nobat: Well, delivery in August is the best we can do for you. The demand for our products has kept rising. If you made your inquiry today, even August delivery wouldn't be possible. But since you made your inquiry three days ago, we'll try to make delivery in August.

Linger: How long will your offer hold good?

Nobat: For three days, as usual. I hope you'll make up your mind soon.

Dialogue 2

Can we meet each other half way?

Mr. Smith a textile dealer from London is met by Ms. Yang in the showroom. Looking at the samples, Mr. Smith negotiates business with Ms. Yang.

Smith: What do you have there, Ms. Yang?

Yang: Some of our new products. Would you like to have a look at the patterns?

Smith: Yes, please.

Yang: Here they are, Mr. Smith.

Smith: I like this printed poplin. How much is it a yard?

Yang: 45 pence per yard, CIF London.

Smith: Your price is higher than I can accept. Could you come down a little?

Yang: What would you suggest?

Smith: Could you make it 40 pence per yard, CIF London?

Yang: I'm afraid we can't .This is the best price we can quote.

Smith: Let's leave that for the time being.

Yang: Are you interested in our pongee?

Smith: Yes. Please show me the latest product.

Yang: Here it is.

Smith: The quality is very good. But nowadays nylon is pushing this material out.

Yang: I don't think so. We've sold a lot this month.

Smith: Well, anyway, I'll book a trial order. The price?

Yang: Same as we offered last time.

Smith: What about the quantity?

Yang: 200 pieces for September shipment.

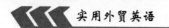

Smith: All right. I'll take the lot.

Yang: How about printed poplin, then?

Smith: There's still a gap of 5 pence. Will you give me a trade discount?

Yang: Sorry. Can we meet each other half way?

Smith: What do you mean?

Yang: Let's close the deal at 43 pence per yard, CIF London.

Smith: You drive a hard bargain, but I'll accept this time.

Yang: We will provide good service and quality.

Smith: That will be deeply appreciated.

Yang: Shall I make out the contract for you to sign tomorrow?

Smith: Fine.

Dialogue 3

The fact is that your price is too high to be workable.

Mr. Jurgen Henke, a representative from a German machinery company, is talking with Mr. Wang into accepting the price for the drillers.

Henke: I'm glad that we've had good discussions about the technical side. Shall we bring in the commercial side of it now?

Wang: Yes. But your price is so high that we can hardly make a counteroffer.

Henke: It pays to buy good machines. Better quality usually means a higher price.

Wang: You're right there.

Henke: You probably know that our drillers are by far the best in Europe, and probably, in the world.

Wang: Yes. And your price is by far the highest.

Henke: It's the quality that counts. Our driller steel is far superior to that used by the Japanese.

Wang: It's no secret that we've had quotations from Japan for similar machines. If your price were just slightly higher, there wouldn't be any problem at all. The fact is that your price is too high to be workable.

Henke: You should take into consideration on our machines' superior quality.

Wang: That we have.

Henke: What's more, our design and technology are completely up-to-date. You'll be assured of efficient service for years to come.

Wang: That's precisely why we prefer to order from your company.

Henke: Well then, can you give us an idea what price you consider workable?

Wang: We hope that you'll take the initiative and bridge the gap.

Henke: Well, well. We'll reduce the price by 5%. I hope this sets the ball rolling.

Wang: I'm afraid the ball can hardly roll very far. Certainly it's a step forward. But the gap is still too wide. I'd suggest another 10%.

Henke: Oh, I'm afraid that won't do. It simply can't stand such a big cut.

Wang: If that's the case, I'm afraid we'll have to go elsewhere.

Henke: Well, I'm not in a position to agree to such a big reduction. I have to get in touch with my head office and let you know their decision in a day or two. Will that be okay with you?

Wang: OK. I hope we can both get something out of this.

Notes

1. to push sales of 推销

2. It's up to sb. to do sth. 轮到某人做某事。

3. go down 下跌

4. make delivery 交货

5. I can't agree with you there. 在这一点上我不能同意您的看法。

6. I grant that yours are of better quality. 我承认你们的质量比较好。

7. How long will your offer hold good? 贵方报价有效期多长？

8. manager 经理，主任，公司内中层领导的职衔

e.g.

general manager 总经理，总主管

export manager 出口(部)经理

international sales manager 国际销售(部)经理

regional manager 区域经理

quality control manager 品质管理主任

9. pattern (s) 式样，样品

10. printed poplin 印花府绸

11. Let's leave that for the time being. 暂时把这个问题搁一下。

12. pongee 类似茧绸的织物(如人造丝等)

13. nylon 尼龙

14. a trial order 试订(货单)

15. lot 批，表示交易数量的一个名称

16. trade discount 同业折扣。对本行业不同买主所给予的折扣生产企业对其产品的经销商、批发商及零售商等以及批发商对零售商所给的折扣都是同业折扣。

17. Can we meet each other half way? 我们能折中一下吗?

18. to drive a hard bargain (over sth.) (对某事)拼命讨价还价。

19. to talk into 说服

20. It's the quality that counts. 重要的是质量

21. set the ball rolling. 使(某活动、谈话)开始起来

22. It simply can't stand such a big cut. 哪能经得住这么大的削价。

23. I'm afraid we'll have to go elsewhere. 恐怕我们得转向他处(进货)。

Section 4　Exercises

1. Translate the following sentences into English:

(1)　应你方要求，我们很高兴作如下报价，5 月 30 日前复到有效。

(2)　上述价格是我们能报的最低价格。

(3)　除非另有说明或协议，所有价格为净价不含佣金。

(4)　兹回复您 6 月 10 日信函，我们很遗憾你方价格过高不能接受。

(5)　这超出了我们的目标价。

(6)　如增加订购数量，价格还可以进一步优惠。

(7)　感谢您 3 月 29 日的回复，很遗憾你们觉得我们报的价格过高。

(8)　考虑到我公司产品品质卓越，对于我们来说几乎不可能再降价了。

2. Translate the following sentences into Chinese:

(1)　We are making the following offer, subject to our final confirmation.

(2)　We could give you a special discount of 5% if the quantity up to 1×40' FCL.

(3)　You can be certain that our price is really competitive.

(4)　Your final price is 10% higher than your competitors.

(5)　Business is not possible unless you make a reduction of 5% in our quotation.

(6)　In view of the fact that we have concluded transactions with all other customers at the price, we cannot reduce it any further.

(7)　We make this allowance because we would like to do the first business with you, but we must stress that it is the utmost that we can help you.

(8)　If 10% discount provided, we'll consider placing one more 40' FCL.

3. Translate the following letter into English:

史密斯先生：

　　感谢您的 5 月 10 日的询盘。应你方要求，现报盘如下：

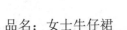

品名：女士牛仔裙

价格：每件 10 美元，FOB 上海

装运日期：不迟于 2014 年 8 月 30 日

支付方式：50%价款以电汇方式预付，其余 50%凭提单副本支付。

由于市场需求不断增长，价格也即将上涨，所以我们希望贵公司能尽早做决定。

期待您的回复。

······ 谨上

4. Translate the following letter into Chinese:

Dear Mr. …,

Thank you for your quotation of June 4.

Although we are interested in your products, we very much regret to find your price is so high that we have almost no profit. As you know, the table lamps manufactured by other Chinese factories are of good quality and the price is about 10% lower than yours. So we hope you can reduce your price by 5% so as to stand up to the competition.

Please take it into serious consideration and your early reply will be appreciated.

Yours faithfully,

5. Compose a dialogue based on the following situation:

Mr. Brown, the manager of a large textiles company in Germany, is interested in Chinese silk scarf. He hopes to get an offer for 1000 pieces of silk scarf.

Mr. Yang, a salesman from AAA Co., in China, makes an offer as request.

But Mr. Brown asks for a 10% reduction on price.

Finally they both accept 5% discount on price.

Section 5　Solution to Problem

1. Making friends and making profits

It is said in Economics: "Maximizing profits is always the goal of enterprise", while the great master of Management, Peter F. Drucker has ever said："The purpose of enterprise is to create a customer." What do you think of these two different views? Do they conflict with each other. Different people have different views, these two views are given by different people from different angles, there is no need to comment whose is right.

Anyway, it is commonly understood no customer no business, the development and

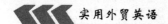

expansion of a business depends on customers, in China a saying is popular, it is "Customer is God", customer has been God, is our customer our friend yet? Obviously customers are also our friends, they are no doubt resources of our profits. From the angle of marketing, we really need to make arrangement for customer lubrication and maintenance.

2. Negotiation is an art of compromise

War is a state of armed conflict between different countries or different groups, for one group involved in the war, the aim is to eliminate the other group. Negotiation is the process of discussing something with someone in order to reach an agreement, China accession to the WTO chief negotiator, the famous diplomat Long Yongtu has even said: "Negotiation is an art of compromise." How do you see Mr. Long's view?

Negotiation, especially business negotiation, is not a war, even there is no need to contend for face and neglect substantial profit. As above mentioned, customer is God or friend, if two business associates may realize this,

one is willing to make concession for the other one, one is thoughtful and considerate of the other one, one knows the other one has to exist and make reasonable profit to survive, both parties can build mutual trust, it is easy to create win-win solution. That is why principle negotiation or value negotiation is highly praised/enthroned by most business persons all around the world.

3. Winning a deal and developing business relationship, which comes first and which comes next?

There are two sayings in China, "Haste makes waste" and "Still water runs long", they could be an analogy to business, we would better not be anxious to earn quick money, develop business relationship attentively, earn money stably, not care for gain and loss of one deal too much. In this sense, penetration pricing is probably better than skimming pricing.

4. Reasonable request, principle and flexibility

—a case of application of negotiation skills

In a business letter, the exporter re-quotes USD48.50/DOZ CIF NY to importer and insists on payment by sight L/C , and gives reasons, at the same time states validity of revised offer is 5 days from the date of writing. Exporter writes as following:

Thank you for your letter dated ×××. We are sorry to tell you that your prices are not appropriate to us. As you know, wages and materials have risen considerably these days.

We are compelled to adjust our prices to cover the increasing cost. USD48.5 per DOZ is our lowest level, which leaves us with only the smallest profit.

Although we have confidence in your integrity, our usual terms of payment by sight L/C remain unchanged in all cases with new clients. So for the time being, we regret our inability to accept your D/P terms. Maybe after several smooth and satisfactory transactions, we can consider other flexible ways.

For your information, the demand for our products has been extremely great recently. This offer is valid for 5 days and we are looking forward to receiving your order at the earliest date.

Apparently the exporter writes this letter in rational and convincing way. His request for new price and time limit of the offer stand to reason, and make importer be unable to refuse easily, he sticks to principle at the same time shows flexibility on term of payment, it may create win-win solution.

5. Does it certainly mean a firm offer if there is a time limit in the offer?

The answer is "No", according to "Convention", the basic conditions of an offer are

(1)   The offer shall be made to one or more specific persons

(2)   Contents of the offer shall be sufficiently definite, i.e., trade terms of the offer shall be complete, clear and final

(3)   The offer shall indicate the intention of the offer or to be bound in case of acceptance. This intention may be indicated by terms as "firm" offer, "offer with engagement", etc. If the offer has a restrictive condition, i.e., "subject to our final confirmation", then it's a non-firm offer regarded as an invitation for offer.

Although a firm offer usually has a time limit in it, it does not mean if only there is a time limit in a offer, the offer is certainly a firm offer. Above mentioned 3 conditions are necessary for a firm offer, especially the last one.

Unit 4

Ordering

Section 1　Introduction

What's an order? (什么是订单？)

An order is a request made by the buyer to the seller for the purchase of a specified quantity of goods, while an order is a proposal made by the seller to the buyer for the selling of certain goods. Usually, an order is a symbol of acceptance, but it may also result in an offer or an inquiry with subsequent quotations. That is to say, the form of an order can be used as a buying offer, an acceptance or a confirmation. An order is just a form to describe the commodity accurately and clearly. So when you receive an order from a customer, you need to identify what it stands for. And then, you can accept it, counter-offer it and confirm it.

According to commercial law, the buyer's order is an offer to buy and the arrangement is not legally binding until the seller has accepted the offer. After that, both parties are legally bound to honor their agreement. In international trade, the exporter may send out a firm offer or a non-firm offer. In the case of the firm offer, the importer will send out his acceptance within the time set if it meets the requirement. The business is concluded. In the case of a non-firm offer, the importer has to place an order with the exporter based on the non-firm offer. The order is considered accepted only when the exporter accepts or confirms the order.

An order may be given by letter, fax, e-mail or at a business meeting. Nowadays importers can also use printed order form which insure that no important information will be neglected.

订单是买方为要求供应具体数量的货物而向卖方提出的要求，或者卖方为出售特定的货物而向买方提出的建议。通常，订单意味着接受，但它也可能会导致发盘或对进一步报价的询盘。也就是说，订单这种形式可以作为购买货物的发盘，接受或确认成交。订单只准确和清楚地描述了商品。所以，当你收到来自客户的订单，你需要确定它代表什么。然后，你可以对订单做出接受、还盘或确认成交。

根据商法的规定，除非卖方接受订单，买方的订单是购买货物的发盘，对双方没有约束力。卖方接受订单后，协议就对双方都具有法律约束力。在国际贸易中，出口商会向进口商发实盘或虚盘。如果发的是实盘，且内容满足进口商的需求，则他会在规定的时间内做出接受，交易就达成了。如果发的是虚盘，则进口商就会依据虚盘的内容向出口商下订单。只有当出口商对此订单表示同意或确认时，这个订单才被视为接受。

订单可以用信函、传真、电子邮件形式发出，或在商务会议中下订单。现今，进口商也使用印制好的订货单，以确保不会疏漏任何重要的条件。

Section 2　Correspondence

1. Writing Skills

A letter of order is composed of the following parts:

(1)　Inform the reader of your order.

(2)　Confirm the specifics (Terms and conditions etc.)

(3)　Inform the reader of the arrangement of your order.

(4)　Urge the reader to deliver goods early.

A letter of repeat order generally is made up of three parts as follows:

(1)　Show your satisfaction for the goods shipped to you by the reader.

(2)　State repeat order for the products on the previous terms and conditions.

(3)　Hope the reader to accept early.

2. Sample Letters

Letter 1 (Placing a Purchase Order)

Purchase Order No. BD/135

Dear Sirs,

We confirm our agreement on purchase of the following goods:

Description: A—I Grade[1] Canned Beef of the following four specifications

　　　A.　225 GM net weight

　　　B.　350 GM net weight

　　　C.　425 GM net weight

　　　D.　450 GM net weight

Quantity: (case)

　　　A.　500

　　　B.　400

　　　C.　400

　　　D.　600

Packing: By standard export case[2] of 120 cans each.

Unit Price: CIF net New York per case in U.S. dollars

    A. 36.20

    B. 40.50

    C. 50.60

    D. 38.40

Payment: 100% by irrevocable letter of credit opened immediately through First National City Bank[3], N.Y., and drawn at sight.

Delivery: For item A and B, Prompt shipment

    For item C and D, One month after receipt of L/C

Shipping marks[4]: On each and every case, the following shipping mark should be stenciled[5].

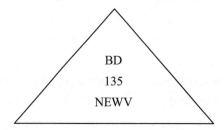

BD Co. Ltd.

Remarks[6]: In addition to the ordinary shipping documents[7], please also submit[8] Certificate of Origin for each shipment.

Letter 2 (A Repeat Order)

Dear Sirs,

    Re: Contract No. WS226-Chinese Silk Goods

We have received the captioned shipment ex S.S.[9] "Victory", and are pleased to inform that all your goods are found quite satisfactory.

As it is certain that the market is in great need of additional quantities, we wish to book with you a repeat order[10] for the following items. Other terms and conditions are the same as stated in Contract No. WS226.

Pattern[11] No.	043	175	196
Quantity	34 000 yards	36 000 yards	50 000 yards

Our urgent need of the goods requires prompt shipment, for any delay in it would cause us inconvenience. If the repeated order can't be shipped from stock, please advise us with all particulars of those available from stock.

Yours faithfully

Letter 3 (Declining an Order)

Dear Mr. Sun,

We thank you for your Order No.115 received this morning for the above goods, but regret that owing to shortage of stocks, we are unable to accept the same[12], nor can our manufacturers undertake to entertain your order for future delivery on account of the uncertainty of raw material.

We will, however, revert to[13] this matter and contact you by cable, once the supply position improves.

Meanwhile, please feel free to[14] send your specific inquiries for any other metal sheets[15] and you can rely on our best attention at all times.

3. Notes to Text

(1)　A—I Grade 甲级

(2)　standard export case 标准出口箱

(3)　First National City Bank 花旗银行，创立于 1812 年，为美国最大的商业银行之一

(4)　shipping mark 运输标志，业务中习惯称装运唛头

(5)　stencil 模板；用模板印刷

(6)　remark 备注

(7)　shipping documents 装运单据

shipping advice 装船通知	shipping agents 装运代理，发货代理人
shipping company 船运公司	shipping container 船运集装箱；集装箱
shipping order 装货单，下货纸	shipping space 舱位，载位，船位
shipping dock 装卸码头	shipping expense 装运费
shipping invoice 货物装运单	shipping notice 装船通知，装运通知
shipping process 装运手续	shipping weight (s.w.) 起运重量

(8)　submit 呈递，呈交；提交

All important problems must be submitted to the Board of Directors for discussion. 一切重要的问题都必须提交董事会讨论。

(9)　ex 从；在……交货

S.S. = S÷S，s÷s，SS，S·S，steamship

ex S.S. "Peace" 由和平轮卸下

ex S.S. "Victory" 由胜利轮装运

(10) book (place) a repeat order with sb. 向……续订；向某人买进

(11) pattern 图案，式样

(12) the same 指前面说过的事情，为避免重复用 the same，这里指订货

(13) revert to 回复，重谈

It would probably be a month before we can revert to the special quality you required. 你们所需质量的产品可能要一个月的时间才能有。

We shall revert to this matter as soon as we can supply from stock. 一旦我们有现货就来谈这件事。

(14) feel free to = do not hesitate 无约束地(做)，可译为务请

When you are in need of further quantities, please fell free to communicate with us. 当你需要更多数量的货物时，务请与我方联系。

(15) metal sheets 金属板

4. Useful expressions

(1) 很高兴随函附上一式两份我方第 AV-13 号订单，订购 10 台爱普生打印机。

We are pleased to enclose Order No.AV-13 in duplicate for 10 sets of EPSON printing machines.

(2) 非常高兴向你方订购以下商品，并希望贵方尽快发货。

We have pleasure of placing the following order with you, and hope you kindly send by fast freight.

(3) 由于我们对质量和价格都满意，现就以下货物向你方订货。

As we find both quality and prices satisfactory, we place an order with you for the following.

(4) 非常抱歉我们不能按 6 个月前的报价接收贵方的订单。

We are regretful that we are unable to accept your order at the prices we quoted six months ago.

(5) 因我方急需此货，请尽力将我们所订货物于 6 月底前按期出运。

As we are in urgent need of the goods, would you please do your utmost to effect shipment of our ordered goods by the end of June as scheduled.

(6) 兹附上我方试订单一份。如果质量合乎要求，我方近期内将寄订单。望能及时处理此订单，不胜感激。

We enclose a trial order. If the quality is up to our expectation, we shall send further orders in the near future. Your prompt attention to this order will be appreciated.

Section 3   Dialogues

Dialogue 1

If the first lot is good, we'd like to repeat the order and have a regular supply.

A: Welcome to our company. It's a pleasure to meet you.

B: The pleasure is all mine. I've long wanted to have a talk with you about the possibility to of business between us.

A: We welcome good business.

B: Good.

A: What are you interested in?

B: White crystal sugar.

A: What's the quantity you have in mind?

B: 10,000 metric tons.

A: Is it your trial order?

B: Yes, since this is the first time.

A: That sounds reasonable.

B: If the first lot is good, we'd like to repeat the order and have a regular supply.

A: Very good.

B: May I have a look at your samples?

A: Sure, we've got several different sugars.

B: (Looking at the sample) This seems of good quality.

A: It's superior white crystal sugar.

B: How do you pack it?

A: We pack sugar in new gunny sacks of 100 kgs, each.

B: Could you give the price?

A: US$150 per M/T.

B: Do you quote C.I.F. or F.O.B.?

A: Our price is on C.I.F. basis.

B: When can you deliver the goods?

A: We can ship them as soon as we receive your L/C.

B: I see.

A: When can we have your firm offer?

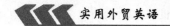

B: How about tomorrow?

A: OK. Please come any time tomorrow morning.

Dialogue 2

I think we should prefer to have an idea of the total cost of the orders.

Mr. White is a buyer from overseas visiting the office of an import & export corporation in Shanghai. Mr. Chou is the manager of the corporation, with Ms. Li as his secretary.

Li: Mr. White is here to see you. Mr. Chou, shall I bring him in?

Chou: Yes, please, and bring me the correspondence file and the last quotations we sent him, will you? Oh, just remind me, Ms. Li, did we offer subject unsold?

Li: No, we offered firm.

Chou: Thank you.

Li: Mr. White.

Chou: Good morning, Mr. White. You've had a good trip, haven't you?

White: Yes, very good journey, thank you. We have had your offer and are very much interested.

Chou: I wonder if you have found that our specifications meet your requirements. I am sure the prices we submitted are competitive.

White: Oh yes, and I have come to place order with you. We like the design of your ivory carvings. My company will send you an official confirmation soon, but there are a few questions still to be settled, for example, the costs for sending the goods.

Chou: Yes, I see, we quoted you ex-warehouse prices. Do you want me to give you the prices F.O.B? That would cover transport from our warehouse to the docks, and all the handing and shipping charges that will include wharfage, porterage, dock dues, and port rates. Leaving you to pay the sea freight and marine insurance. Is that what you want?

White: No, I think we should prefer to have an idea of the total cost delivered right to our port.

Chou: Then what about a C.I.F. price? That would cover the cost of the goods to make them seaworthy, a comprehensive insurance, all the forwarding and shipping charges, and the freight paid to your port.

White: But there will be a few things left for us to pay.

Chou: Yes, the charges for your forwarding agent for clearing the goods, paying the customs duties, and arranging delivery to your site. I can get C.I.F. prices worked out by our shipping department while we go on talking. Ms. Li, take these price quotations to the shipping department and get them to work out C.I.F. prices for Mr. White, will you?

White: I would like to ask you next, Mr. Chou, about delivery. How soon can it be effected?

Chou: Will you take partial deliveries? I mean, we could let you have, say, one-third of the order immediately from stock, and this can be dispatched just as soon as we can get shipping space. In this case, I suggest you make your order on shipping schedule divided in 3, each with an interval of 3 weeks.

White: Good.

Chou: And the final consignment would be forwarded at some future time, when the goods are available from the mills.

White: Excuse me, but I think we should like to have a definite date for the last shipment.

Chou: Of course, you can stipulate in your order saying "final shipment not later than such a date". Some date on which we could agree, which could be met by the mills supplying us.

White: Good, let us know the best they can do.

Chou: That depends on their production program and the orders they have on their books. I shall inquire, now about yourself, you are not pressed for time, aren't you?

White: Oh no.

Chou: Good. Well, while Ms. Li is typing out these quotations, perhaps you will have something to drink with me.

White: Thank you very much, I should like to.

Notes

1. long 此处意为：很久以来，一直(盼望，想)
2. white crystal sugar 白糖
3. metric tons 吨
4. gunny sacks 麻袋
5. firm offer 不可撤销的订单
6. Did we offer subject unsold? 我们报的是虚盘吗？
7. marine insurance 海运保险
8. with the clause from warehouse to warehouse 仓至仓条款
9. each time with an interval of 3 weeks 每次间隔 3 周
10. consignment 货物
11. available 可得的
12. stipulate 规定，确认 the contract stipulates payment by L/C
13. forward 运输，交货
14. be pressed for 缺少，缺乏
15. the best sb. can do 最大限度能做到的

16. place order with 向……订货

17. cover transport 包含运费

18. seaworthy 适合海运的

19. partial delivery 分批装运

20. definite date 具体时间

21. How soon can it be effected? 此货最快可在何时发运?

Section 4　Exercises

1. Translate the following sentences into English:

(1) 目前我方库存有限, 如果你方在 5 月 30 日之前订购, 我们可以提供 1000 箱。

(2) 由于订货太多, 如果您今天下单, 最早的交货时间是今年 11 月。

(3) 若贵方能保证在 8 月 30 日之前将货物由深圳运至新加坡, 则我很高兴向贵方订购下列货物。

(4) 兹回复贵方 3 月 9 日花生报价函, 现订购如所附订单所示。

(5) 我们很高兴地告知已接受你方第 123 号订单。现寄上第 456 号销售确认书一式两份, 请会签并寄回一份供我方存档。

2. Translate the following sentences into Chinese:

(1) We have received your catalogue and price list, and now we order the following goods at the named prices.

(2) Thank you for your Order No. 443. We accept it and will dispatch the goods in early June.

(3) Can you duplicate our Order No.656?

(4) Thank you very much for your order of May 5 for 500 cases of canned beef. We are pleased to confirm our acceptance as shown in the enclosed Sales Contract.

(5) Unfortunately, Style No. 101 you ordered is now out of stock, but we recommend No. 102 as a substitute which is very close to your choice in quality and slightly lower in price.

(6) As wages and prices of materials have risen considerably, we regret we are not in a position to book the order at the prices we quoted half a year ago.

3. Translate the following letter into English:

敬启者:

感谢你方 8 月 15 日寄来的报价单和样品。我们对价格和质量非常满意, 现订购 2000 件, 详见随附订单。

由于我方急需该货物，请尽快安排运输。如果该订单项下没有现货，请即告知我方。因该笔订单金额较小，我们建议采用电汇的付款方式。

等待你方的早日确认。

此致

4. Translate the following letter into Chinese:

Dear Mr. …,

Thank you for your order No. 223 and we are very pleased to start the first cooperation with you. We will do our best to execute your order and assure the quality, shipping date, and other terms you asked for will receive the best attention.

Besides, we will fax you later this afternoon the sales confirmation No.89990. Please kindly fax back with your duly signature.

Thank you for your kind attention to all the above and look forward to your L/C soon.

Yours faithfully,

5. Compose a dialogue based on the following situation:

Mr. Jones received the bicycles ordered from DDD Co., and was quite satisfied with them, so he wants to book a repeat order. But Mr. Yang, a salesman from DDD Co., cannot accept the order at the price quoted before. So they are discussing the terms of the order.

Section 5　Solution to Problem

When you receive the following letter, what would you do?

We have received your quotes in triplicate for the subject parts. We appreciate your prompt attention.

We wish to order from you the items in your quote and will apply for governmental approval to import them. This will take considerable time, so please start manufacturing them for delivery within two to three months.

Your compliance will be appreciated.

When you receive above letter, you would better take the following into account then decide.

(1)　Regular customer with pretty good credit situation? The same thing happened before? It is worth doing as request?

(2)　Trade term: DDP or not?

(3)　Payment: L/C? When L/C arrives?

Unit 5

Contracts

Section 1　Introduction

1. Definition of Contracts (合同的定义)

A contract is an agreement between two or more competent parties in which an offer is made and accepted. It is an agreement which sets forth binding obligations of the relevant parties, which is enforceable by law. If one of the parties fails to keep the promises, the other is entitled to legal recourse against him. The agreement can be formal, informal, written or oral. Some contracts are required to be in writing in order to be enforced. This term, in its more extensive sense, includes every description of agreement, or obligation, whereby one party becomes bound to another to pay a sum of money, or to do or omit to do a certain act. In its more confined sense, it is an agreement between two or more persons, concerning something to be done, whereby both parties are bound to each other, or one is bound to the other.

合同是由两个或两个以上的当事人经过发盘和接受而达成的契约。它是对有关当事人规定了约束性责任的一种协定，由法律强制保证实施。如果一方未履行承诺，则另一方有权向他行使法律追索权。这种协定可以是正式的，也可以是非正式的，书面的或口头的。从广义的角度看，合同包括协议的各个方面，双方的义务，根据该契约，一方有义务向另一方支付一定数额的货款，或必须履行某种义务，或可以免除某种义务。从狭义的角度看，合同则是两个或两个以上的当事人之间为实施某一经济目的而确定相互的权利和义务所达成的关系。

2. Types of Contracts (合同的形式)

Internationally, there is no specific limit in the form of a contract. The buyer and the seller can adopt contract, confirmation, agreement, memorandum and so on. At present, two of former are most used, which have their own canonical format.

在国际上，对书面合同的形式没有具体的限制，买卖双方可采用正式的合同书、确认书、协议、备忘录等形式。目前采用最多的是前两种形式，并有一定的规范格式。

(1)   Contract (合同书)

A contract refers to a written document made by one party involved in the contract according to the terms and conditions agreed upon and signed by both parties with a legal effect. Each party holds one or several copy (copies) of the contract after signing, as the basis of their enjoying the rights and assuming the obligations. In international trade, when the contract is made out by the importer, it is called purchase contract; and when made out by the exporter, sales contract.

合同书简称合同，是指交易双方当事人中的一方当事人按已经达成一致意见的各项交易条件制成书面文件并经双方当事人签字的具有法律效力的书面凭证。签字后的合同有双方当事人各执一份或者几份，作为其享受权利和履行责任的依据。在国际贸易中，由进口商制作的合同称为购货合同，由出口商制作的合同称为售货合同。

(2)   Confirmation (确认书)

A confirmation is shortened as S/C, which refers to a valid written document made by one party involved in the confirmation according to the terms and conditions agreed upon and signed by himself, and then sent to the other party for confirmation and signature. One copy of the signed confirmation should turn back to the maker after signing by the other party. The confirmation is simplified format of the contract, which can be less detailed than a contract, coving only the essential terms of the transaction. Its form of signature is also simple. This is usually used between long-term trading partners.

确认书缩写为 S/C，是指交易双方当事人中的一方当事人按已经达成协议的各项交易条件制成书面文件并签字，然后提交对方当事人并签字的具有法律效力的书面凭证。确认书经对方当事人确认并签字后，其中一份退还给制作人。确认书实际是合同的简化形式，其细节比合同少，仅包含了交易的重要条件，其签字的形式也简单。确认书经常用于长期的贸易伙伴之间的交易。

3. Contents of Contracts (合同的内容)

As a complete and effective business contract, it is, in most cases, comprised of the three principal parts, i.e., the head, the body and the tail.

作为完整和有效的贸易合同，应该由三个部分组成：约首、约文和约尾。

①   The Head (约首)

A. Title of The Contract (合同名称)

B. Preamble (前文/序言)

    a. Date of Signing (订约日期)

    b. Place of Signing (订约地点)

    c. Contract Number (合同号)

    d. Signing Parties And Their Addresses (订约当事人及其地址)

    e. Recitals Or Whereas Clause (订约缘由)

②   The Body (约文)

A. Definition Clause (定义条款)

B. Basic Conditions (基本条款)

    a. Name of Commodity and Specifications (货物品名和规格)

    b. Quantity (数量)

    c. Unit Price and Total Amount (单价和总金额)

    d. Packing and shipping Marks (包装和唛头)

    e. Terms of Payment (支付条件)

    f. Insurance (保险)

    g. Time of shipment (装运时间)

    h. Port of Shipment and Destination (装运港和目的港)

    i. Liabilities for Breach of Contract (违约责任)

    j. Solutions to The Disputes (解决争议的办法)

C. General Terms and Conditions (一般条款)

    a. Duration (合同有效期限)

    b. Termination (合同的终止)

    c. Force Majeure (不可抗力)

    d. Assignment (合同的让与)

    e. Arbitration (仲裁)

    f. Governing Law (适用的法律)

    g. Jurisdiction (诉讼管辖)

    h. Notice (通知手续)

    i. Entire Agreement Clause (完整条款)

    j. Amendment (合同的修改)

    k. Others (其他)

③   The Tail (约尾)

A. Number of Originals (合同份数)

B. Effectiveness of The Language (合同文字的效力)

C. Effectiveness of The Contract Annexes (合同附件的效力)

D. Signature and Seal (签名和盖印)

Samples of Contract (合同样本)

SHENFAN Machinery Equipment IMP & EXP COMPANY
SALES CONTRACT

Contract NO.: 04012E
Date: Jan. 23, 2004
Signed at: Shenzhen, China

THE SELLERS: SHENFAN Machinery Equipment IMP &EXP COMPANY
No. 5 ME Street, Shenzhen 510000, China　Tel/Fax: 0755-783256
THE BUYERS: John Williams Trading Company
No. 75 Coastal Road, New York, NY10000, USA Tel/Fax: +1-221-4881300

The undersigned Sellers and Buyers have confirmed this contract in accordance with the terms and conditions stipulated below:

1. Description of Goods, Quantity, Unit Price and Amount:

No.	Descriptions	Unit	Quantity	Unit Price	Amount
1	Drilling Machine A12 (specifications as per the Appendix)	set	30	FOB Guangzhou, China	
				USD1000.00	USD30,000.00
				Total: USD30,000.00	

Total Value (in words): SAY US DOLLAR THIRTY THOUSAND ONLY.

*The price terms are based on INCOTERMS 2000

2. Manufacturer and Country of Origin: XINYA Machine Tool Works, China.

3. Packing: In strong wooden case(s) and be good for long-distance ocean transportation.

4. Insurance: To be covered by the Buyer.

5. Date of Shipment: Within 45 days after the issuing date of L/C.

6. Port of Shipment: Guangzhou, China　　**Port of Destination**: New York, USA

7. Partial shipment: Not allowed　　**Transshipment**: Not allowed

8. Payment: By irrevocable sight L/C issued before March 1, 2004 in favor of the Seller and payable against the presentation of the documents in Clause 9.

9. Documents:

Full set clean on board Bill of Lading made out to order and blank endorsed;

Commercial Invoice in 3 originals and 2 copies;

Packing List in 3 originals and 2 copies;

Certificate of Quality & Quantity in 3 originals and 2 copies;

Beneficiary's certified copy of fax dispatched to the Buyer with 48 hours after shipment advising name of vessel, date, quantity, weight and value of shipment.

Beneficiary's certificate certifying that one set of copy of the above documents has been sent

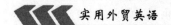

to the Buyer by express mail within 15 days after the date of shipment.

10. Shipping Advice

The Seller shall, within 48 HOURS after shipment, advise the Buyer by fax of the Contract number, Invoice number, B/L number, description of goods, quantity, invoiced value, gross weight, name of vessel and date of shipment.

11. Inspection and Claims

Except those claims for which the insurance company or the owners of the vessel are liable, should the quality of specification or quantity be found not in conformity with the stipulations of the contract, the Buyer may lodge claim against the Seller supported by survey report issued by an inspection institute agreed upon by both parties. Claim for quality discrepancy should be lodged by the Buyer within 30 days after the arrival of the goods at the port of destination, while for quantity/weight discrepancy claim should be lodged by the Buyer within 15 days after the arrival of the goods at the port of destination. If the Seller fails to respond within 30 days after receipt of the aforesaid claim, the claim shall be reckoned as having been accepted by the Seller.

12. Force Majeure

The Seller shall lose no time to advise the Buyer of delay in shipment or non-delivery of the goods due to Force Majeure during the process of manufacturing or in the course of loading and express to the Buyer within 14 days with a certificate of the incident issued by local government authorities. In such case, the Seller is still liable to take all possible measures to expedite the shipment. Should the incident last over 10 weeks, the Buyer shall have the right to treat the contract as null and void.

13. Arbitration

All disputes in connection with this Contract of the execution thereof shall be settled through friendly negotiation. Should no settlement be reached, the case may then be submitted for arbitration to the Arbitration Committee of the China Council for the Promotion of International Trade and be subject to the rules and procedures of the said Arbitration Committee. The Arbitration shall take place in Beijing, the People's Republic of China. The arbitration result of the Committee shall be final and binding upon both Parties. Neither Party shall seek recourse to a court or other authorities to appeal for revision of the arbitration. The arbitration fee and attorneys' charges shall be borne by the losing Party.

This Contract shall be made in original and duplicate, one for each Party, and shall be binding on both Parties under the terms and conditions stipulated herein upon being signed in the presence for witnesses.

Representative of the Sellers

WANG LI

（signature）

(Authorized Signature)

Representative of Buyers

M. LEE

（signature）

(Authorized Signature)

Samples of Confirmation (确认书样本)

SALES CONI'IRMATION
售货确认书

To Messrs,

Date:
日期：
No.:
编号：
Signed at：
签约地点：

The undersigned sellers and buyers have agreed to close the following transactions according to the terms and conditions stipulated below:

经买卖双方同意成交下列商品订立条款如下：

(1) Commodity:
商品：

(2) Specification:
规格：

(3) Quantity:
数量：

(4) Unit Price:
单价：

(5) Total Value:
总值：

(6) Time of Shipment:
装运期：

(7) Packing:
包装：

(8) Loading Port and Destination:

装运港和目的港：

(9) Shipping Marks:

唛头：

(10) Terms of Payment:

Terms of payment: by 100% value confirmed irrevocable letter of credit by draft at sight with transshipment and partial shipments allowed, to reach the Sellers _____ days before month of shipment, with shipment validity arranged till the 15th day after the month of shipment, and remain valid for negotiation in the loading port until the _____ day after the shipment validity.

付款条件：凭 100%保兑的、不可撤销的信用证附带即期汇票付款，允许分批装运和转船，要求在装船期前_____天到达卖方，有效期至装船期后 15 天，且在装船有效期后_____天在装货港议付仍然有效。

(11) Insurance:

保险：

The Buyers

买方

The Sellers

卖方

China National Textiles

Import & Export Corporation

Shanghai Silk Branch

中国纺织品进出口公司

上海丝绸分公司

Section 2　Correspondence

1. Writing Skills

A letter of contract is composed of the following parts:

(1)　Confirm the order or inform the seller of your order.

(2)　Tell the reader that how much copies of the contract you have sent. Ask the reader to countersign the contracts and send one copy back for your file.

(3)　Remind the reader the matters needing attention and promise the performance of your duties.

(4)　Thanks for the reader's cooperation and put forward your hope.

2. Sample Letters

Letter 1 (Seller to Buyer)

Dear Sirs,

We are very pleased to receive your order No. BD/135 Canned Beef. We accept the order and are enclosing you our Sales Confirmation No. 345 in duplicate[1] of which please countersign[2] and return one copy to us for our file[3]. We trust you will open the relative L/C at an early date.

As to the Items A and B, we shall arrange delivery as soon as we get your L/C, and Items C and D we shall ship accordingly[4].

Hoping the goods will turn out[5] to your entire satisfaction and we may have further orders from you.

Yours faithfully,

Letter 2 (Seller to Buyer)

Dear Sirs,

Your Order No. HZ1034 for Silk Textiles

We are pleased to confirm the above order from you and are sending you our Sales Confirmation No. HZ1034 in duplicate, one copy of which is to be countersigned and returned for our file.

It is understood that a letter of credit in our favor[5] covering the captioned merchandise will be established on or about[6] the 25th of the month. The stipulations in the relative credit should strictly conform to[7] the terms stated in our Sales Confirmation in order to avoid the trouble of subsequent amendments.

We appreciate your cooperation and trust that the first partial shipment which is to be effected early month will turn out to your complete satisfaction.

Letter 3 (Buyer to Seller)

Dear Sirs,

Contract No. ZH7452

Enclosed we are sending you Contract No. ZH7452 in duplicate. Please return to us one of them by airmail, complete with your signature.

We are glad to inform you that we shall open the covering letter of credit very soon. Please advise us when the goods are ready for shipment, so that we can arrange the shipping space and insurance.

Sincerely,

Encl. : Contract No. ZH7452

3. Notes to Text

(1) in duplicate 一式二份

in triplicate 一式三份   in quadruplicate 一式四份

一式四份及以上也常说 in four copies, in five copies, … 或 in four fold, in five fold, …

(2) countersign 副署，连署；会签

When the Sales Contract has been signed by the seller, it will be countersigned by the buyer. 销售合同经卖方签署后，须经买方会签。

(3) for one's file = for one's record(s) 以便某方存档

(4) accordingly 按照(所说的)情形

Our contract stipulates that payment should be made by irrevocable letter of credit payable by sight draft, so you must act accordingly. 合同规定应以不可撤销的信用证支付，因此你方必须照办。

(5) in one's favor 以某人为受益人

(6) on or about: The expression "on or about" or similar will be interpreted as a stipulation that an event is to occur during a period of time, from five calendar days before the specified date to five calendar days after the specified date, both start and end dates included

On or about December 25: From December 21 to December 29

(7) conform to = conform with = in conformity with 与……一致

4. Useful expressions

(1) 正如合同中具体定明，有关信用证必须于装货前 15 天到达卖方，也就是说，5 月份装运的货物的信用证必须不迟于 4 月 15 日到达我方手中。

As it specifically stipulated in the contract, the relevant L/C should reach the seller 15 days before shipment, that is, the L/C covering the goods to be shipped in May should reach us not later than April 15.

(2) 执行合同中产生的争执应通过友好协商加以解决。

Any dispute arising out of this contract shall be settled through friendly negotiation.

(3) 此商品应用适合于海运的新木箱包装。

The commodity shall be packed in new wooden cases suitable for ocean transportation.

(4) 卖方保证合同中订购的仪器以一流的工艺和最好的材料制成。

The seller guarantees that the instrument contracted for will be made of the best materials with first-class workmanship.

(5) 机器的各个方面将符合于合同所规定的质量要求和规格。

The machines will correspond in all respects with the quality and specifications as stipulated in the contract.

(6) 我们有权取消由于买方不能履行的合同。

We are entitled to cancel the contract which became overdue owing to the buyer's non-performance.

Section 3   Dialogues

Dialogue 1

Are we anywhere near a contract yet?

Miss Zhao, from Xi'an Machinery Import & Export Corporation, has secured an order from an American importer for her corporation's garden tools. She is now negotiating the terms of the contract with Mr. Jackson from an importing firm.

Zhao: Well, Mr. Jackson. It seems to me that we've come quite a long way, but there are still a few points left over to clear up.

Jackson: Yes, let's go over the terms and conditions of the contract. If you have any comments about them, do not hesitate to say so.

Zhao: Good, now the price: 1000 sets of garden tools, quality and design as shown in our catalogue at USD6.50 each set CIF NEW YORK. So the business is closed at this price.

Jackson: Yes, that's right. As to packing, we hope you can pack the goods in wooden cases.

Zhao: Oh, Mr. Jackson. As I told you before, cartons are as seaworthy as wooden cases and even have more advantages over the latter, for instance, they are easier to handle and cheaper in cost. We have never received any complaint about it from our clients. You can take it from me that they are strong enough to stand rough handling.

Jackson: All right, cartons then. Well, the shipment I understand is to be made before December, isn't it? We can't accept any delay.

Zhao: Yes. Rest assured that shipment will be effected according to the contract stipulations. But if my memory serves me right, "Transshipment via Hong Kong allowed" is what we agreed upon, isn't it?

Jackson: Ah, yes, I remember. Now, how about the terms of payment?

Zhao: Payment is to be made by irrevocable L/C as I suggested?

Jackson: I sincerely hope you are able to make a last minute change on this aspect.

Zhao: Sorry, that's impossible. As I said, 60 days is the result of great concession made on our part, and I think we'd better keep what has been agreed upon.

Jackson: Well, I guess there is no way out. I'll see about the opening of the L/C as soon as I get home.

Zhao: Thanks. The next point is insurance. I'm sure you are quite familiar with our usual terms. If you have no objection, let's take it as agreed.

Jackson: No objection at all. I remember it is to be covered by the seller for 110% of the invoice value against All Risks and War Risk.

Zhao: Right, Mr. Jackson. Anything else you would like to discuss?

Jackson: Okay, there is the last thing to make clear. How do we resolve the case when both parties hold different opinions on the standard of the goods?

Zhao: Oh, suppose we have a dispute, we can resolve the case by submitting the dispute to arbitration by the Chinese International Trade Arbitration Commission.

Jackson: All right. I'm glad our discussion has come to s successful conclusion. Are we anywhere near a contract yet? I hope we can sign it very soon.

Zhao: I'll contact you as soon as the formal contract is ready.

Jackson: Thank you.

Dialogue 2

A contract cannot be changed after both parties have signed it.

Now Miss. Zhao and Mr. Jackson are taking one more look before signing the contract.

Zhao: Now, we've finally reached a basic agreement on the problems that need to be worked out. Shall we sign the contract now?

Jackson: Just a minute. Generally speaking, a contract cannot be changed after both parties have signed it. So we'd better make sure one more time that we've got them right.

Zhao: That's a good idea.

Jackson: First of all, about the format of our contract. There are two of the originals of the contract both in Chinese and English. So they're equally authentic in terms of law. Here's a copy for you to check.

Zhao: Thank you. I have no objections. It contains basically all we have agreed upon during our negotiations. To make sure no important items have been overlooked, let's check if all the stipulations are in conformity with the terms we agreed on.

Jackson: Okay, let's start from the name of the commodity, specifications, quantity, unit price. Well, it looks good enough to me, you've done a good job.

Zhao: Thank you. Since your company enjoys a good reputation, we want to make sure we keep your business.

Jackson: We always think our commercial reputation is of primary importance, and promise that the execution of the contract will not be compromised, no matter what happens.

Zhao: It's really nice to get to know all of you, shall we sign the contract now?

Jackson: Yes, I've been looking forward to this moment.

Zhao: Let me propose a toast to the success of negotiations and to our future cooperation. Cheers!

Jackson: Cheers! Let's congratulate ourselves on having brought this transaction to successful conclusion.

Notes

1. secure an order from sb. 获得订单

2. leave over 留下；剩下

3. clear up 完成；解决

4. go over 检查；重温

5. business is closed 达成交易

6. pack sth. in wooden cases 使用木箱包装

7. seaworthy 适合海运

8. stand rough handling 经得起野蛮装卸

9. rest assured 放心

10. contract stipulation 合同条款

11. if my memory serves me right 如果我没有记错

12. agree upon 就……达成一致

13. irrevocable L/C 不可撤销信用证

14. make concession 让步

15. on our part = on our side 我方

16. usual terms 一般条款

17. resolve the case 解决问题

18. come to a successful conclusion 得到圆满的结果

19. formal contract 正式合同

20. reached a basic agreement on/ about 关于……基本达成一致

21. format of contract 合同格式

22. the original of the contract 合同正本

23. they're equally authentic in terms of law 它们在法律上具有同等效力

24. have no objections 没有异议
25. be in conformity with… 与……一致
26. keep business 保持、维持业务
27. commercial reputation 商业信誉
28. be of primary importance 放在首位
29. execution of the contract 履行合同
30. not be compromised 严格执行
31. propose a toast to sth. 为……干杯庆祝

Section 4　Exercises

1. Translate the following sentences into English:

(1)　感谢我们双方的努力，终于成功达成交易。

(2)　随附 990 号售货确认书两份，请签署后用航空信函寄回一份给我方。

(3)　由于我方急需该批货物，请问可否提前交货？

(4)　我们保证会尽力执行本合同以使贵方满意。

(5)　如合同中所规定的，相关信用证应于装运日前 20 天开至我方。

2. Translate the following sentences into Chinese:

(1)　We have duly received the Sales Confirmation No.990，and now return to you one copy with our countersignature.

(2)　We appreciate your cooperation and trust that the goods delivered will turn out to your complete satisfaction.

(3)　If your goods are of superior quality, exquisite workmanship, and reasonable price, we will place a large order with you in the future.

(4)　The stipulations in relative credit should strictly conform to the terms stated in our Sales Confirmation in order to avoid the trouble of subsequent amendments.

(5)　We have some stock of the goods you ordered last time，and shall be able to meet your requirements if you wish to duplicate your last order.

3. Translate the following letter into English:

×××先生：

567 号售货确认书已收到，随附一份我方已会签的合同，请查收。这是我们第一次合作。相信在我们双方的共同努力下，本次交易一定会进展顺利。

相关的以你方为受益人的信用证已通过中国银行开立，很快会到达你方。

如果这批货物质量好，受欢迎的话，我方还会继续订购。

…… 谨上

4. Translate the following contract terms into Chinese:

This Contract is made by and between the Buyer and the Seller, whereby the Buyer agrees to buy and the Seller agrees to sell the under-mentioned commodity according to the terms and conditions stipulated below:

Commodity and Specification	Quantity	Unit price	Amount
Baby quilt (100% cotton)	600pcs	CIFC5 DUBAI USD20/pc	USD72000.00
Total	600pcs		USD72000.00

Total Contract Value: Say US dollars seventy two thousand only.

TIME OF SHIPMENT:

Within 60 days upon receipt of the L/C which accords with relevant clauses of this Contract.

PORT OF LOADING AND DESTINATION:

From Dalian, China to Dubai, UAE

Transshipment and partial shipment are prohibited.

INSURANCE:

To be effected by the Seller for 110% of invoice value covering All Risks and War Risks as per CIC of PICC dated 01/01/1981.

INSPECTION:

The certificate of quality issued by SGS in Shanghai shall be taken as the basis of delivery.

5. Compose a dialogue based on the following situation:

Mr. Smith, manager of the import company, received the sales confirmation from the seller, but he found that many terms do not conform to the order, such as the packing, payment and shipment terms etc. So he calls Mr. Yang, manager of the sales department of the export company, to discuss these points.

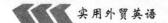
Section 5   Solution to Problem

Could the signed pro forma invoice be used as contract in business practice?

Outwardly, except the marked "pro forma", pro forma invoice is like an ordinary commercial invoice containing the general particulars, for example, marks, number of goods, descriptions, quantities, quality, price, and etc. However, in nature, it is a different form of invoice which treats "Hypothetical" sales as if they have actually and contractually taken place. Pro forma invoices are required for various reasons. Primarily the importer requires them to comply with the regulations in force in his country, importers may apply for the necessary Import License or Foreign Exchange with them. Moreover, the importer can require them in advance for information, or letter of credit purposes.

Anyway the importer who asks for a pro forma invoice is in fact making an inquiry, and the exporter who sends the pro forma invoice is actually making an offer. Let's cite related articles of "Convention".

Article 11 of "Convention", a contract of sale need not be concluded in or evidenced by writing and is not subject to any other requirement as to form. It may be proved by any means, including witnesses.

Article 13 of "Convention", for the purposes of this Convention "writing" includes telegram and telex.

Article 23 of "Convention", a contract is concluded at the moment when an acceptance of an offer becomes effective in accordance with the provisions of this Convention.

Pro forma invoice with definite intention of acceptance and signature of the importer could be regarded as a contract between both parties of importer and exporter.

 # Unit 6

Terms of Payment

Section 1   Introduction

1. Payment Instruments in International Trade (国际贸易中的支付工具)

International settlement changes from cash settlement to non-cash settlement, along with the development of international trade. Thereinto, the bill has played a more and more important role. In international trade, instruments for settlement mainly include the bill of exchange, cheque and promissory notes. Among them, bill of exchange is more frequently used.

随着国际贸易的发展，国际结算由现金结算发展到非现金结算，其中票据起到了越来越重要的作用。在国际贸易中，用于结算的票据主要包括汇票、支票和本票。其中，汇票运用更频繁。

Bill of Exchange or Draft (汇票)

(See Fig. 6-1 Sample of Bill of Exchange, Fig. 6-2 Blank Bill of Exchange and Fig. 6-3 Filled Bill of Exchange) (参见图 6-1 汇票样本、图 6-2 空白汇票和图 6-3 填制好的汇票)

(Sample A)

```
No. 1022
$ 20 000                                        London, 10th January, 2006-03-19
     On demand pay to Bill Green or bearer the sum of USD Twenty Thousand only.
                                                      (Signed) Tom White
To: Mr. David Smith
    New York
```

（例一）

```
编号：1022
汇票金额：20 000 美元                            伦敦：2006 年 3 月 19 日
     见票时付比尔·格林或持票人贰万美元整
                                              （签字）汤姆·怀特
此致
大卫·史密斯
纽约
                                              敬礼
```

(Sample B)

```
No: 123/67

Exchange for $ 8 000                           Guangzhou, China, 5th March, 2006
At 60 days sight of this First of exchange (the SECOND of the same and date being unpaid) pay to or to the
order of Guangzhou ABC Import and Export Corporation the sum of USD eight thousand only.
To: A&C Import and Export Co. Ltd.
    23 Washington Street
    New York, USA              Guangzhou ABC Import and Export Corporation
                                               Manager

                                             (Signed)
```

（例二）

```
发票号：123/67

汇票金额：8 000 美元                            中国广州，2006 年 3 月 5 日
     凭本汇票（副本未付）于见票后 60 天付广州 ABC 进出口公司或其指定人捌仟美元整（大写）。
此致
A&C 进出口公司
华盛顿大街 23 号                                广州 ABC 进出口公司
美国纽约
   （发票号：123/67）                                经理（签字）
```

图 6-1　Sample of Bill of Exchange(汇票样本)

BILL OF EXCHANGE

No._____

For

At_____sight of THIS SECOND BILL of EXCHANGE

(first of the same tenor and date unpaid) pay to_____or order the sum of

Value received and charge the same to account of _____

_____

Drawn under_____

L/C No._____dated_____

To.

_____

_____

图 6-2   Blank Bill of Exchange(空白汇票)

BILL OF EXCHANGE

No.   T03617   Date: OCT.24,2004

For USD 89 705.50

At _____sight of THIS SECOND BILL of EXCHANGE

(first of the same tenor and date unpaid) pay to BANK OF CHINA   or order the sum of

SAY US DOLLARS EIGHTY NINE THOUSAND SEVEN HUNDRED AND FIVE POINT FIFTY ONLY

Drawn under   NATIONAL PARRIS BANK （CANADA）MONTREAL

L/C No.   TH2003   Dated   OCT.06th,2004

To.

NATIONAL PARIS BANK

24 MARSHALL VEDONCASTER MONTREAL，CANADA

SUZHOU KNITWEAR AND MANUFACTURED GOODS

IMPORT&EXPORT TRADE CORPORATION

李莉

图 6-3   Filled Bill of Exchange(填制好的汇票)

1)   Definition of Bill of Exchange (汇票的定义)

A bill of exchange, also called draft, is defined as an unconditional order in writing, addressed by one person to another, signed by the person giving it, requiring the person to whom it is addressed to pay on demand, or at a fixed or determinable future time, a sum certain in money, to or to the order of a specified person, or to bearer.

汇票是由一人向另一人签发的无条件的书面命令，要求接受命令的人在见票时或在指定的或可以确定的将来某一日期，支付一定的金额给特定的人或其指定的人或持票人。

2)   Contents of Bill of Exchange (汇票的内容)

A. "Draft" or "bill of exchange" must appear on the bill (标明 "汇票" 字样)

B. An unconditional order in writing (无条件的书面命令)

C. A sum certain in money (一定的金额)

D. The parties to a bill of exchange (汇票的当事人)

A bill of exchange involves three parties:

Drawer: The person who writes the order and gives directions to the person to make a specific payment of money. He is usually the exporter or his banker in import and export trade; usually, he is also a creditor of the drawee.

Drawee (Payer): The person to whom the order is addressed and who is to pay the money. He is usually the importer or the appointed bank under a letter of credit in import and export trade. In addition, when a time bill has been accepted by the drawee, he becomes an acceptor who is the same person as the drawee. The drawer and the acceptor must be different persons.

Payee: The person (individual, firm, corporation, or bank) to whom the payment is ordered to be made. The payee is usually the exporter himself or his appointed bank in import and export trade. The payee may also be the bearer of the bill. The payee may be the original payee in the bill, or may be some parties to whom the original payee has transferred the instrument.

一张汇票中主要涉及三个当事人：

出票人：签发命令要求另一人支付一定金额的人。在进出口贸易中，他通常是出口商或出口地银行，并且他也经常是受票人的债权人。

受票人(付款人)：接受命令并将付款的人。在进出口贸易中，他通常是进出口商或信用证下的指定银行。当受票人承兑一张远期汇票时，他就成为承兑人。出票人和承兑人必须是不同的人。

受款人(收款人)：接受付款的人(个人、商号、公司或银行)。在进出口贸易中，受款人经常就是出口商自己或他指定的银行。受款人也可能是持票人。受款人可以是汇票中的原有受款人，也可以是原有受款人所转让汇票的人。

E. Date of issuing (出票日期)

F. Tenor of payment (付款时间)

G. Place of payment (付款地点)

H. Place of issuing (出票地点)

3)　Classification of Bill of Exchange (汇票种类)

On the basis of different criteria, bills of exchange may be classified into several types:

根据不同的标准，汇票可以分为以下几种：

A. Clean Bill and Documentary Bill (光票和跟单汇票)

In the transfer of the bill of exchange, if the bill of exchange is accompanied by shipping documents, it is a documentary bill, if not, it is a clean bill. In international trade, mostly it is the documentary bill, occasionally the clean bill is used to collect payment in small or sundry charges, such as commission, interest, sample fee and cash in advance, etc.

按汇票流通时是否随附货运单据，分为跟单汇票和光票。随附货运单据的汇票，称为跟单汇票。不随附货运单据的汇票，称为光票。在国际贸易中的货款结算，大多数使用跟单汇票。偶尔也使用光票收取小额费用或杂费的付款，如佣金、利息、样品费和代垫费用等。

B. Sight (or Demand) Bill and Time (or Usance) Bill (即期汇票和远期汇票)

According to the time when the bill falls due, bills of exchange may be divided into sight (or demand) bill or a time (or usance) bill. A sight bill should be paid at the first presentation of the bill. In case of a time bill, the drawee does not make immediate payment, is required to accept it at first sight and pay it at a fixed or determinable future time, in other words, it requires acceptance before payment. The fixed or determinable future time may be a certain number of days after acceptance: a. At … days after sight, such as "60 days after sight"or"30 days sight"; b. At … days after the date of draft, such as "90 days after date of this draft"; c. at fixed date in the future, such as "On May 12, 2006".

汇票按付款期限的不同，可分为即期汇票和远期汇票。汇票上规定见票后立即付款的称为即期汇票。汇票上规定受票人先承兑，然后在指定的或将来一个可确定的日期付款的，换句话说，要求先承兑后付款的称为远期汇票。在指定的或将来一个可确定的日期是承兑以后的若干天：a.付款人见票后若干天付款，如见票后 30 天或 60 天；b.出票后若干天付款，如出票后 90 天付款；c.将来某一指定日期，如于 2006 年 5 月 12 日付款。

4)   Operation of Bill of Exchange (汇票的使用)

The operation process of draft includes: to draw, presentation, acceptance, payment, endorsement, dishonor and recourse.

汇票的使用程序包括：出票、提示、承兑、付款、背书、拒付及追索。

A. To draw/Issue (出票)

To draw is to fill up by the drawer the particulars in a bill of exchange the date of drawing, the name of the drawee, the time and amount of the payment, etc. The draft is signed by the drawer and then sent to the payee.

出票是指出票人在汇票上填写付款人、付款金额、付款日期和地点以及受款人等项目，经签字后交给受款人的行为。

B. Presentation (提示)

The act of taking the bill to the drawee and demanding that he makes the payment or accepts the bill is known as presentation. For a sight bill, payment should be made at the same time when the presentation is made, and for a time bill, the drawee is required to accept the bill when the bill is presented to him.

提示是指持票人将汇票提交付款人要求承兑或付款的行为。付款人看到汇票叫见票，

实用外贸英语

如是即期汇票，付款人见票后应立即付款；如是远期汇票，付款人见票后先办理承兑手续，到期时付款。

C. Acceptance (承兑)

The formal act whereby the drawee adopts the bill as his own obligation is known as acceptance. Acceptance is the written signification by the drawee of his assent to the order of the drawer. This is accomplished in the regular manner by writing the word "Acceptance", with the date and the signature of the drawee, across the face of the bill. When the bill is accepted by the drawee, he is then known as an acceptor.

承兑是指付款人对远期汇票表示承担到期付款责任的行为。承兑手续是由付款人在远期汇票正面写上"承兑"字样，注明承兑日期，并由付款人签字，交给持票人。付款人承兑汇票后，即为承兑人。

D. Payment (付款)

Under a sight bill, the drawee is required to make the payment when the bill is presented to him while for a time bill, the drawee is required to accept the bill when the bill is presented to him and make the payment at the maturity of the bill. When paid, the bill is retained by the payer while the receipt is made and signed by the holder of the bill.

对即期汇票，在持票人提示时，付款人即应付款，不需要经过承兑手续；对远期汇票，付款人经过承兑后，在汇票到期日付款。付款人付清款项后，汇票上的一切债权债务即告结束。

E. Endorsement (背书)

The bill of exchange is negotiable and transferable as the payee on most bills is to "to the order of …". Negotiation and transfer is effected with endorsement. If the payee on the bill is to "to the bearer", then negotiation and transfer is done with mere delivery of the bill. Endorsement is done when the payee has signed his name on the back of the bill with or without additional words conveying instructions or qualifying liability.

Generally speaking, there are three main endorsements, i.e. demonstrative endorsement, blank endorsement, and restrictive endorsement.

汇票在转让时，除来人抬头的汇票，只需交付汇票即可转让外，指示性抬头汇票转让时必须办理背书。背书是转让汇票权利的一种法定手续，是由汇票持有人在汇票背面签上自己的名字，或加上受让人的名字，注明背书日期并把汇票交给受让人的行为。

一般来说，汇票背书主要有三种：指示性背书、空白背书和限制性背书。

2. Modes of Payment in International Trade (国际贸易支付方式)

In order to prevent risks in export or import transactions, different methods of payment have been developed. The modes of payment in international trade can be generally divided into three categories, illustrated as follows: remittance, collection and letter of credit.

为了预防交易中种种可能的风险，人们采用了不同的支付方式。总地来说，国际贸易支付方式可以分为三大类：汇付、托收和信用证。

1)   Remittance (汇付)

(1)   Definition of Remittance (汇付的定义)

Remittance is a process that the payer instructs his bank or other institutions to have a payment made to the payee. Remittance belongs to commercial credit. Four parties are involved in the remittance business: the remitter, the payee, the remitting bank and the paying bank. In international sales of goods, remittance service is often used for payment of advance payment, cash with order, open account, down-payment, payment in installments and commission etc.

汇付是指付款人通过银行或其他途径将款项汇交收款人。汇付属于银行信用。在汇付业务中，通常有四个当事人：汇款人、收款人、汇出行和汇入行。在国际贸易中，汇付方式常用于预付货款、随订单付款和赊销、支付定金、分期付款以及佣金等费用的支付。

(2)   Types of Remittance (汇付的种类)

Remittance can be made by mail, telegraph and draft.

汇付方式包括信汇、电汇和票汇三种。

A. Mail Transfer (M/T) (信汇)

Mail Transfer is a process that the remitting bank, at the request of the remittance, sends instructions by mail to the paying bank asking it to make a certain amount of payment to the payee. The cost of this method is less, but the speed is slower.

信汇是汇出行应汇款人的申请，将信汇委托书寄给汇入行，授权解付一定金额给收款人的一种付款方式。信汇的成本较低，但速度较慢。

B. Telegraphic Transfer (T/T) (电汇)

Telegraphic Transfer (T/T) is a process that the remitting bank, at the request of the remittance, sends a cable to its correspondent bank in the country concerned instruction, to make a certain amount of payment to the payee. The payee can receive payment promptly, but the charges for this type of transfer are relatively high.

电汇是汇出行应汇款人的申请，电报通知另一国家的代理行指示解付一定金额给收款人的一种汇款方式。电汇方式下收款人可以迅速收到汇款，但费用较高。

C. Demand Draft (D/D) (票汇)

Demand Draft (D/D) is a process that the remitting bank, at the request of the remitter, draws a demand draft on its branch or correspondent bank instructing it to make a certain amount of payment to the payee on behalf of the remitter.

票汇是指汇出行应汇款人的申请，代汇款人开立以其分行或代理行为解付行的银行即期汇票，支付一定金额给收款人的一种汇款方式。

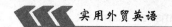

(3) Terms of Payment by Remittance in Contract

When remittance is used as the payment mode agreed upon, it should state clearly the time, amount and types of remittance, etc. in the contract.

e.g. The Buyer shall pay 100% of the sales amount in advance by T/T (M/T or D/D) to reach the Sellers not later than Oct. 10, 2008.

当约定采用汇付作为支付方式时，应在合同的支付条款中规定清楚汇付的时间、金额、具体汇付的方式等项内容。

例如：买方应不迟于 2008 年 10 月 10 日将 100%的成交金额用电汇(信汇或票汇)方式汇付给卖方。

2) Collection (托收)

(1) Definition of Collection (托收的定义)

Collection is a process that the exporter's bank receives an exporter's collection order and documents, and then presents the documents to the importer and collects funds for the seller by the importer's bank. Collection also belongs to commercial credit. Four parties are involved in the collection business: the principle, the remitting bank, the collecting bank and the payer.

托收是指出口商出具汇票连同单据委托其所在地银行通过进口地银行向进口商收取货款。托收也属于商业信用。在托收业务中，包含四个基本当事人：委托人、托收银行、代收行和付款人。

(2) Types of Collection (托收的种类)

Collection of two types: clean collection and documentary collection. Clean collection is a collection not accompanied by commercial documents. Documentary collection means collection of: a. financial documents accompanied by commercial documents; b. commercial documents not accompanied by financial documents. The documentary collection is widely used in international trade. Documentary collection falls into two kinds: documents against payment (D/P) and documents against acceptance (D/A). Documents against payment call for transfer of shipping documents against actual payment. Documents against acceptance call for delivery of documents against acceptance of the draft drawn by the exporter.

托收分为光票托收和跟单托收两种。光票托收是指资金单据的托收，不附有商业单据。跟单托收是指：a.资金单据的托收，附有商业单据；b.商业单据的托收，不附有资金单据。在国际贸易中大多采用跟单托收。跟单托收又分为付款交单和承兑交单两种。付款交单要求凭付款才移交货运单据，而承兑交单要求凭承兑出口商开具的汇票才转交货运单据。

① Document against Payment (D/P) (付款交单)

Under D/P, the exporter is to ship the goods ordered and deliver the relevant shipping documents to the buyer abroad through the remitting bank and the collection bank with instructions not to release the documents to the buyer until the full payment is effected.

According to the different time of payment, document against payment can be further divided into D/P at sight and D/P after sight.

在付款交单支付方式下，出口人交出单据后指示托收行和代收行在国外的买方付清货款后才交出单据。根据付款时间的不同，付款交单可分为即期付款交单和远期付款交单。

A. D/P at sight (即期付款交单)

Under this term, the seller draws a sight draft, and sends it with the shipping documents to the collecting bank. Then the collecting bank presents the sight of draft and shipping documents to the buyer. When the buyer sees them he must pay the money at once, then he can obtain the shipping documents. The procedure of which can be seen in the following: See Fig.6-4 Procedures of D/P at sight.

在这种方式下，卖方开具即期汇票并通过银行向买方提示，买方见票后马上付款，只有付清货款后才能领取单据。即期付款交单程序如图 6-4 所示。

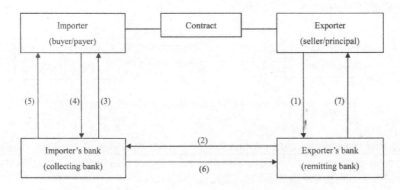

图 6-4　Procedures of D/P at sight(即期付款交单程序图)

Remarks (说明)：

(1)　According to the contract, the exporter loads the goods and draws a sight draft, then sends the draft together with shipping documents to his bank for collecting a documentary bill on his behalf. (出口商根据合同规定装货后，开立即期汇票连同货运单据交托收行，委托代收货款)

(2)　The remitting bank sends the documentary bill to a correspondent bank overseas-the collecting bank for collecting money. (托收行将汇票连同货运单据一起寄交进口地代办银行委托代收)

(3)　The collecting bank represents the bill and documents to the importer for payment. (代收行向买方提示汇票与单据)

(4)　The importer makes payment. (进口商付款)

(5)　The collecting bank hands over the document to the importer. (代收行交单给进口商)

(6)　The collecting bank notifies the remitting bank of crediting the money to their account. (代收行办理转账并通知托收行款已收妥)

(7)　The remitting bank makes payment to the exporter. (托收行向出口商交款)

B. D/P after sight (远期付款交单)

Under D/P after sight, the seller draws a time (or usance) draft. The collecting bank presents the time draft and shipping documents to the buyer. When the buyer sees them he just accepts the time bill and then effects payment at maturity of the draft. When receiving the money from the buyer, the collecting bank hands over the shipping documents to him. The procedure of D/P after sight is shown as follows: See Fig. 6-5 Procedures of D/P after sight.

在远期付款交单方式下，卖方开立远期汇票。代收行将此汇票向买方提示汇票和货运单据。买方见票后仅须承兑汇票，等汇票到期支付货款。代收行收到货款后，即向他交付单据。远期付款交单的程序如图 6-5 所示。

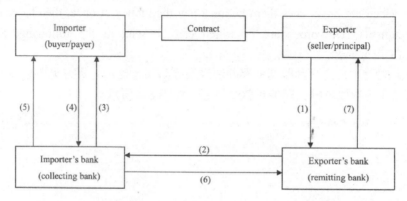

图 6-5　Procedures of D/P after sight(远期付款交单程序图)

Remarks (说明):

(1)　According to the contract, the exporter loads the goods and draws a sight draft, then sends the draft together with shipping documents to his bank for collecting a documentary bill on his behalf. (出口商根据合同规定装货后，开立远期汇票连同货运单据交托收行，委托代收货款)

(2)　The remitting bank sends the documentary bill to a correspondent bank overseas-the collecting bank. (托收行将汇票连同货运单据一起寄交进口地代办银行委托代收)

(3)　The collecting bank represents the bill and documents to the importer for acceptance. After the importer accepts the draft, the collection bank takes back the draft and documents. (代收行向进口商提示汇票与单据，让其承兑。进口商承兑汇票后，代收行收回汇票)

(4)　The importer makes payment when it falls due. (进口商到期付款)

(5)　The collecting bank hands over the document to the importer. (代收行交单给进口商)

(6)　The collecting bank notifies the remitting bank of crediting the money to their account. (代收行办理转账并通知托收行款已收到)

(7)　The remitting bank makes payment to the exporter. (托收行向出口商交款)

②　Document against Acceptance (D/A) (承兑交单)

Under documents against acceptance, the exporter releases the documents on the condition that the importer has made acceptance on the draft. The exporter makes presentation to the importer through the bank of the time draft and the shipping documents after the shipment, the collecting bank will release the documents to the importer after the importer has make the acceptance, and the importer will make the payment only at the expiry of the draft. The procedure of D/A is shown as follows: See Fig. 6-6 Procedures of D/A.

在承兑交单方式下，代收行向进口人交付单据是以进口人对汇票承兑为条件。即承兑交单是指出口人在装运货物后开具远期汇票连同货运单据，通过银行向进口人提示，进口人承兑汇票后，代收行即将货运单据交给进口人，进口人在汇票到期时才履行付款义务。承兑交单程序如图 6-6 所示。

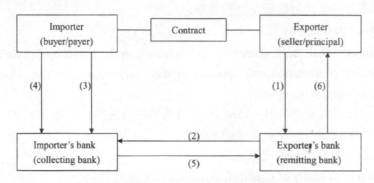

图 6-6 Procedures of D/A(承兑交单程序图)

Remarks (说明):

(1) According to the contract, the exporter loads the goods and draws a time draft, them send the draft together with shipping documents to his bank for collecting a documentary bill on his behalf. (出口商根据合同规定装货后，开立远期汇票，连同货运单据交托收行，委托代收货款)

(2) The remitting bank send the documentary bill to a correspondent bank overseas-the collecting bank. (托收行将汇票连同货运单据一起寄交进口地代办银行委托代收)

(3) The collecting bank presents the bill and documents to the importer for acceptance, after that, the collecting bank takes back the draft and gives the shipping documents to the importer. (代收行向买方提示汇票与单据，进口商在汇票上承兑。代收行收回汇票，同时将货运单据交给进口商)

(4) The importer makes payment when time falls due. (进口商到期付款)

(5) The collecting bank notifies the remitting bank of crediting the money to their account. (代收行办理转账并通知托收行款已收到)

(6) The remitting bank makes payment to the exporter. (托收行向出口商交款)

(3) Terms of Payment by Collection in Contract(合同中的汇付条款)

When collection is used as the payment mode agreed upon, it should state clearly the types of draft, terms of releasing documents of the bank, time of payment, etc. in the contract.

当约定采用托收作为支付方式时，应在合同的支付条款中规定清楚汇票类型、交单条件付款时间等项内容。

① Terms of Payment by D/P at Sight (即期付款交单支付条款)

e.g. Upon first presentation the Buyers shall pay against documentary draft drawn by the Sellers at sight. The shipping documents are to be delivered against payment only.

例如：买方凭卖方开具的即期跟单汇票于见票时立即付款，付款后交运输单据。

② Terms of Payment by D/P after Sight (远期付款交单支付条款)

e.g. The Buyers shall duly accept the documentary draft drawn by the Sellers at 30 days after sight upon first presentation and make the payment on its maturity. The shipping documents are to be delivered against payment only.

例如：买方对于卖方开具的见票后 30 天付款的跟单汇票，于提示时应立即承兑，并应于汇票到期日即予付款，付款后交运输单据。

③ Terms of Payment by D/A (承兑交单支付条款)

e.g. The Buyers shall duly accept the documentary draft drawn by the Sellers at 30 days after sight upon first presentation and make the payment on its maturity. The shipping documents are to be delivered against acceptance.

例如：买方对于卖方开具的见票后 30 天付款的跟单汇票，于提示时应立即承兑，并应于汇票到期时即予付款，承兑后交运输单据。

3) Letter of credit (L/C) (信用证)

(1) Definition of Letter of Credit (信用证的定义)

According to The Uniform Customs and Practice for Documentary Credits, 2007 Revision, ICC Publication No. 600 ("UCP600"), documentary credit means any arrangement, however named or described, that is irrevocable and thereby constitutes a definite undertaking of the issuing bank to honor a complying presentation. "To honor" means: a. to pay at sight if the credit is available by sight payment. b. to incur a deferred payment undertaking and pay at maturity if the credit is available by deferred payment. c. to accept a bill of exchange ("draft") drawn by the beneficiary and pay at maturity if the credit is available by acceptance.

That is to say letter of credit is a conditional undertaking of payment in writing, recorded a sum certain in money, issued by a bank to the exporter on request and instruction of the importer. The payment by letter of credit refers to the credit given by banks, it is not money, but the issuing bank or the bank concerned promise to make payment by banks' credits. The issuing banks provide credits, not money, so letter of credit belongs to banker's credit.

The parties involved in letter of credit include the applicant (or opener), the issuing bank (or opening bank), the beneficiary, the advising bank (or notifying bank), the negotiating bank, the paying bank, the accepting bank, the reimbursing bank and so on.

国际商会《跟单信用证统一惯例(UCP600)》(2007 年修订版)给信用证的定义是：信用证是指一项不可撤销的安排，无论其名称或描述如何，该项安排构成开证行对相符交单予以承付的确定承诺。承付是指：a.如果信用证为即期付款信用证，则即期付款。b.如果信用证为延期付款信用证，则承诺延期付款并在承诺到期日付款。c.如果信用证为承兑信用证，则承兑受益人开出的汇票并在汇票到期日付款。

信用证是银行根据进口人的请求和指示向出口人开立的一定金额的，有条件的承诺付款的书面文件。信用证支付方式是银行的信用，而不是资金，开证行或相关银行以自己的信用做出付款保证。开证行提供的是信用，不是资金，所以信用证属于银行信用。

信用证中涉及的当事人包括开证申请人、开证行、受益人、通知行、议付行、付款行、承兑行、偿付行等。

(2)　Operation of Documentary Letter of Credit by Negotiation (跟单议付信用证业务)

As documentary letter of credit by negotiation is commonly used in international trade, let's discuss its procedure of operation. (See Fig. 6-7 Procedures of Documentary L/C by negotiation)

由于在国际贸易中最常使用跟单议付信用证，现介绍跟单议付信用证的业务流程。(如图 6-7 跟单议付信用证业务流程所示)

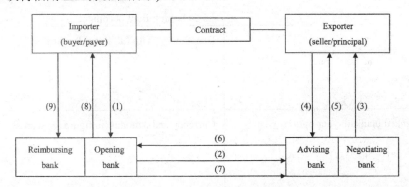

图 6-7　Procedures of Documentary L/C by negotiation(跟单议付信用证业务流程)

Remarks (说明):

(1)　The buyer makes application for a letter of credit with his bank and signs the opening bank's agreement form (See Fig. 6-8 Application form for establishment of L/C). The opening bank approves the application and issues the actual letter of credit document. (进口商向当地银行(开证行)申请开立信用证(如图 6-8 所示为信用证开证申请书)，并与开证行签订协议。开证行同意其申请后开出信用证。

(2)　The opening bank forwards the letter of credit to the advising bank. (开证行将信用证寄给通知行)

(3)　The advising bank delivers the letter of credit to the beneficiary. (通知行将信用证转递给受益人)

(4)　Having examined the letter of credit, the beneficiary (seller) ships the goods to the buyer. After that, the beneficiary prepares documents, draws a draft and presents them to his bank. (受益人(出口商)经审核信用证认可后，即向买方发货。受益人发货后，备妥信用证规定的单据，送交当地银行议付)

(5)　The beneficiary's bank negotiates the documents and pays funds to the beneficiary in accordance with the letter of credit. (受益人银行(议付行)确认单据后，按照信用证规定将垫款给受益人)

(6)　The negotiating bank forwards the documents to the opening bank. (议付行将单据寄给开证行索款)

(7)　The opening bank receives the documents and checks them. If the documents are in order and comply with the letter of credit, the opening bank credits the negotiating bank's account. (开证行经审核单据无误后，付款给议付行)

(8)　The opening bank notifies the buyer to make payment for documents. (开证行通知进口人付款)

(9)　After making payment, the buyer receives the documents and take delivery of the goods. (进口人付款并取得货运单据后，即可提货)

 实用外贸英语

表6-8 Application form for establishment of L/C(信用证开证申请书)

IRREVOCABLE DOCUMENTARY CREDIT APPLICATION
开立不可撤销跟单信用证申请书　　　Date 日期_____
TO: HANGZHOU UNITED RURAL COMMERCIAL BANK CO.，LTD.

	Credit No.信用证号码
☐ Issued by mail ☐ With brief advice by teletransmission ☐ Issued SWIFT	Expiry Date and Place _____ ☐ in the country of Beneficiary ☐ at Issuing Bank's counter
Applicant TEl:　　　　FAX:	Beneficiary (with full name & address) TEL:　　　　FAX:
Advising Bank(if blank, at your option) SWIFT NO.:	Currency and Amount (in figures & words)

Partial shipments ☐ allowed ☐ not allowed	Transshipment ☐ allowed ☐ not allowed	Credit available with _____By ☐ sight payment ☐ acceptance
Shipment from For transportation to Not later than		☐ negotiation ☐ deferred payment against the documents detailed herein
Terms ☐ FOB　　☐ CFR　　☐ CIF ☐ FCA　　☐ CPT　　☐ CIP ☐ OR OTHER TERMS_____		☐ and beneficiary's draft(s) at _____ sight　drawn on for_____of invoice value.

Documents required: (marked with "×")

☐ Signed Commercial Invoice in ___ originals and in ___ copies indicating L/C No. and Contract No.____

☐ 3/3 set of clean on board Ocean Bill of Lading made out to _____ and blank endorsed, marked "freight ( ) prepaid/( ) to collect", ( ) showing freight amount and notifying _____.

☐ Clean Air Waybill consigned to_____ marked "freight ( ) prepaid/ ( ) to collect" notifying _____.

续表

□ Insurance Policy/Certificate in full set for _____ of the invoice value, blank endorsed, showing claims payable at _____ in the currency of the draft, covering _____.

□ Packing List in ___ originals and in ____ copies indicating quantity, gross and net weight and Contract No., Seal No., Container No, B/L no. and Insurance policy No.

□ Certificate of Quantity / Weight in ____ originals and in ____ copies issued by

□ Certificate of quality in ____ copies issued by □ manufacturer / □ public recognized surveyor /

□ _____.

□ Certificate of Origin in ____ originals issued by _____.

□ Beneficiary's certified copy of fax / telex dispatched to the applicant within ____ day(s) after shipment advising L/C No, name of vessel, date of shipment, name of goods, quantity, weight and value of goods.

□ Other documents, if any:

Description of goods / □ See Attachments:

  COMMODITY:

  UNIT PRICE:

  QUANTITY:

  TOTAL AMOUNT:

  Additional instructions: 附加条款

□ All banking charges outside the Issuing Bank including reimbursing charges are for account of Beneficiary.

□ Documents must be presented with in ____ days after date of issuance of the transport document but within the validity of the Credit.

□ Both quantity and Credit amount _____% more or less are allowed.

□ This is a usance L/C payable at sight basis by the Issuing Bank or the Paying Bank nominated by the Issuing Bank. Discount interest and other banking fees are for account of us.

□ Other terms and conditions, if any:

本信用证为履行第_____号进口合同开立，开证前实存开证保证金为开证金额_____%，即(币种及金额大写)人民币_____，其余信用证金额申请减免保证金。

本笔开证业务受编号为_____的《减免保证金开证额度合同》的约束。

声明：我公司已对本申请书及其背面承诺书各印就条款进行审慎研阅，对各条款含义与贵行理解一致。

我公司在此签章表示对本申请书及背面承诺书印就条款的接受，愿受其约束。

申请人的外币及人民币账户：   申请人(签章)

开户行：

外币账号：   法定代表人

人民币账号：   或授权代理人 年   月   日

续表

同意受理。本信用证为假远期信用证的，融资利率为对外付款日当天的_____(大写)个月 LIBOR 加____点差。
银行(签章)
负责人或授权代理人　年　月　日

(3) Types of Letter of Credit (信用证的种类)

a. Documentary L/C and Clean L/C (跟单信用证和光票信用证)

b. Irrevocable L/C and Revocable L/C (不可撤销信用证和可撤销信用证)

c. Confirmed L/C and Unconfirmed L/C (保兑信用证和不保兑信用证)

d. Payable L/C, Acceptable L/C and Negotiable L/C (付款信用证、承兑信用证和议付信用证)

e. Sight L/C and Usance L/C (即期信用证和远期信用证)

f. Transferable L/C and Non-transferable L/C (可转让信用证和不可转让信用证)

g. Revolving letter of credit (循环信用证)

h. Reciprocal L/C (对开信用证)

i. Back to back L/C (对背信用证)

j. Anticipatory L/C (预支信用证)

k. Standby L/C (备用信用证)

(4) Terms of Payment by Letter of Credit in Contract

When letter of credit is used as the payment mode agreed upon, it should state clearly the date of opening L/C, opening bank, beneficiary, types of L/C, amount, tenor of payment of draft, period of validity, expiry place, etc. in the contract.

当约定采用信用证作为支付方式时，应在合同的支付条款中规定清楚开证时间、开证行、受益人、信用证的类型、开证金额、汇票的付款日期、有效期和到期地点等项内容。

① Terms of Payment by sight L/C (即期信用证支付条款)

e.g. The Buyer shall open through a bank acceptable to the Seller an Irrevocable Letter of Credit payable at sight to reach the seller 30 days before the month of shipment, valid for negotiation in China until the 15th day after the date of shipment.

例如：买方通过一家卖方可接受的银行，于装运月份 30 天前开立不可撤销即期信用证并送达卖方，有效期至装运日后 15 天在中国议付有效。

② Terms of Payment by time L/C (远期信用证支付条款)

e.g. The Buyer shall open through a bank acceptable to the Seller an Irrevocable Letter of Credit at 30 days after sight to reach the seller by the end of Aug. 2007, valid for negotiation in China until the 15th day after the date of shipment.

例如：买方通过一家卖方可接受的银行，于 2007 年 8 月底前开立不可撤销见票后 30 天付款的信用证并送达卖方，装运日后 15 天在中国议付有效。

Section 2 Correspondence

1. Sample Letters

Letter 1 (Buyer Instructs Bank)

Dear Sirs,

We enclose an application form for documentary credit[1] and shall be glad if you will arrange to open for our account with your office in London an irrevocable letter of credit for £...infavor of the Urban Trading Company, the credit to be valid until Oct. 30.

The credit which evidences shipment of 3,000 tons of steel may be used against presentation of the following documents: Bills of Lading in triplicate, one copy each of Commercial Invoice, Packing List[2], Certificate of Insurance and Certificate of Origin. The company may draw on your London office at 60 d/s[3] for each shipment.

Yours faithfully,

Encl.: Application for Irrevocable Documentary L/C

Letter 2 (Bank Agrees to Open a Credit)

Dear Sirs,

As instructed in your letter of 2 May we are arranging to open a letter of credit with our office in London in favor of the Urban Trading Company, valid until 30 October.

Please check our enclosed fax opening the credit to ensure that it agrees to your instructions. As soon as the credit is used we shall debit your account with the amount notified to us as having been drawn against the L/C.

We shall see to it that your instructions are carefully carried out.

Yours faithfully,

Letter 3 (Buyer Notifies Seller)

Dear Sirs,

We are glad to inform you that we have now opened an irrevocable letter of credit through the Bank of London, for £...in your favor.

Please make sure that the shipment is effected within September, since punctual delivery[4] is

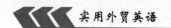

one of the important considerations in dealing with our market. We are awaiting your Shipping Advice[5].

Yours faithfully,

Letter 4 (Urging Establishing of L/C)

Dear Sirs,

Our Sales Confirmation No. TE151

Reference is made to the 1,000 cartons of Canned Asparagus under the subjected sales confirmation, we wish to draw your attention to the fact that the date of delivery is approaching, but up to the present we have not received the covering Letter of Credit. Please do your utmost to expedite[6] its establishment, so that we may execute the order within the prescribed time[7].

In order to avoid subsequent[8] amendments, please see to it that the L/C stipulations are in exact accordance with the terms of the contract.

We look forward to receiving your favorable response at an early date.

Yours faithfully,

(reply)

Dear Sirs

Your Sales Confirmation No. TE151

We have received your faxes dated 20th of April and 8th of May, urging us to establish the L/C for the captioned sales confirmation.

We are very sorry for the delay in opening the L/C, which was due to an oversight[9] of our staff. However, upon receipt of your fax of May 8, we immediately opened the covering credit with Bank of China, and trust the same is now in your hand. Please allow us to express again our regret for the inconvenience that has been caused to you.

Yours faithfully,

Letter 5 (Amendment to L/C)

Dear Sirs,

Re: L/C No. 345 Issued by First National City Bank

We have received the above L/C established by you in payment-for your Order No. 678 covering 200 cases of …

When we checked the L/C with the relevant contract, we found that the amount in your L/C is insufficient[10]. The correct total CIF New York value of your order comes to US$2,750.00 instead of US$2,550.00. The difference is US$200.00.

Your L/C allows us only half a month to effect delivery. But when we signed the contract we have agreed that the delivery should be made within one month upon receipt of the Letter of Credit.

As to packing, the contract stipulates that the goods should be packed in carton and reinforced[11] with nylon straps[12] outside, but your L/C required metal straps[13] instead. We think we should arrange the packing according to the contract.

In view of the above, you are kindly requested to increase the amount of your L/C by US$200.00, extend the shipment and validity to September 15, 30 respectively, as well as amend the term of packing. Meanwhile please advise us by fax.

Yours faithfully,

2. Notes to Text

(1) documentary credit 跟单信用证

(2) packing list 装箱单，货物明细单

(3) at 60 d/s = at 60 days' sight 见票 60 天付款

(4) punctual delivery 准时交货

We always keep excellent quality, low price and punctual delivery time. 我们始终保持优良的品质，低廉的价格，准时交货时间。

If you can guarantee punctual delivery, we shall place a large order with you. 若贵方能保证及时交货，我们就下大宗的订单。

(5) shipping advice = advice of shipment = shipment notice = notice of shipment 装船通知

(6) expedite 加快(进程等)，促进(措施等)，迅速处理(事物等)

(7) prescribed time 约定的期限

Acceptance must take place within a prescribed time. 承诺必须在规定的期间内做出。

(8) subsequent 继……之后的，随后的，后来的

(9) oversight 疏忽出错，忽略

(10) insufficient 不足的

(11) reinforce 加固

(12) nylon strap 尼龙绳

(13) metal strap 金属绳

3. Useful Expressions

(1) 作为一项特殊照顾，我们接受付款交单方式支付你方这笔订货。

As a special accommodation, we will accept document against payment for this trial order.

(2) 我方同意以托收方式开出以你方为受益人的即期跟单汇票支付货款，不以信用证支付。

We agree that payment is made by documentary draft at sight drawn in your favor on collection basis instead of L/C.

(3) 我们承诺交货时付款。

We guarantee that payment will be made on delivery.

(4) 对于你方以电汇方式不晚于 11 月 30 日预付全部货款，我方表示感谢。

We should express thanks that you pay the total amount to us in advance by T/T not later than 30 November.

(5) 我们从应付的总额中扣除 3%的佣金，现随信附寄 1000 美元的汇款单以结清账款。

We have deducted a commission of 3% from the total amount due and enclose a remittance bill for US$1,000 in full settlement of account.

(6) 随信附上即期汇票 57.29 美元以补齐差额，收到后请回复。

Enclosed is Demand Draft for the difference of US$57.29. Please let us have your acknowledgement of receipt.

(7) 如发票无误，请立即汇款为盼。

If the invoice is correct, your prompt remittance will be appreciated.

(8) 请尽快寄给我方支票以结清去年年底之前的账款，谢谢。

Please kindly send us the check for the settlement of your account to the end of last year at your earliest convenience.

(9) 按你方要求，我们破例接受即期付款交单，但只此一回下不为例。

In compliance with your request, we exceptionally accept delivery against D/P at sight, but this should not be regarded as a precedent.

(10) 由于金额小，我们同意向你方开出即期跟单汇票。

As the amount involved is rather small, we agreed to draw on you by documentary sight draft.

(11) 很抱歉，贵方订单中规定的付款条件不能为我方所接收。

We regret to say the payment terms stipulated in your order are unacceptable to us.

(12) 请将 15%的首笔付款电汇给我们，余额分三次付清。

Please remit the 15% down payment to us by T/T. Payment of the balance is to be made in three installments.

(13) 开立信用证费用很高，会影响到像我方这样小公司的资金周转，因此最好采用付款交单或承兑交单的方式。

It is expensive to open an L/C and ties up the capital of a small company like ours. So it is better for us to adopt D/P or D/A.

Section 3   Dialogues

Dialogue 1

Payment by L/C is our usual practice

Becker: Mr. Santinelli, we have settled the price, quality and quantity of the transaction. Now, let's come to the terms of payment. What do you say?

Santinelli: For payment, we only accept confirmed irrevocable letter of credit payable against draft at sight and with partial shipment and transshipment allowed clause.

Becker: Oh, that will tie up too severely. Would you give us some favorable terms, such as D/A, for the sake of our future cooperation?

Santinelli: I have to say sorry, Mr. Becker. Payment by L/C is our usual practice. As a matter of fact, L/C protects the importer as well as the exporter.

Becker: That is true, but opening an L/C is rather complicated. I wonder if D/P is acceptable to you, then.

Santinelli: I am afraid we must insist on our usual form.

Becker: You see opening an L/C with a bank involves a deposit. That will tie up our funds.

Santinelli: You might consult with your bank and see if the required deposit can be reduced to a minimum.

Becker: Nevertheless, bank charges still occur. How about 50% by L/C and the rest by D/P?

Santinelli: I am awfully sorry. I am afraid I cannot promise even that. We usually require payment by confirmed irrevocable L/C, payable against shipping documents.

Becker: Well, it seems that I have no other choice but to accept the payment by sight L/C. The season is drawing near, you know, so we'd like to take delivery at the end of June.

Santinelli: If so, you must open the L/C a month earlier.

Becker: Very well. I'll arrange for the L/C as soon as I get home. Thank you very much.

Santinelli: I'm glad to be of help.

Dialogue 2

Could you agree to payment by D/A?

Ms. Lin is taking Mrs. Jones to see a factory. Before they start, they're talking in the lounge.

Jones: There are a few minutes before we visit the factory. May I ask you a question?

Lin: Go ahead, please.

Jones: Could you agree to payment by D/A? This is a sample order.

Lin: Occasionally we do. But yours is a normal case, isn't it?

Jones: As you know, it doesn't pay to open an L/C with a bank for such a small amount.

Lin: We'll consider that when we make you the firm offer.

Jones: Thanks.

Lin: I hope after the first supply your customers will place regular orders.

Jones: For regular orders, couldn't you agree to payment by L/C at 60 days' sight?

Lin: I'm afraid not. Our usual practice is L/C at sight.

Jones: I see.

Lin: Here comes the car to pick us up.

Jones: Let's go.

Lin: Fine.

Notes

1. confirmed irrevocable letter of credit：保兑不可撤销信用证。Confirmed L/C：保兑信用证。Irrevocable L/C：不可撤销信用证

2. draft at sight(=sight draft)：即期汇票，即见票即付的汇票

3. partial shipment：分批装运

4. transshipment：转船，转运

5. D/A：Documents against Acceptance, 承兑交单

6. D/P：Documents against Payment, 付款交单

7. deposit：存款，保证金

8. tie up：占用。e.g. He tied up the phone for an hour.

9. The season is drawing near, you know, so we'd like to take delivery at the end of June. 销售季临近，所以我们想在六月底收货。drawing near：临近；take delivery：提取货物，收货

10. It doesn't pay to…：不值得，不合算。

11. Here comes the car to pick us up. 接我们的车来了。e.g. Here comes the bus.

Section 4   Exercises

1. Translate the following sentences into English:

(1) 买方应不迟于 2014 年 10 月 10 日将 100%的货款以电汇方式预付至卖方。

(2) 买方通过一家卖方可接受的银行于 1998 年 8 月底前开立不可撤销见票后 30 天付款的信用证，并送达卖方，装运日后 15 天在中国议付有效。

(3) 我方已收到贵方由中国银行开出的以我方为受益人的第 3299 号保兑的不可撤销的信用证。

(4) 本信用证项下金额于议付后自动循环两次。

(5) 为保证如期迅速装运，请开立有关信用证，此信用证须在装船前 20 天到达我方。

(6) 我们只能接受远期 60 天信用证作为付款方式。

2. Translate the following sentences into Chinese:

(1) Your confirmed, irrevocable L/C No.7766 issued by the Bank of China has arrived.

(2) In order to avoid subsequent amendments to L/C, please see to the following.

(3) Upon first presentation the Buyers shall pay against documentary draft drawn by the Sellers at sight. The shipping documents are to be delivered against payment only.

(4) The Buyers shall duly accept the documentary draft drawn by the Sellers at 30 days after sight upon first presentation and make the payment on its maturity. The shipping documents are to be delivered against payment only.

(5) We can accept D/P at sight, but this should not be regarded as a precedent.

(6) If you insist on L/C, we have no choice but charge you 3% as handing fee.

3. Translate the following letter into English:

×××先生：

我们上次从贵公司购买农产品时采用信用证方式支付，但是这给我公司带来了很大的负担。从开立信用证到收回货款，资金至少要占用 3 个月的时间。

如果贵公司能简化支付方式，相信一定会有助于我们今后的合作。我们建议支付方式改为货到后凭单付款。

如能仔细考虑以上建议并尽早回复，我们将不胜感激。

4. Translate the following letter into Chinese:

Dear Mr. …,

With reference to our fax dated the March 15, requesting you to establish the letter of credit

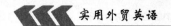

covering the mentioned order, we have not received the covering L/C up to the present.

As the goods have been ready for shipment, it urges you to take immediate action. Please do your utmost to expedite its establishment.

We look forward to receiving your favorable response at an early date.

Yours faithfully,

5. Compose a dialogue based on the following situation:

Mr. Yang, a salesman from export company, insists on paying by L/C.
Mr. Jones, the buyer, cannot accept L/C. but insists on paying D/A at 30 days after sight.
Finally they agree on payment by D/P at sight.

Section 5   Solution to Problem

Is L/C highly versatile and all-powerful?

No, it is not. It has advantages, unavoidably it has disadvantages.

1)   Advantages

(1)   guaranteed

Because of banker's credit, exporter has opening bank's guarantee of payment, importer has opening bank's guarantee of issuance of L/C and payment for exporter instead of importer on the condition of import's application and deposit. It resolves the contradiction between both parties of importer and exporter, which they don't believe in each other.

(2)   financing and efficient

Under L/C, importer usually deposits a small part of the total amount of L/C in opening bank, opening bank lends credit to importer and opens L/C covering total amount of L/C, it is actually financing for importer, negotiating bank could also give exporter a sum of money in exchange for documents, it is similar to a loan on security/mortgage, this is so called negotiation, exporter is even more able to get a packing loan from negotiating bank before shipment, it is actually financing for exporter, it's able to quicken the rotation of exporter's capital. L/C facilitates trade, efficiency of trade could be improved.

Under L/C, it's impossible for exporter to postpone shipment, importer could take delivery

(3)   preferential/favorable

If payment by L/C, it's possible for importer to get better trade conditions on other clauses, for example, importer probably asks to advance shipment.

2) Disadvantages

(1) uneconomic

Under L/C, importer has to pay opening bank deposit for L/C opening, the amount of deposit is dependent on his credit status, no matter how much is it, importer's capital is frozen in opening bank, it isn't rotated, while under sight D/P, it wouldn't happen; Exporter has to pay negotiating bank discounting interests, pay negotiating bank documents forwarding fee, and pay advising bank notifying fee, moreover, if there are discrepancies in documents and opening bank is willing to accept defective documents, exporter has to pay discrepancy fee.

(2) risky

Under L/C it becomes a pure transaction of documents, exporter is able to get payment, if only documents are strictly in conformity with stipulations in L/C, even though exporter effects shipment of fake goods or puts nothing in the cartons and lades cargo on board the ship; If discrepancies occur in documents, payment is likely to be refused, exporter's draft is possibly to be dishonored.

(3) complicated

Operation and procedure are complicated, relevant parties are more than other modes of payment.

Part 2   Fulfillment of Contract

Unit 7

Shipment

Section 1　Introduction

1. Delivery Conditions (装运条款)

Delivery conditions include the time of delivery, and in some cases including the time of loading and unloading, and the charges resulting from loading and unloading operations, the port of shipment, the port of destination, partial shipments and transshipment, shipping documents, etc.

装运条款主要包括装运时间，有时包括装卸时间、装卸费用、装运港和目的港、分批和转船的规定等内容。

(1). Time of Shipment (装运时间)

The time of shipment refers to the time limit during which the seller shall ship the goods on the specified the means of transport. There are the following ways to stipulate the time of shipment in the contract.

装运时间又称装运期，通常是指卖方应在规定的时间或期限内将货物装上指定运输工具。在进出口合同中对装运时间的规定方法，主要有以下几种。

① Stipulate the definite time of delivery (明确规定具体期限)

e.g. Shipment on or before March 15th, 2006 (2006 年 3 月 15 日前装运)

　　Shipment during January/February/March 2006 (2006 年 1/2/3 月装运)

　　Shipment on or before April 30st, 2006 (装运期不迟于 2006 年 4 月 30 日装运)

② Stipulate a period of fixed time, the seller can arrange shipment during whichever date (规定了某一段装运时间，卖方可以选择其中任何一天装运)

e.g. Shipment during March 2006 (2006 年 3 月份装运)

Shipment during January/February/March 2006 (2006 年 1/2/3 月装运)

Shipment within 15 days after receipt of remittance (收到货款后 15 天内安排装运)

③ Stipulate shipment within…days after receipt of the letter of credit (规定在收到信用证后××天内安排装运)

　　e.g. Shipment within 45 days after receipt of L/C (收到信用证后 45 天内安排装运)

Shipment within 1 months after receipt of L/C (收到信用证后 1 个月内安排装运)

In order to prevent the buyer from opening L/C late, when the clause "shipment within … days after the date of receipt of L/C" is used, it is necessarily accompanied by another clause "The relevant L/C must reach the seller not later than …". In this way a somewhat indefinite clause is made more or less definite.

在使用"收到信用证后××天内安排装运"条款时，还必须加上"信用证不得迟于……到达我处"。从某种意义上说，也是对装运时间的限制。

(2) Port of Shipment and Port of Destination (装运港和目的港)

Generally, either a definite one port, or two or more ports can be stipulated as port of shipment (or port of destination) in the contract. The points that we should pay attention to when stipulating the port of shipment in an export contract: A. The port of shipment shall be close to the origin of the goods. B. We should take into consideration the loading and unloading, and specific transportation conditions and the standards of freight and various charges at home and abroad. When we determine the port of destination, we must pay attention to the following points: A. We should not accept the port in the country with which our government does not permit to do business. B. The stipulation on the port of destination shall be definite and specific. C. If we have to choose a port which has no direct liner to stop by or the trips are few, we should stipulate "transshipment to be permitted" in the contract. D. The port of destination shall be the one at which the vessel may safely arrive and be always afloat. E. Facilities in the port of loading or unloading are also very important and therefore reasonable attention should be given to issues such as loading and unloading facilities, freightage and additional freightage, etc. F. Pay attention to the names of foreign ports.

一般在合同中可规定一个明确的港口，也可规定两个或两个以上的港口作为装运港(或目的港)。当在出口时规定装运港应特别注意的问题：A.选择靠近商品产地的装运港。B.要考虑国内外装运港口的装卸条件、具体的运输条件、收费标准等。当规定目的港时，应注意以下问题：A.如果我国政府规定不能与某个国家做外贸业务，那么，就不能选择该国的港口为目的港。B.对于目的港的规定必须明确具体。C.如果我国没有直达船或直达船很少，就应该在合同中写清楚允许转船。D.所选择的目的港必须适合货船的停靠。E.码头的装卸设备也很重要，因此，必须注意码头的装卸设备、货运条件、额外费用等问题。F.应注意国外目的港的重名问题。

(3) Partial shipments and Transshipment (分批装运和转运)

In case of an export business covering a large amount of goods, it is necessary to make shipment in several lots by several carriers sailing on different dates. That is partial shipment.

According to the relevant stipulations of the UCP (Uniform Customs and Practice for Documentary Credits), Transport documents which appear on their face to indicate that shipment has been made on the same means of conveyance and for the same journey, provided they indicate the same destination, will not be regarded as covering partial shipments, even if the transport documents indicate different dates of issuance and/or different ports of shipments, places of taking in charge, or dispatch.

In case where such kind of clause as "partial shipment is allowed" is stipulated in the contract (such as, shipment during March and April in two equal monthly lots), then, the seller should strictly follow the stipulations of the contract. According to the relevant stipulations of the "Uniform Customs and Practice for Documentary Credits", if any installment is not shipped within the period allowed for that installment, the credit ceases to be available for that and any subsequent installments, unless otherwise stipulated in the credit.

分批装运是指一笔成交的货物分若干批于不同航次装运。

按《跟单信用证统一惯例》的有关规定，如果运输单据表面注明货物是使用同一运输工具并经过同一路线运输的，而且运输单据注明的目的地相同，那么即使每套运输单据注明的装运日期不同及/或装货港、接受监管地、发运地不同，也不作为分批装运。

如果在合同中规定了分批装运条款(例如，3 月和 4 月分两批每月平均装运)，那么，卖方应严格按合同规定执行。按《跟单信用证统一惯例》的有关规定，除非另有规定，否则其中任何一批未按规定装运，则本批及以后各批均告失效。

Transshipment in ocean transport, is the movement of goods in transit from another at the ports of transshipment before the goods reach the port of destination.

If transshipment is necessary in case of no direct or suitable ship available for shipment, clause in these regard can be included in the contract. According to the relevant stipulations of the "Uniform Customs and Practice for Documentary Credits", unless the credit stipulates otherwise, partial shipment and transshipment are allowed. But contractual laws in some country stipulate that partial shipment and transshipment, if not stipulated in the contract, shall not be deemed to be allowed. It, therefore, should be clearly stipulated in the relevant contract.

一般来说，分批装运和转运对卖方有利，卖方可以争取主动。如果没有直达船或无合适的船舶运输，而需要转运的可以要求在合同中订立允许装船条款。按《跟单信用证统一惯例》的有关规定，除非信用证有相反的规定，可允许分批装运和转船。但按有些国外合同法，如果没有在合同中规定分批装运和转运条款，那么将不等于可以分批装运和转运。因此，一般应对此条款明确规定。

(4)　Advice of Shipment (装运通知)

In the case of concluding a shipment contract in international trade, the seller, after the goods is placed on board the vessel, should at the agreed time, notify the buyer of the contract No., the name and weight of the goods, the invoice amount, the vessel's name and the date of shipment so that the buyer can make necessary arrangements for taking delivery of the goods and

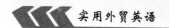

purchasing the relevant insurance (where applicable). (See Fig. 7-1 Sample of Shipping Advice and Fig.7-2 Example of Shipping Advice)

在国际贸易中，如果订立的是装运合同，则卖方应在货物装船后再约定时间将合同号、货物品名、重量、发票金额、船名及装船日期等内容告知买方，以便买方做好接卸货物的准备和办理保险(如果需要)。(如图 7-1 装运通知样本和图 7-2 装运通知实例所示)

SHIPPING ADVICE

FAX: Invoice No.: _____

TELEX: L/C No.: _____

TEL: S/C No.: _____

MESSRS:

Dear Sirs:

We hereby inform you that the goods under the above mentioned credit have shipped. The details of the shipment are as follows:

Commodity: _____

Quantity:_____

Amount:_____

Bill of Lading No.:_____

Ocean Vessel:_____

Port of Shipment:_____

Port of Destination:_____

Date of Shipment:_____

We hereby certify that the above content is true and correct.

Company name:

  Address: Signature:

图 7-1 Sample of Shipping Advice(装运通知样本)

SHANGHAI TEXTILES IMPORT & EXPORT CORPORATION

27. CHUNGSHAN ROAD E.1.

SHANGHAI CHINA

TEL: 8621-65342517   FAX: 8621-65724743

SHIPPING ADVICE

Nov. 20th,2001

Messre: **CRYSTAL KOBE LTD.,**

Dear Sirs，

      Re: Invoice No.: **STP015088**   **L/C No.: L-02-I-03437**

We hereby inform you that the goods under the above mentioned credit have been shipped. The details of the shipment ae stated below.

Commodity:	**LADIE'S 55% ACRYLIC 45% COTTON KNITED BLOUSE**
Quantity:	**120 CARTONS**
Amount:	**USD 23,522.50**
Ocean Vessel:	**ZHELU V.031118SE**
Bill of lading No.:	**CSA1505**
E.T.D.:	**On / or about Nov. 25th, 2001**
Port of Loading:	**SHANGHAI**
Destination:	**NEW YORK**

We hereby certify that the above content is true and correct.

SHANGHAI TEXTILES IMPORT & EXPORT CORP.

× × ×

图 7-2　Example of Shipping Advice(装运通知实例)

2. Modes of International Transportation (国际货物运输方式)

As to the modes of transportation in international practice, there are many modes to carry the goods purchased, such as ocean transport, railway transport, air transport, river and lake transport, postal transport, road transport, pipelines transport, land bridge transport and international multimode transport and so on. As ocean transport is the most widely used form of transportations in international trade, the author mainly introduce it in this text.

So far as foreign trade is concerned, goods transport is mostly (over 80% of world trade in volume terms) done by ocean vessel, which can be divided into liners and chartering.

国际货物运输有多种方式：海洋运输、铁路运输、航空运输、江河运输、邮政运输、公路运输、管道运输、大陆桥运输以及国际多式联运等。因为海洋运输是国际贸易运输中采用最广泛的一种形式，故本文重点介绍海运方式。

在国际贸易货物运输中，大多数(80%以上)都是由远洋运输船舶来完成的，海上货物运输可分为班轮运输和租船运输。

3. Shipping Documents (货运单据)

International attaches so great importance to shipping documents that, to a certain degree, it can be called trade of documents, or "symbolic" trade. As a rule, every contract of sale stipulates the kinds of shipping documents required. Generally, commercial invoice, bill of lading, insurance policy or certificate, packing list, and weight memo etc., are called shipping documents. In addition, other documents required by the buyers and related to the matter of duty to be paid on the imported goods, sometimes, are also included in shipping documents, they are the pro forma, consular invoice, certificate of origin, certificate of value, certificate of inspection. This unit mainly deals with bill of lading, commercial invoice, pro forma invoice, packing list, weight memo.

国际贸易对单证的要求非常高，从某种程度上讲国际贸易是一种单证的交易，"象征性交货"，因为货运单证代表着对货物的所有权。一般来说，每一笔销售合同都要规定各种所需要的单证。商业发票、提单、保险单、装箱单、重量单等通常称为货运单证。此外，货运单证还包括买方所要求的以及与对进口货物征收关税有关的单证，如形式发票、领事发票、产地证书、价值证书、检验证书等。本单元将主要涉及商业发票、形式发票、提单、装箱单、重量单和检验证书。

(1) Bill of Lading (提单)

Bill of lading is a document given by a shipping company, representing both a receipt for the goods shipped and a contract for shipment between the shipping company and the shipper. It is also a document of title to the goods, giving the holder or the assignee the right to possession of the goods. (See Fig. 7-3 Sample of Bill of Lading and Fig. 7-4 Example of Bill of Lading)

提单是轮船公司签发的单证，既代表承运货物的收据，又代表承运人和托运人之间的运输合同。它也是代表货物所有权的证件，它给予持有人或受让人提货的权利。(如图 7-3 所示为空白海运提单，如图 7-4 所示为填制好的海运提单。)

Shipper	B/L NO.
Consignee	**PIL** **PACIFIC INTERNATION LINES (PTE) LTD** (Incorporated in Singapore)
Notify Party	**COMBINED TRANSPORT BILL OF LADING** Received in apparent good order and condition except as otherwise noted the total number of container or other packages or units enumerated below for transportation from the place of receipt to the place of delivery subject to the terms hereof. One of the signed Bills of Lading must be surrendered duly endorsed in exchange for the Goods or delivery order. On presentation of this document (duly) Endorsed to the Carrier by or on behalf of the Holder, the rights and liabilities arising in accordance with the terms hereof shall (without prejudice to any rule of common law or statute rendering them binding on the Merchant) become binding in all respects between the Carrier and the Holder as though the contract evidenced hereby had been made between them. **SEE TERMS ON ORIGINAL B/L**

Vessel and Voyage Number	Port of Loading	Port of Discharge
Place of Receipt	Place of Delivery	Number of Original Bs/L

PARTICULARS AS DECLARED BY SHIPPER – CARRIER NOT RESPONSIBLE

Container Nos/Seal Nos. Marks and/Numbers	No. of Container / Packages / Description of Goods	Gross Weight (Kilos)	Measurement (cu-metres)

FREIGHT & CHARGES	Number of Containers/Packages (in words)
	Shipped on Board Date:
	Place and Date of Issue:
	In Witness Whereof this number of Original Bills of Lading stated Above all of the tenor and date one of which being accomplished the others to stand void. for **PACIFIC INTERNATIONAL LINES (PTE) LTD**

图 7-3　Sample of Bill of Lading(海运提单样本)

BILL OF LADING

SHIPPER YUNNAN ELECTRON I/E CORP. 211 RENMING ROAD KUNMING YUNNAN CHINA			B/L NO. LD-DRGBL01
CONSIGNE TO ORDER			**COSCO** 广州远洋运输有限责任公司 **GUANGZHOU OCEAN SHIPPING CO., LTD.**
NOTIFY PARTY U.S GLOBAL ELECTRONCO., LTD. 308 SEASHORE ROAD NEWYORK, PA 19446 U.S.A			
PLACE OF RECEIPT GUANGZHOU CY	OCEAN VESSEL DONGFENG		ORIGINAL
VOYAGE NO. V.208	PORT OF LOADING GUANGZHOU		**Combined Transport BILL OF LADING**
PORTOF DISCHARGE NEWYORK	PLACE OF DELIVERY		

MARKS	NOS. & KINDS OF PKGS.	DESCRIPTION OF GOODS	G.W.(kg)	MEAS(m³)
U.S GLOBAL ELECTRON CO., LTD NEWYORK U.S.A CX-TRMSQ06 NO. 1-500	500 CARTONS	MICROWAVE NV-123	5	0.25

TO TAL NUMBER OF CONTAINERS SAY FIVE HUNDRED CARTONS ONLY
OR PACKAGES (IN WORDS)

FREIGHT PREPAID
L/C NO. ETN-CXLC06

FREIGHT & CHARGES	REVENUE TONS		RATE	PER	PREPAID	COLLECT
EX. RATE	PREPAID AT	PAYABLE AT		PLACE AND DATE OF ISSUE		
	TOTAL PREPAID	NUMBER OF ORIGINAL B(S)L THREE		GUANGZHOU 31-AUGUST-06		

LOADING ON BOARD THE VESSEL		李立 COSCO GUANGZHOU OCEAN SHIPPING CO., LTD.
DATE 31-AUGUST-06	BY COSCO GUANGZHOU OCEAN SHIPPING CO., LTD. 李立	

图 7-4　Example of Bill of Lading(海运提单实例)

Classification of Bill of Lading (提单的种类)

There are several types of Bills of Lading which are categorized in different ways.

根据不同的方法提单可分为如下几种类型。

A. On board B/L and received for shipment B/L (已装船提单和备运提单)

B. Clean B/L and unclean B/L (清洁提单和不清洁提单)

C. Straight B/L, Order B/L and Blank B/L (记名提单、指示提单和不记名提单)

D. Direct B/L, Transshipment B/L and Through B/L (直达提单、转船提单和联运提单)

E. Long form B/L and Short form B/L (全式提单和略式提单)

F. Liner B/L and Charter party B/L (班轮提单和租船提单)

G. Other types of B/L (其他类型的提单)

Besides the above-mentioned types of B/L, there are some other types such as: container B/L, on Deck B/L, stale B/L, house B/L, antedated B/L and advanced B/L.

除了上述提单外，还有其他一些种类的提单，如集装箱提单、舱面提单、过期提单、运输代理行提单、倒签提单和预借提单。

(2) Airway Bill (航空运单)

The airway bill, also called air consignment note, is a document or consignment note used for the carriage of goods by air supplied by the carrier to the consignor.

空运提单，也称为航空托运单，是用来证明货物已由承运人通过航空方式交给收货人。

Airway Bill has the following features:

①   It is a transport contract signed between the consignor/shipper and the carrier/ airline.

②   It is a receipt from the airline acknowledging the receipt of the consignment from the shipper.

③   The airway bill is an internationally standardized document mostly printed in English and in the official language of the country of departure, which facilitates the on-carriage of goods going through 2 to 3 airlines in different countries to the final destination. Generally, there are usually 12 copies of each airway bill for distribution to the various parties, such as the shipper, consignee, issuing carrier, second carrier (if applicable), third carrier (if applicable), airport of destination, airport of departure, and extra copies for other purposes (if required). Copies 1, 2 and 3 are the originals. The No. 1 Original waybill is retained by the airline for filing and accounting purposes—"For the carrier". This is signed by the consignor. The No. 2 Original waybill is to be carried with the consignment and delivered to the consignee at the destination—"For the consignee". This is signed by the carrier, as well as the consignor, and is sent with the goods to the consignee. The No. 3 Original waybill is for the shipper, who may present it to the negotiating bank as a shipping document evidencing shipment having been made—"For the consignor". This is signed by the carrier and sent back to the consignor.(See Fig. 7-5 Airway Bill)

航空货运单

999				

Shipper's Name and Address | **Shipper's Account Number**

999—

NOT NEGOTIABLE **中国民航** **CAAC**

AIR WAYBILL AIR CONSIGNMENT NOTE
ISSUED BY：THE CIVIL AVIATION ADMINIASTRATION OF CHINA
BEIJING CHINA

Copies 1, 2 and 3 of this Air Waybill are originals and have the same validity.

Consignee's Name and Address | **Consignee's Account Number**

It is agreed that the goods described herein are accepted in apparent good order and condition（except as noted）for carriage SUBJECT TO THE CONDITIONS OF CONTRACT ON THE REVERSE HEREOF. THE SHIPPER'S ATTENTION IS DRAWN TO THE NOTICE CONCERNINC CARRIER'S LIMITATION OF LIABILITY. Shipper may increase such limitation of liability by declaring a higher value for carriage and paying a supplemental charge if required.

ISSUING CARRIER MAINTAINS CARGO ACCIDENT LIABILITY INSURANCE

Issuing Carrier's Agent Name and City

Agent's IATA Code | **Account No.**

Accounting Information

Airport of Departure（Addr. of First Carrier）and Requested Routing

to	By First Carrier	Routing and Destination	to	by	to	by	Currency	CHGS Code	WT/NAL		Other		Declared Value for Carriage	Declared Value for Customs
									PPD	COLL	PPD	COLL		

Airport Destination	Flight/Date	For Carrier Use only	Flight/Date	Amount of Insurance	INSURANCE if carrier offers insurance, and such insurance is requested in accordance with conditions on reverse here of, indicate amount to be insured in figure in box marked amount of insurance.

Handling Information

（for USA only）Those commodities licensed by U.S. for ultimate destination...Diversion contray to U.S. law is prohibited.

No. of Pieces RCP	Gross Weight	Kg Lb	Rate Class Commodity Item No.	Chargeable Weight	Rate Charge	Total	Nature and Quantity of Goods (incl. Dimensions or Volume)

Prepaid	Weight Charge	Collect	Other Charges

Valuation Charge	AWA：50

Tax

Total Other Charges Due Agent
50

Shipper certifies that the particulars on the face hereof are correct and that insofar as any part of the consignment contains dangerous goods, such part is properly described by name and is in proper condition for carriage by air according to the applicable Dangerous Goods Regulations.

Total Other Charges Due Carrier

....
Signature of Shipper or his Agent

Total Prepaid	Total Collect

Currcency Conversion Rates	CC Charges in Dest. Currency

Executed on （date）   at （place）   Signature of Issuing carrier or its Agent

For Carrier's use only at Destination	Charges at Destination	Total Collect Charges

999—

图 7-5   Airway Bill(空运单)

①　空运提单是托运人/发货人与承运人/航空公司之间签订的货物运输协定。

②　空运提单是航空公司开给托运人的托运货物的收据。

③　空运提单通常都是按国际标准用英语和起运地的语言印制,这样方便途中经由2～3 个不同国家转到目的地。一般来说,空运提单可以有 12 份以便交给不同的有关当事人,如托运人、收货人、承运人、第二承运人(如果有的话)、第三承运人(如果有的话)、目的地机场、起飞机场以及其他用途(如果有的话)。每份空运提单有三份正本。第一份由托运人签署交给承运人或其代理人保存作为运输契约凭证。第二份由承运人与托运人共同签署,连同货物备交收货人作为核收货物的依据。第三份由承运人签署,于收到货物后,交付托运人作为收到货物的运输契约的证明。(如图 7-5 所示为空运单)

(3)　Commercial Invoice (商业发票)

An invoice is a statement sent by the seller to the buyer giving particulars of the goods being purchased, and showing the sum of money due. There are various invoices, such as commercial invoices, banker's invoices, consular invoices, customer invoices and pro forma invoices. Among these, the commercial invoice is the most common one and has to be provided for each and every consignment as one of the documents evidencing shipment. It is a document which contains identifying information about merchandise sold for which payment is to be made. All invoices should show the name and address of the debtor, terms of payment, description of items, the price. (See Fig. 7-6 Sample of Commercial Invoice)

发票是卖方对他所出售的货物开出的包括各项细节的清单,并作为向买方收取货款的凭证。发票的形式多种多样,有商业发票、银行发票、领事发票、海关发票和形式发票。在这些发票中,商业发票使用得最为广泛,几乎每一单运输都要求提供商业发票作为证明货物已交运的单证之一。商业发票是一种载有买方必须付款的所售货物的识别情况的单证。所有商业发票应写明债务人的名称和地址、支付条款、商品名称、价格。(如图 7-6 所示为商业发票样本)

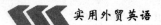

×××**IMPORT & EXPORT CO.**
商业发票
COMMERCIAL　INVOICE

Consigner:		发票号码 Inv. No. …………………….. 日期 Date: ……………… 贸易方式　(Term　of　Trade)
Address:		
Postcode:	Phone/Fax No.:	运单号 Air waybill No. 承运人　　———DHL——— Carrier 毛重/净重 Net / Gross WT (KG) 体积大小尺寸……………公分 Dimensions
Consignee:		
Company name:		
Address:		
Postcode:	Country:	
Contact person:	Phone / Fax No. :	

详细的商品名称 Full Description of Goods	数量 No. of Items	单价 Item Value	报关总价 Total Value for Customs

图 7-6　Sample of Commercial Invoice 商业发票样本

出口理由……

Reason for Export…

本人认为以上提供的资料属实和正确，货物原产地是……

I declare that the above information is true and correct to the best of my knowledge and that the goods are of…origin

谨代表上述公司

For an on behalf of the above named company

姓名（正楷）　　　　　　　　　　　　签名

Name (in print)……………………………Signature…………………………………..

职务　　　　　　　　　　　　　　　公章

Position in Company………………．………..Stamp……………………………………

(4)　Pro forma Invoice (形式发票)

Pro forma invoice is a document such as an invoice, issued as a temporary statement, but ultimately to be replaced by a final statement which can only be issued at a later date. Outwardly, except the marked "pro forma", it is like an ordinary commercial invoice containing the general particulars, for example, marks, number of goods, descriptions, quantities, quality, price, etc. However, in nature, it is a different form of invoice. It is not a formal document but a document without engagement, which is binding neither on the import nor the export. (See Fig. 7-7 Sample of Pro forma Invoice)

Pro forma invoices are required for various reasons. Primarily the importer requires them to comply with the regulations in force in his country. The governments of countries which carry out strict control policies usually enforce import license system or import quota system. Importers must apply for the necessary import license or foreign exchange. Often their application has to be supported by an informal invoice—a pro forma invoice, issued by the foreign exporter.

形式发票是指一种凭证，只作为临时单证使用，数天后由开具的最终发票所代替。从外观上看，除注明"形式"字样外，它和一般的商业发票一样，包含一些常规项目，如唛头、货物的件数、货名、数量、质量、价格等。但是，从本质上讲，形式发票是一种不同形式的发票，它不是正式文件，对买卖双方都无约束力。(如图 7-7 所示为形式发票样本)

需要使用形式发票的原因有多种，其中最重要的是进口商需要形式发票以便适应其本国现行的规章制度。实行严格贸易管制国家的政府通常都实行进口许可证制度或进口配额制。进口商必须申请必要的进口许可证或外汇，他们的申请往往须提供外国出口商签发的非正式发票——形式发票为依据，该发票须列明商品名称、规格、单价等。

优来特国际有限公司

YoLite Industrial Co., Ltd.

Add: A605,Dashidai building,Jiangbei,Ningbo, 315021 China
Tel: +86-574-87666169   Fax: +86-574-87667367
web: http://www.yolite.com   email: reflective@reflective.cn

PROFORMA INVOICE

Name:	Sc		Date:	2011-9-8
Address:			No.:	YL11A177
S-120 30 Stockholm, Sweden			Email:	
Attn.: **Git**	Phone No.:		Fax No.:	

ITEM No.	Description & Specification	Q'ty	U/Price (USD)	Amount(USD)
	Euromaster 110829			
	Reflective slapwrap	2000	0.83	1660
	3c logo , EN13356			
		TOTAL		**$1660.00**

图 7-7　Sample of Pro forma Invoice(形式发票样本)

Total Amount:	**Say US Dollar ONE THOUSAND SIX HUNDRED SIXTY Total.**
Delivery Term:	**TO DOOR BY TNT**
DeliveryTime:	**10-15 DAYS**
Payment Term:	**100% T/T in advance**

RECEIVING BANK:

    HSBC BANK NEW YORK

    SWIFT BIC: MRMDUS33

BENEFICIARY BANK:

    SHANGHAI PUDONG DEVELOPMENT BANK, OFFSHORE BANKING UNIT

    ADD: NO. 12, ZHONGSHAN DONG YI ROAD, SHANGHAI

    SWIFT BIC: SPDBCNSHOSA

BENEFICIARY:

    ACCOUNT NUMBER: OSA11443639473135

    NAME: YOLITE INDUSTRIAL COMPANY LIMITED

    ADDRESS: DASHIDAI 105# RENMIN RD NINGBO, CHINA

    TEL: 86-574-87666169, 86-574-87667367

图 7-7   Sample of Pro forma Invoice(形式发票样本)(续)

(5) Packing List (装箱单)

Packing list is a document made out by a seller when a sale is effected in international trade. It shows numbers and kinds of packages being shipped, total of gross, legal and net weights of the packages, and marks and numbers on the packages. It is used to make up the deficiency of an invoice. It also enables the consignee to declare the goods at customs office, distinguish and check the goods when they arrive at the port of destination, thus, facilitates the clearance of goods through customs. What's more, packing lists can facilitate settling insurance claims in case of loss or damage. (See Fig. 7-8 Sample of Packing List)

装箱单是国际贸易中卖方售货时出具的单据，用以说明所发运货物的数量、种类、毛重，每件货物的法定净重以及标志和号数的单证。它用于补充发票的不足之处，以便收货人在货物抵达目的港后区分和核对货物并向海关申报货物。这样可以加快货物的清关过程。并且，在货物失落或受到损坏时，可凭装箱单向保险公司索赔。(如图 7-8 所示为装箱单样本)

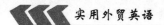

John Williams Agricultural Machinery Co., LTD.
No.75 Coastal Road, Forest District, New York, NY10000, USA
Tel/Fax: +1-221-4881300

PACKING LIST

Invoice No.: _____

Date: _____

S/C No.: _____

The Buyer: _____

_____

_____   SHIPPING MARK:

C/NOS.	Description	Quantity	N.W.	G.W.	Measurement

Packing:

Shipment From   To

John Williams Agricultural Machinery Co., LTD.

XXX

图 7-8　Sample of Packing List(装箱单样本)

(6)　Weight Memo(重量单)

Weight memo is a document made out by a seller when a sale is affected in foreign trade. It indicates the gross weight, net weight of each package. It is used to makeup the deficiency of an invoice. It is also used to facilitate the customs formalities and the general check of the goods by the consignee on their arrival at the destination. Packing list and weight memo usually come out in a combined form. (See Fig. 7-9 Sample of Weight Memo)

重量单是对外贸易中卖方售货时出具的单据，用以说明每件货物的毛重和净重的证件。它用于补充发票的不足之处，以便收货人在货物到达目的港后核对货物和加快办理海关手续。装箱单和重量单通常合二为一，做成一个单证。(如图 7-9 所示为重量单样本)

ISSUER NORTHERN ENERGY CORPORATION LIMITED NO.166 CAMPBELL STREET QLD AUSTRALIA		**WEIGHT　LIST**				
TO DATONG COAL MINE GROUP CO. LTD XINPINGWANG　COUNTY　SHANXI　CHINA		INVOICE NO. 7966616		DATE NOVEMBER 20 2013		
Marks and Numbers	**Number and kind of package Description of goods**	**Quantity**	**Package**	**G.W**	**N.W**	**Meas.**
DATONG COAL CO SC-529 RRRI-601225 QINHUANGDAO	STEAM COAL GROSS CALORIFIC VALUE AT MIN 6300-6100 KCAL/KG (ADB) 2000MT IN BULK	2000 MT	IN BULK		2000 MT	
TOTAL: 2000MT						
SAY TOTAL: TWO　THOUSAND　MT　ONLY						
NORTHERN ENERGY CORPORATION LIMITED 　　XXX **SHIPPING MARK:**						

图 7-9　Sample of Weight Memo(重量单样本)

Section 2　Correspondence

Letters regarding shipment are usually written for the following purposes:

(1)　to urge an early shipment;

(2)　to amend shipping terms;

(3)　to give shipping advice;

(4)　to dispatch shipping documents, etc.

1. Sample Letters

Letter 1 (Shipping Instructions)

Dear Sirs,

Re: Your Sales Confirmation No. C215 Covering 4,000 Dozen Shirts

We have acknowledgement for your letter dated 19th August in connection with the above subject.

In reply, we have the pleasure of informing you that the confirmed, irrevocable Letter of Credit No. 7634, amounting to[1] £ 500 has been opened this morning through the District Bank, Ltd, Manchester. Upon receipt of the same, please arrange shipment of the goods booked by us without the least delay. We are informed by the local shipping company that s/s "Browick" is due to sail from your city to our port on or about the 10th September and, if possible, please try your best to ship by that steamer.

Should this trial order prove satisfactory to our customers, we can assure you that repeat orders in increased quantity will be placed.

Your close co-operation in this respect will be highly appreciated. In the meantime we await your shipping advice by cable.

Sincerely,

Letter 2 (Urging for Prompt Shipment)

Dear Sirs,

We have received your letter of June 17, with regard to our Purchase Contract No. 80616 for 3,000 sets of Double Offset Ring Spanners[2], we write to inform you as follows:

According to the contract stipulations, the aforesaid goods should be shipped in three equal lots in April, June and August, but up to the present moment even the first lot has not been shipped. Our end-users are waiting for the goods and they are very much surprised that you should have been much behind with the delivery.

Please do your utmost to ship the first and the second lots together by the June; otherwise our clients will feel dissatisfied with your delay (in shipment), so we would probably have to cancel the order by covering their requirements elsewhere.

Upon receipt of this letter please let us know by cable the exact date of shipment.

Yours faithfully,

Letter 3 (Booking Shipping Containers)

Dear Sirs,

We have 50 cases of medicines and chemical reagents[3] at the above address ready for dispatch to any European Main Ports[4], and shall be glad if you will arrange for your shipping container to collect them. Each case weighs 60 kgs.

As our client requires us to ship the goods not later than July 15, please quote for a shipping container from Hong Kong to the above mentioned port before that deadline.

Your early quotation will be highly appreciated.

Sincerely,

(Reply)

Dear Sirs,

Thank you for your inquiry of 5 June, asking us to quote shipping container to any EMP for 50 cases of medicines and chemical reagents.

The shipping containers we provide are of two sizes, namely[5] 10 ft, and 20 ft and built to take loads up to two to four tons respectively. They can be opened at both ends, thus making it possible to load and unload the same time. They are both watertight[6] and airtight[7] and can be loaded and locked at the factory, if necessary.

There is also a saving in freight[8] charges when separate consignments intended for the same port of destination are carried in one container and an additional saving on insurance because of the lower premiums[9] charged for container shipped goods.

We enclose a copy of our tariff[10] and look forward to receiving your instructions.

Yours faithfully,

Letter 4 (Shipping Advice)

Dear Sirs,

We are pleased to inform you that the following goods under our Contract No. CC1200 have now been shipped by s.s. Feng Qing sailing tomorrow from Guangzhou to Sydney.

Order No. C120 10 Bales Grey Cotton Cloth

Order No. C135 10 Bales White Cotton Cloth

Copies of the relative shipping documents are enclosed, thus you may find no trouble in taking delivery[11] of the goods when they arrive.

We hope this shipment will reach you in time and turn out to your entire satisfaction.

Yours faithfully,

Encl. Our Invoice No. 12345 in duplicate

Packing List No. 34567 in duplicate

Non-negotiable Bill of Lading No. 4578

Insurance Policy No.3569

Survey Report No. FT136

2. Notes to Text

(1) amount to 合计为，等于

The weight amounts to 78,000 pounds. 重量合计为 7.8 万磅。

Your reply amounts to a refusal of our request. 你的答复等于拒绝我们的请求。

(2) double offset ring spanners 梅花扳手

(3) medicines and chemical reagents 医药化学试剂

(4) European Main Ports = EMP 欧洲主要口岸

按照航运公会统一规定，EMP 包括意大利的热那亚(Genoa)、法国的马赛(Marseilles)、比利时的安特卫普(Antwerp)、荷兰的鹿特丹(Rotterdam)、英国的伦敦(London)、德国的汉堡(Hamburg)、丹麦的哥本哈根(Copenhagen)等港口。

(5) namely 即；也就是

(6) watertight 防水的

(7) airtight 不漏气的，密封的

(8) freight 货物(特指装载于车船、飞机上的)

freight charges 运费

freight agency 运货代理商

freight forwarder 运输公司

freight rate 运费率

freight service 货运

freight tariff 运费表

(9) premium 保险费

(10) tariff 运费表；关税；关税率

tariff compact 关税协定

tariff diminishing 关税减让

tariff quota 关税配额

tariff rate 关税税率

(11) take delivery 提货

3. Useful expressions

(1) Mode of Shipping 运送方式

① 为保证最快交货，我方要求对上述订单用航空货运。

To ensure fastest delivery, you are requested to forward the above order by air freight.

② 由于商品种类的关系，我方只能用卡车(火车等)来运送。

Because of the type of merchandise, we can only ship by truck (rail, etc.).

③ 如果客户要求选择卡车以外的运输工具，就必须负担额外费用。

If the customer wishes to choose a carrier other than truck, he must bear the additional charges.

(2) Time of Shipment 装运期

① 我们坚持在原定日期内交货，若迟交保留拒收的权利。

We must insist on delivery within the time dated, and reserve the right to reject the goods, should they be delivered late.

② 在 4 月至 6 月间货物分三次均装。

Shipment is to be made during April to June in three equal lots.

③ 收到你方信用证 30 天内发货。

Goods will be shipped within 30 days after receipt of your L/C.

④ 由于唯一停靠我港的月班直轮刚刚驶离，货物只能下月装船。

As the only direct steamer which calls at our port once a month has just departed, goods can only be shipped next month.

⑤ 由于你方迟开信用证，无法按合同要求及时装船，只能推迟到 9 月和 10 月。

Owing to your delay in opening the relative L/C shipment cannot be made in time as contracted and should be postponed to September and October.

⑥ 我方订购的皮鞋应在 6 月份交货，现已延误多日。

Our order of leather shoes, which should have been delivered in June, is now considerably overdue.

(3) Advising Shipment 通知装运

① 货物一俟装运，我方即电告你方。

We shall advise you by cable as soon as the goods are shipped.

② 欣告你方……轮已顺利装载，希望达到目的港时货物良好。

We have the pleasure to inform you that the shipment per S.S. … has gone forward and hope that it will arrive at the destination in perfect condition.

③ 货已装上……轮，在香港转……轮。

The cargo has been shipped on S.S. …for transshipment at Hong Kong into S.S. …

④ 由于工厂遇到了不可预见的困难，我们抱歉无法按信用证规定的日期装船，但工厂已保证 1 个月内备妥货物。

Owing to the unforeseen difficulties on the party of our mills, we regret being unable to ship the goods within the time limit of your credit. But the mills have promised that they will get the goods ready for shipment in one month's time.

(4) Sending Shipping Documents 寄装运单据

① 按合同要求，货物装运后，我们航邮寄上全套不可转让单据。

In compliance with the terms of the contract, we forward you by airmail a full set of non-negotiable documents immediately after the goods are loaded.

② 按要求，我们另封寄上我方第 92838 号合同项下贵方第 5757 号订单所定 1200 包坯布的有关单据，即第 6687 号发票两份，第 5629 号保险单两份，第 2030 号不可转让提单一份。

As requested, we are sending you under separate cover two copies of our Invoice No. 6687, two copies of Insurance Policy No. 5629 and one copy of non-negotiable B/L No. 2030 covering the consignment of 1,200 bales of grey cloth for your Order No. 5757 under our Contract No. 92838.

(5) Urging Shipment 催促装船

① 必须强调，装船期限于预定的日期，不允许延期。

Emphasis has to be laid that shipment must be made within the prescribed time limit, as further extension will not be considered.

② 请认真对待这一订单，盼早日收到装船通知。

We recommend this order to your particular attention, and await your early advice of shipment.

③ 你方必须在指定的时间内将货物装上……号轮，否则空舱费将由你方承担。

You must deliver the goods on board S.S. …within the time limit as instructed, otherwise dead freight, if any, should be borne by you.

④　长时间地延误交货已给我方带来很大的不便。我们坚持要求立即发货，否则，将不得不取消原订合同的订货。

We have been put to considerable inconvenience by the long delay in delivery. We must insist on immediate delivery; otherwise, we shall be compelled to cancel the orders in accordance with the stipulation of the contract.

⑤　装船预定在……(时间)之前完成，贵方如能提前，我方将十分感激。

Shipment is stipulated to be made before …, and if possible, we should appreciate your arranging to ship the goods at an earlier date.

Section 3　Dialogues

Dialogue 1

We will do our best to advance the shipment,
but your L/C should be opened early September.

Mr. Peterson is urging Ms. Huang to advance the shipment in order to catch the Christmas sales in the United States.

Peterson: If I remember correctly, time of delivery is another point on which we differ.

Huang: That's right. Let's go into details.

Peterson: OK. I hope you can have these goods delivered before the end of September. We'd like them to be there in time for our Christmas sales.

Huang: Christmas doesn't come until almost the end of the year, does it?

Peterson: But, in the United States the Christmas season begins about a month before December 25.

Huang: Well, I'm afraid it'll be difficult for us to advance the time of shipment. Our manufacturers are fully committed at the moment.

Peterson: I hope you'll try to get them to step up production.

Huang: As new orders keep pouring in, the workers are working three shifts to step up production.

Peterson: If that's the case, there's nothing more to be said.

Huang: I'm sorry.

Peterson: What's your last word as to the date then?

Huang: I said by the middle of October. This is the best we can promise.

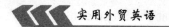

Peterson: All right, I'll take you at your word.

Huang: Good. Let's call it a deal. We'll do our best to advance the shipment, but your L/C should be opened early September.

Peterson: I promise.

Dialogue 2

We may agree to have the goods transshipped at Hong Kong around mid-October.

Edward: Hello.

Wang: Hi, Mr. Edward, I am just calling to inquire about the shipment of the products we order from you as our customer is in urgent need of the delivery for new season sale.

Edward: Mr. Wang, I am sorry that we were just informed that lately there has been much congestion in shipping. There are very few direct steamers sailing for your port. So is there any chance transshipment is allowed?

Wang: Well, transshipment will prolong the delivery and is likely to cause damage. So, we still hope a direct shipment could be arranged.

Edward: Now the trouble is that it is very difficult to book shipment space. I'm afraid we can do little about this.

Wang: You surely know that transshipment adds to the expenses and sometimes may delay the arrival. If the goods can not be put on the market on time, then good quality and competitive price would mean nothing.

Edward: Yes, we really understand your position. Anyhow, we'll try. We'll see whether we can get the cooperation of the China National Chartering Corporation. It has a good reputation for meeting the clients varied demands.

Wang: Thank you very much indeed! Can you let me know the result as soon as possible?

Edward: No problem.

Wang: All right. We are expecting good news from you.

(The next day)

Edward: Mr. Wang, I was just informed by the China National Chartering that liner space for China is fully booked up and goods have to be transshipped if you insist on October shipment.

Wang: We prefer direct shipment, of course, but if you can't get hold of a direct vessel, we may agree to have the goods transshipped at Hong Kong around mid-October. If you could manage to catch this vessel, everything would be all right.

Edward: It's very difficult for us to accept a designed on-carrier. There are so many factors that might make the goods miss the intended departure. Besides, are you sure the vessel will call at Guangzhou? And is she already carrying a full load?

Wang: Let's hope for the best, but prepare for the worst. If the worse comes to the worst, please ship the goods to Zhuhai. How about Zhuhai as an optional port of destination?

Edward: Good. Then, what would you say if we put it like this: "Shipment by first available steamer in October. Port of destination in Guangzhou or Zhuhai. Transshipment at Hong Kong allowed."

Wang: Fine. It seems I have no alternative. Thank you, Mr. Edward. I'm sorry if the arrangements cause you any inconvenience.

Edward: Oh no, we're only too glad to help you in any way we can.

Notes

1. Christmas Sales 圣诞节销售

2. Our manufacturers are fully committed at the moment. 我方厂家现已承约过多。

3. As new orders keep pouring in. 新的订单源源而来。

4. I'll take you at your word. 我就按你说的做吧。

5. new season sale 新的销售季

6. direct steamers 直轮

7. transshipment 转运；转载

8. prolong the delivery 延迟装运

9. shipping space 仓位

10. be put on the market on time 及时投入市场

11. China National Chartering Corporation 中国租船公司

12. book up 订满

13. on-carrier 二程船

14. call at 停靠

15. We're only too glad to help you in any way we can. 我们很高兴能够尽一切力量来帮助您。

Section 4　Exercises

1. Translate the following sentences into English:

(1)　希望贵方注意，截至目前我们还没有收到你方有关 228 号合同货物的装运信息。

(2)　所订货物已分三批运往你方。

(3)　如果此次延误给贵方造成任何不便，我方将十分抱歉，希望此事不会影响我们的良好关系。

(4) 一旦货物已发运，我们会将装运通知传真给您。

(5) 由于没有轮船直达你方港口，我们希望您能接受在香港转运。

(6) 除非另有说明，该唛头适用所有运输。

2. Translate the following sentences into Chinese:

(1) We will ship the remaining 3,000 pieces by the first boat available after receipt of your amendment to the L/C.

(2) We shall be appreciated it if you will effect shipment as soon as possible, thus enabling our buyers to catch the brisk demand at the start of the season.

(3) We are pleased to inform you that the cargo has been shipped on S/S "DONGFENG" which sails for your port tomorrow, and hope that it will arrive in perfect condition.

(4) In compliance with the terms of contract, we will forward you a full set of non-negotiable copies of documents immediately after the goods are shipped.

(5) Because the shipping space has been fully booked up to the end of next month, we would suggest that you allow us to ship the half of the goods via Hong Kong.

3. Translate the following letter into English:

格林先生：

很高兴通知您，下述货物已经装船完毕。

订单号：CW-8899

品名：袜子

数量：2000 打

包装：每个纸箱 20 打，共 100 箱

提单号：CN300900

船名：东风号

航次号：9889W

预计出发时间：2014 年 5 月 30 日

预计到达时间： 2014 年 6 月 15 日

装运港：上海

目的港：洛杉矶

希望上述货物能准时、完好地到达。同时期待不久的将来能与贵公司有更愉快的合作。

…… 谨上

4. Translate the following letter into Chinese:

Dear Mr. …,

Referring to our order No. 356 for 10 tons of vegetable, so far we have no definite information from you about delivery time, although the shipment is approaching and our L/C was opened as early as in April.

Your delay will put us to too much trouble, since this is a kind of seasonal goods, our customers are in urgent need of the whole lot to be ready for the selling season. We must now ask you to do your utmost to dispatch the goods without delay. Otherwise we have the right to cancel the order and lodge claims for our losses.

Please give us your definite reply within 3days.

Yours faithfully,

5. Compose a dialogue based on the following situation:

Mr. Peterson is in urgent need of the goods to be ready for Christmas sales, so he wants the goods to be shipped in advance. But Mr. Zhang thinks it difficult to advance the time of shipment. They are discussing the definite time of delivery.

Section 5　Solution to Problem

1. What should be included in shipping advice?

To some extent, the following letter acts as shipping advice, but what it lacks?

Thank you for your extension of your L/C No. 5757. Today we shipped the above consignment on board S.S. "Nellore" which sails for your port tomorrow.

Enclosed please find one set of the shipping documents covering this consignment, as follows:

(1) One nonnegotiable copy of B/L

(2) Invoice in duplicate

(3) Packing list in triplicate

(4) One copy of Manufacturer's Certificate of Quality

(5) One copy of Insurance Policy

We are glad to have filled your order after long delay and trust that the goods will reach you in time to meet your urgent need and that they will turn out to your complete satisfaction.

We will fill your future orders promptly and carefully.

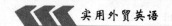

Consignee cares much more than above contents, he still wants information of estimated time of arrival, port agent in destination and so on.

2. Is Combined Transport Document (C.T.D. or M.T.D. for Multimodal Transport Document) a document of title?

Combined Transport document (C.T.D. or M.T.D. for Multimodal Transport Document) is a document, covering at least two different modes of transport, which evidences the combined transport contract and indicates that the multimodal transport operator shall take over the goods and shall be responsible for delivering according to the clauses in the contract.

Combined Transport B/L, which covers at least ocean marine transport (or inland waterway transport) and at least other one mode of other transport, is one kind of Combined Transport Documents.

According to Rule 3 and Rule 4 of "Uniform Rules For a Combined Transport Document (ICC Publication No. 298 1975)" and Article 5 and Article 6 of "United Nations Convention on International Multimodal Transport of Goods 1980" C.T.D. (or M.T.D.) could be issued negotiable or non-negotiable, it means C.T.D. (or M.T.D.) could be a document of title, of cause, it also could be not a document of title.

3. Could Bill of Lading (B/L) be used in inland waterway transport and to negotiate payment?

We generally regard B/L as Ocean (Marine) Bill of Lading, anyway, Bill of Lading could be used in inland waterway transport and to negotiate payment.

Article 28 of UCP 500 (Uniform Customs and Practice for Documentary Credits 500), if a credit calls for a road , rail, or inland waterway transport document, banks will, unless otherwise stipulated tin the credit, accept a document of the type called for , however named ...

Article 24 of UCP 600 (Uniform Customs and Practice for Documentary Credits 600), A road, rail or inland waterway transport document, however named...

Unit 8

Insurance

Section 1   Introduction

At present, according to the different transportation methods, there are ocean marine transport insurance, overland transport insurance, air transport insurance and parcel post transport insurance in our country. Among all these, ocean marine transportation insurance is mostly and widely used in international trade practical business. Even though they have different obligations, their basic principles and guarantees provided by the insurance companies are nearly the same. In this unit we are going to discuss ocean marine transportation insurance.

目前，我国办理的进出口货物运输保险业务，按照运输方式的不同，主要分为海洋运输货物保险、陆上运输货物保险、航空运输货物保险和邮包运输保险等，其中业务量最大、涉及面最广的是海洋运输货物保险。尽管各种不同货物运输保险的具体责任有所不同，但它们的基本原则、保险公司保障的范围等基本一致。在这一单元中，我们将重点讨论海上运输保险。

1. Risks, Losses and Expenses (风险、损失和费用)

According to the loss or damage caused by risks included in different coverage and the expenses involved, the insurance company is responsible for indemnifying the insured goods. Obviously, risk, loss and coverage are closely related to each other.

保险公司按照不同险别包括的风险所造成的损失和发生的费用承担赔偿责任。所以在保险业务中，风险、损失和险别三者有着密切的联系。

(1)   Risks (风险)

Marine risks in connection with cargo in transit can be classified into two types: perils of the sea and extraneous risks.

海洋货物运输的风险主要分为海上风险和外来风险两大类。

①   Perils of the Sea (海上风险)

Perils of the sea are caused by natural calamities and fortuitous accidents.

Natural calamities—Disasters such as heavy weather, thunder and lightning, flood, earthquake, tsunami, volcanic eruption, etc.

Fortuitous accidents—Accidents such as ship grounded, stranded, sunk, collision, capsized, fire, explosion, missed, etc.

海上风险是由海上发生的自然灾害和外来风险引起的。

自然灾害：是指恶劣气候、雷电、洪水、地震、海啸、火山爆发等灾难。

意外事故：是指船舶搁浅、触礁、沉没、碰撞、倾覆、失火、起火、爆炸、船只失踪等事故。

② Extraneous Risks (外来风险)

Extraneous risks are caused by extraneous reasons, consisting of general extraneous risks and special extraneous risks.

General extraneous risks include: theft or pilferage, short-delivery and non-delivery, rain, shortage, contamination, leakage, breakage, train of odor, dampness, heating, rusting hooking, etc.

Special extraneous risks include: war risks, strikes, non-delivery of cargo, refusal to receive cargo, confiscation of cargo, emergence of aflatoxin, etc.

外来风险由各种外来原因所引起，包括一般外来风险和特殊外来风险。

一般外来风险包括：偷窃、短少或提货不着、雨淋、短量、污染、渗漏、破损、串味、受潮、受热、锈损和钩损等。

特殊外来风险包括：战争、罢工、交货不到、拒绝收货、没收、产生黄曲霉素等风险。

(2) Losses (损失)

Marine losses are the damages or losses of the insured goods incurred by perils of the sea. According to the extent of damage, losses in marine insurance fall into two types: total loss and partial loss. The former may be subdivided into actual total loss and constructive total loss; the latter, general average and particular average.

海损一般是指海运保险货物在海洋运输中由于海上风险所造成的损坏和灭失。根据损失的不同程度可分为全部损失和部分损失。前者可再分为实际全损和推定全损。后者可分为共同海损和单独海损。根据货物所遭受的损失可分为:

① Total Loss (全部损失)

Total loss refers to the loss of the entire shipment caused by risks

全部损失是指由于遭遇风险引起的全部运输货物的全部损失。

A. Actual total loss (实际全损)

The actual total loss occurs in the following cases: a. The insured goods have been totally lost or damage. b. The insured goods have been totally lost original use and valueless on arrival. c. The insured's ownership of the insured goods have been irreparably derived completely. d. The carrying ship has missed to a certain period and there is still no message.

出现下列情况就认为已经发生实际全损: a. 被保货物的实体已经灭失。b. 被保险货物遭到严重损害，已经丧失原有的用途和价值。c. 被保险人对保险货物的所有权已无可挽回地被完全剥夺。d. 载货船舶失踪，达到一定时期仍无音讯。

B. Constructive total loss (推定全损)

Constructive total loss is found in the case where an actual total loss appears to be unavoidable or the cost to be incurred in recovering or reconditioning the goods together with the forwarding cost to the destination named in the policy would exceed their value on arrival.

推定全损是指该批被保险货物受损后，实际全损已经不可避免，或者恢复受损货物并将其送到保险单所注明的目的地所需的费用将超过货物的价值。

② Partial Loss (部分损失)

Partial loss refers to the loss of part of a consignment. According to different causes, partial loss can be either general average or particular average.

部分损失是指货物的损失只是部分的。根据损失产生的原因不同，部分损失可分为共同海损和单独海损。

A. General average (共同海损)

General average is a partial, deliberate and reasonable sacrifice of the ship, freight or goods undertaken when the whole ship was threatened by a peril of the sea or some other hazard, for the common interests or safety. In this case, the general average will be shared proportionally among all the interests affected and all those whose property does not suffer any loss.

共同海损是指载货运输的船舶在海上运输途中遭遇自然灾害、意外事故或其他特殊情况，使航行中的船东、货主及承运人的共同安全受到威胁，为了解除共同危险，维护各方的共同利益并使航程继续完成，由船方有意识地采取的合理的抢救措施所直接造成的某些特殊牺牲或支出的额外费用等。

B. Particular average(单独海损)

Particular average means a partial loss suffered by part of the cargo and solely borne by the owner of the lost property.

单独海损是指被保险货物遭遇海上风险受损后，其损失未达到全损程度，且由受损方单独承担的损失。

(3) Expenses (费用)

Losses sustained by the insured because of the risks come from not only the loss of the goods or the damage done to the goods, but also from the expenses the insured sustained in rescuing the goods in danger. The main expenses include:

被保险货物遭遇保险责任范围内的事故，除了使货物本身受到损毁导致损失外，还会产生费用方面的损失。这些费用主要有：

① Sue and labor expense (施救费用)

② Salvage charges (救助费用)

③ Particular Charges (特别费用)

④ Forwarding Charges (续运费用)

2. Marine Insurance Coverage (海上保险险别)

According to People's Insurance Company of China Ocean Marine Cargo Clauses, the insurance is mainly classified into two groups: Basic Insurance Coverage and Additional Insurance Coverage.

根据《中国人民保险公司海洋运输货物保险条款》，保险可分为两大类：基本险和附加险。

(1) Basic Insurance Coverage (基本险别)

① Free from Particular Average (F.P.A.) (平安险)

According to PICC's Ocean Marine Cargo Clauses revised in January 1, 1981, F.P.A. insurance covers:

A. Total or Constructive Total Loss of the whole consignment hereby insured caused in the course of transit by natural calamities—heady weather, lightning, tsunami, earthquake and flood.

B. Total or Partial Loss caused by accidents—the carrying conveyance being grounded stranded, sunk or in collision with floating ice or other objects as fire or explosion.

C. Partial loss of the insured goods attributable to heavy weather, lightning and/or tsunami, where the conveyance has been grounded, stranded, sunk or burnt, irrespective of whether the event or events took place before or after such accident.

D. Partial or total loss consequent on falling of entire package or packages into sea during loading, transshipment or discharge.

E. Reasonable cost incurred the insured in salvaging the goods or averting or minimizing a loss recoverable under the Policy, provided that cost shall not exceed the sum insured of the consignment so save.

F. Losses attributable to discharge of the insured goods at a port of distress following a sea peril as well as special charges arising from loading, warehousing and forwarding of the goods at an intermediate port of call or refuge.

G. Sacrifice and Contribution to General Average and Salvage Charges.

H. Such proportion of losses sustained by the ship owners as is to be reimbursed by the Cargo Owner under the Contract of Affreightment "Both to Blame Collision" clause.

根据 1981 年 1 月 1 日修订的《中国人民保险公司海洋运输货物保险条款》的规定，平安险负责赔偿：

A. 被保险货物在途中由于恶劣气候、雷电、海啸、地震、洪水自然灾害造成整批货物的全部损失或推定全损。

B. 由于遭受搁浅、触礁、沉没、互撞、与流冰或其他物体碰撞以及失火、爆炸意外事故造成货物的全部或部分损失。

C. 在运输工具已经发生搁浅、触礁、沉没、焚毁意外事故的情况下，货物在此前后又在海上遭受恶劣气候、雷达、海啸等自然灾害所造成的部分损失。

D. 在装卸或转运时由于一件或数件整件货物落海造成的全部或部分损失。

E. 被保险人对遭受承保责任内危险的货物采取抢救、防止或减少贪损的措施而支付的合理费用，但以不超过该批被救货物的保险金额为限。

F. 运输工具遭遇海难后，在避难港由于卸货所引起的损失，以及在中途港、避难港由于卸货、存仓以及运送货物所产生的特别费用。

G. 共同海损的牺牲、分摊和救助费用。

H. 运输契约订有"船舶互撞责任"条款，根据该条款规定应由供货方偿还船方的损失。

② With Average/With Particular Average (W.A./W.P.A.) (水渍险)

W.P.A. covers wider than F.P.A. Aside from the risks covered under F.P.A. conditions as above, this insurance also covers partial losses of the insured goods caused by heavy weather, lightning, tsunami, earthquake and/or flood.

水渍险的负责赔偿范围比平安险广。除了上述平安险的各项责任以外，水渍险还负责被保险货物在运输途中由于恶劣气候、雷电、海啸、地震、洪水等造成的部分损失。

③ All Risks (一切险)

The cover of All Risks is the most comprehensive of the three. Aside from the risks covered under F.P.A. and W.P.A. conditions as above, this insurance also covers all risks of loss of or damage to insured goods whether partial or total, arising from external causes (general extraneous risks) in the course of transit.

在三种基本险别中，一切险承保的范围最为广泛。除了包括上述平安险和水渍险的各项责任以外，该保险还负责被保险货物在运输途中由于外来因素(一般外来风险)所致的全部或部分损失。

(2) Additional Insurance Coverage (附加险)

No additional risks can be purchased to insure goods independently. Additional risks include general additional risks and special additional risks. Since the scope of cover of general additional risks is already included into that of All Risks, it is not necessary for the goods to be insured by additional risks if it is insured by All Risks.

附加险不能单独投保。附加险有一般附加险和特殊附加险之别。一般附加险由于已经包含在一切险的承保范围内，所以若已投保了一切险就不需要再加保一般附加险。

① General Additional Risks (一般附加险)

General additional risks under C.I.C. fall into the following eleven kinds:

中国人民保险公司承保的一般附加险有下列 11 种：

A. Theft, pilferage and non-delivery clause (偷窃、提货不着险条款)

B. Fresh water and/or rain damage clause (淡水雨淋险条款)

C. Shortage clause (短量险条款)

D. Intermixture and contamination clause (混杂、玷污险条款)

E. Leakage clause (渗漏险条款)

F. Clash and breakage clause (碰损、破碎险条款)

G. Taint of odor clause (串味险条款)

H. Sweat and heating clause (受潮受热险条款)

I. Hooks damage clause (钩损险条款)

J. Breakage of packing clause (包装破裂险条款)

K. Rust clause (锈损险条款)

② Special Additional Risk (特殊附加险)

Special additional risk differs from general addition risk in that the former covers loss or damage caused by some special extraneous reasons such as politics, law, regulations and wax. On the other hand, like general additional risk, special additional risks can not be used to insure goods alone either. Special additional risks include:

特殊附加险承保由于政治、军事、国家政策法令以及其他特殊外来原因引起的风险所造成的损失。它同一般附加险一样，不能单独投保。特殊附加险常见的有以下几种：

A. War Risk (战争险)

B. Strike Risk (罢工险)

C. On deck risk (舱面险)

D. Import duty risk clause (进口关税险)

E. Rejection risk (拒收险)

F. Aflatoxin risk (黄曲霉素险)

G. Failure to delivery clause (交货不到险)

H. Ocean Marine Cargo War Risk Fire Risk Extension Clause for Storage of Cargo at destination Hong Kong, including Kowloon or Macao [出口货物到香港(包括九龙在内)或澳门存仓火险责任扩展条款]

3. Insurance documents

An insurance policy or an insurance certificate is issued when goods are insured. An insurance policy (or a certificate) forms part of the chief shipping documents. A policy also functions as collateral security when an exporter gets an advance against his bank credit.

货物保险后，将由保险公司签发保险单或保险凭证。保险单或保险凭证是主要的装运单证。在信用证下，保险单还可作为抵押担保从银行获得垫付贷款。

(1) Insurance policy (保险单)

Insurance policy, issued by the insurer, is a legal document setting out the exact terms and conditions of an insurance transaction—name of the insured, the name of the commodity insured, the amount insured, the name of the carrying vessel, the precise risks covered, the period of cover and any exceptions there may be. It also serves as a written contract of insurance between the insurer and the person taking out insurance. (See Fig. 8-1 Sample of Insurance Application of Export transportation and Fig. 8-2 Sample of Insurance Policy)

保险单是保险人签发的一种具有法律效力的单证，它严格规定了一笔保险业务的条款和条件——被保险人姓名、保险货物名称、保险金额、载货船只名称、承保险别、保险期限和可能发生的免责事项。它也是保险人和被保险人之间订立的书面契约。(参见图 8-1 出口运输险投保单样本和图 8-2 保险单式样)

(2) Insurance Certificate (保险凭证)

Insurance certificate is a kind of simplified insurance policy. The insurance certificate only indicates the name of the insured, name of the insured cargo, quantity, mark, conveyance, place of shipment, place of destination, insurance cover, and insurance amount. But the rights and obligations of two parties are omitted. The insurance certificate has the same legal validity as the insurance policy. (See Fig. 8-3 Sample of Insurance Certificate and Fig. 8-4 Filled of Insurance Certificate)

保险凭证是一种保险证明，实际上是简化的保险单。它包含保险单上的必要项目，如品名、数量、唛头、运输工具、装运地点、目的港、保险险别、保险金额等。但它并不列出保险人和被保险人的权利和义务，保险凭证与保险单具有同样的效力。(参见图 8-3 保险凭证式样和图 8-4 填制好的保险凭证)

(3) Open Policy (预约保单)

Open policy is of great importance for export business, it is convenient method for insuring the goods where a number of consignments of similar export goods are intended to be covered. An open policy covers these shipments, as soon as they are made, under the previous arrangement between the insured and the insurance company.

对于出口商来说，这种预约保单非常重要，如果是为一大宗货物投保的话，这种预约保单特别方便。根据投保人与保险公司签订的合同，一经起运，保险人即自动承保。

(4) Combined Certificate (联合凭证)

When the goods are exported to Hong Kong, and some countries in Southeast Asia, the insurance company sometimes adds the coverage and insurance amount on the commercial invoice which is made out by a foreign trade company. This is a certificate which combines the invoice with the insurance policy. It is the simplest insurance certificate in use.

当货物出口香港以及部分东南亚地区时，保险公司将承保的险别、保险金额和保单号加注在出口公司开列的商业发票上。这是商业发票与保险单相结合的一种凭证，是最为简单的一种保险单。

(5) Endorsement (保险更改批单)

After insurance has been taken out, if the insured wants to replenish or change the contents of the policy, he may apply to the company for the same. After agreement by the company, another certificate which indicates the relative amendment will be issued. This certificate is called endorsement.

在保险办完之后，如果投保人想要更改保险条款，他可向保险公司提出申请。经与保险公司协商之后，发出另一份已修改过的保单，这就是保险更改批单。

中国人民保险公司上海分公司

出口运输险投保单

编号　0381143

兹将我处出口物资依照信用证规定拟向你处投保国外运输险计开：

被保险人	（中　文）苏州毛织品进出口贸易公司		过户
	（英　文）SUZHOU KNITWEAR AND MANUFACTURED GOODS IMPORT&EXPORT TRADE CORPORATION		

标记或发票号码	件　数	物资名称	保险金额
AS　　　PER INVOICE No. T0367	367捆	全棉抹布 COTTON TEATOWELS	USD 96696
运输工具 （及转载工具） PUDONG VOY. 053	约　　　　　启 2004 年　10月24日 于　　　　　运		赔款偿 付地点　加拿大蒙特利尔
运输路程 自　上海　经　到 蒙特利尔		转　载 地　点	
要保险别： FOR 110% OF INVOICE VALUE COVERING ALL RISKS PER C.I.C.I 1/1981			投保单位签章 苏州毛织品进出口贸易公司 李莉 2004年　10月　20日

图 8-1　Sample of Insurance Application of Export transportation(出口运输险投保单样本)

中国人民保险公司

THE PEOPLE'S INSURANCE COMPANY OF CHINA

总公司设于北京　　　　一九四九年创立

Head Office: BEIJING　　Established in 1949

发票号码	保险单	保险单号次
Invoice No. BP2000/05-010	**INSURANCE POLICY**	No.PC010-037650

中国人民保险公司(以下简称本公司)

This Police of Insurance witnesses that The People's Insurance

Company of China (hereinafter called "The Company")

根据

at the request of　　LIAONING TEXTILES IMPORT & EXPORT CORP

(以 下 简 称 被 保 险 人) 的 要 求 ， 由 被 保 险 人

(hereinafter called the "Insured") and in consideration of the agreed premium

向 本 公 司 缴 付 约 定 的 保 险 费 ， 按 照 本 保 险 单

paying to the Company by the Insured, Undertakes to insure the undermentioned

承 保 险 别 和 背 面 所 载 条 款 与 下 列 特 款 承 保

Goods in transportation subject to the conditions of this Policy as per Clauses

下 述 货 物 运 输 保 险 ， 特 立 本 保 险 单 。

printed overleaf and other special clauses attached hereon.

标　记 Marks & Nos	包装及数量 Quantity	保险货物项目 Description of Goods	保险金额 Amount Insured
AS PER INVOICE NO.	180DOZ	WOOLEN SWEATER	USD27600.00

总保险金额: **SAY** UNITED STATES DOLLARS TWENTY-SEVEN THOUSAND SIX-HUNDRED **ONLY**

Total Amount Insured

保费　　　　　费率　　　　　　　　装载运输工具

Premium　　as　arranged　Rate　as　arranged　Per conveyance S.S　CHANGQING

开航日期　　　　　　　自　　　　　　　至

Sig on or abt　　AS PER B/L　　　From　　DALIAN.CHINA　To HONGKONG

承保险别　　投保一切险和战争险，按照中国人民保险公司 1981 年 1 月 1 日生效的有关海洋货物运输条款为准。

Conditions　ALL RISKS AND WAR RISKS AS PER AND SUBJECT TO THE RELEVANT DCEAN MARINE CARGO CLOUSES OF THE PEOPLE'S INSURANCE COMPANY OF CHINA DATED 1/1, 1981.

所保货物，如遇出险，本公司凭本保险单及其他有关证件给付赔款。

Claims, if any, Payable On, surrender of this Policy together with other relevant documents.

所保货物，如发生本保险单项下负责赔偿的损失事或事故，应立即通知本公司下述代理人查勘。

In the event of accident whereby loss or damage may result in a claim under this policy immediate notice applying for survey must be given to the company's Agent as mentioned hereunder.

中国人民保险公司

THE PEOPLE'S INSURANCE CO.OF CHINA

赔款偿付地点

Claim payable at　　HONGKONG

日期

DATE　　　9/12, 2008

图 8-2　Sample of Insurance Policy(保险单式样)

华泰保险
Huatai Insurance

安达集团 合作联盟
ACE Group Strategic Partner

CERTIFICATE OF LIABILITY INSURANCE		DATE (MM/DD/YY) 09/04/2006

PRODUCER	THIS CERTIFICATE IS ISSUED AS A MATTER OF INFORMATION ONLY AND CONFERS NO RIGHTS UPON THE CERTIFICATE HOLDER. THIS CERTIFICATE DOES NOT AMEND, EXTEND OR ALTER THE COVERAGE AFFORDED BY THE POLICIES BELOW.

INSURED	COMPANIES AFFORDING COVERAGE
	COMPANY A Huatai Insurance Company of China Limited
	COMPANY B /
	COMPANY C /
	COMPANY D /

COVERAGE

THIS IS TO CERTIFY THAT THE POLICIES OF INSURANCE LISTED BELOW HAVE BEEN ISSUED TO THE INSURED NAMED ABOVE FOR THE POLICY PERIOD INDICATED, NOTWITHSTANDING ANY REQUIREMENT, TERM OR CONDITION OF ANY CONTRACT OR OTHER DOCUMENT WITH RESPECT TO WHICH THIS CERTIFICATE MAY BE ISSUED OR MAY PERTAIN, THE INSURANCE AFFORDED BY THE POLICIES DESCRIBED HEREIN IS SUBJECT TO ALL THE TERMS, EXCLUSIONS AND CONDITIONS OF SUCH POLICIES. LIMITS SHOW MAY HAVE BEEN REDUCED BY PAID CLAIMS.

TYPE OF INSURANCE	POLICY NUMBER	POLICY EFFECTIVE DATE (MM/DD/YY)	POLICY EXPIRATION DATE (MM/DD/YY)	LIMITS IN THOUSANDS	
GENERAL LIABILITY ☐COMMERCIAL GENERAL LIABILITY ☒PRODUCTS LIABILITY ☐CLAIM MADE ☒OCCURRENCE				GENERAL AGGREGATE	
				PRODUCTS AGGREGATE	
				PERSONAL & ADV INJURY	
☐ BROAD FORM VENDORS ☒DESIGNATED FORM VENDORS				EACH OCCURRENCE	
				FIRE DAMAGE (ANY ONE FIRE)	
				MED EXP(ANY ONE PERSON)	

PRODUCTS COVERED

DESCRIPTION OF OPERATIONS/LOCATIONS/VEHICLES/SPECIAL ITEMS

CERTIFICATE HOLDER Additional Insured:	CANCELLATION SHOULD ANY OF THE ABOVE DESCRIBED POLICIES BE CANCELLED BEFORE THE EXPIRATION DATE THEREOF, THE ISSUING COMPANY WILL ENDEAVOR TO MAIL___DAYS WRITTEN NOTICE TO THE CERTIFICATE HOLDER NAMED TO THE LEFT. BUT FAILURE TO MAIL SUCH NOTICE SHALL IMPOST NO OBLIGATION OR LIABILITY OF ANY KIND UPON THE COMPANY, ITS AGENTS OR REPRESENTATIVE.
CERT. No.: 01	AUTHORIZED REPRESENTATIVE

图 8-3   Sample of Insurance Certificate(保险凭证式样)

Date of Issue: M/D, Y

CERTIFICATE OF INSURANCE

VENDOR

This is to certify that the following insurance has been effected with this Company :

CERTIFICATE HOLDER

NAMED INSURED

LOCATION

ADDITIONAL INSURED   Address:

                                  with respect to their interests as the Insured's Vendor only.

COVERAGE   Against the Named Insured's legal liability for bodily injury or property damage
                                  caused by goods sold, supplied or distributed by the named insured.

PRODUCTS INSURED

LIMIT OF LIABILITY   A.　Each Occurrence US$
                                  B.　Aggregate per policy period US$

POLICY PERIOD   From 00:00 am of   to 24:00 pm of   Beijing Standard Time

POLICY FORM

COVERAGE TERRITORY

JURISDICTION   "Jurisdiction" means the country or countries where we will have a duty to defend the
                                  insured against any "claim" or "suit" seeking damages.

SPECIAL PROVISION

POLICY NO.:   CERT NO.: 01

In term of our credit arrangements with the Insured, the premium under the said Policy will be paid as arranged. The
risk insured is covered by this Company subject to the terms and conditions of the said Policy. This Certificate is
issued as a matter of information only and does not amend, extend or alter the coverage of the said Policy.

For and on Behalf of the Company
HUATAI Insurance Company of China, Limited

_____
Authorized Signature

图 8-4　Filled of Insurance Certificate(填制好的保险凭证)

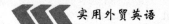

Section 2 Correspondence

1. Sample Letters

Letter 1 (Buyer's Insurance Request)

Dear Sirs,

Please insure[1] us against all risks US$100,000, value of 5,000 sets of "Butterfly" Sewing Machines shipped at Shanghai, on board S.S. "Fengching", sailing for New York on May 20th. Please send us the policy, together with a note for the charges.

Yours faithfully,

Letter 2 (Seller Insuring for Buyer)

Dear Sirs,

Regarding your instructions dated May 8, we have insured your shipment of 5,000 sets of "Butterfly" Sewing Machines shipped from Shanghai on board S.S. "Fengching", sailing for New York on May 20th, as per the policy enclosed. Please remit US$1,200 to our account for this policy by bank check.

Yours faithfully,

Letter 3 (Inquiry of Insurance)

Dear Sirs,

We shall recently have a consignment of cement under the captioned order No. 432, valued at US$40,000 CIF Hong Kong, to be shipped from New York by a vessel of New York Lines Ltd.

We desire to have the shipment insured against all risks. The insurance is from our warehouse at the above address to the port of Hong Kong. Would you please let us know as soon as possible the terms and conditions[2] on which you can provide cover for risks mentioned?

We look forward to the insurance policy, and the earlier the better.

Sincerely,

Letter 4 (Reply to an Inquiry of Insurance)

Dear Sirs,

We acknowledge with thanks the receipt of your letter of November 28th. We are pleased that you would like to insure with us the consignment of 10 cases of cotton shirts by the Hawaii Shipping line from Honolulu to Rome.

We will cover insurance W.P.A. & War Risk according to usual practice in the absence of definite instructions from you. The premium for this cover is at the rate of 1.5% of the value declared. We enclose here the relevant literature of our company for your reference. We are sure that you will find our rate is most favorable.

If our rate is acceptable to you, please let us know it so that our insurance policy can reach you timely.

Looking forward to hearing from you early.

Yours faithfully,

2. Notes to Text

(1) insure 投保

为某人投保：insure/ cover the goods for sb. / on one's behalf/ for and on one's behalf

We have insured the warehouse against fire. 我们给仓库上了火险。

(2) terms and conditions 条件(商业上表示贸易条件和合同条款的习惯总称)

We will come to business with you on the terms and conditions agreed with you. 我方将按照与你方商议好的条件与你方成交。

3. Useful expressions

(1) 我们希望这批货物在贵地投保。我们将非常感谢贵方代我方为这批货物投保一切险，保险金额为发票金额的 110%。

We hope to have the consignments insured at your end, and we will be appreciative of your kind arrangement to insure them on our behalf against All Risks for invoice value plus 10%.

(2) 据我们所知，该保险公司接收投保纸板箱装货物的偷窃、提货不着险。万一发生偷窃，保险公司将予以赔偿，敬请放心。

As far as we know, the insurance company accepts coverage of the goods packed in cardboard cartons against TPND. In case of theft, you may rest assured that insurance company shall compensate for any losses.

(3) 我们急于知道，贵方是否考虑我们每月定期运货从而同意给我们优惠保费率。

We are keen to know if you may allow us a special rate for our regular monthly shipments.

(4) 已收到你方 6 月 13 日来函，感谢你方希望我公司为贵方的货物在运输途中可能受到的损失承保。

Thank you for your letter of June 13th, requesting us to insure your goods against the possible damage in transit.

(5) 我们接收中国人民保险公司提供的 5%保险费率的报价，并要求你为运往印度孟买的 300 吨花费投保平安险。

We accept the quotation of insurance premium of 5% by the People's Insurance Company of China, and request you for arrangement to cover insurance FPA with you on the delivery of 300 ton fertilizer to Bombay, India.

(6) 保险费随保险范围的不同而不同，如果货物需要投保附加险，则额外的保费由买方支付。

The premium varies with the extent of insurance. Should the goods be insured against additional risks, the extra premium should be borne by the buyer.

(7) 请安排增加我们的粮食库存投保金额，从目前的 5000 美元增至 6000 美元，立即生效。

Would you arrange to increase the sum of insurance on our stock of grain from the present figure of USD5,000 to USD6,000 with effect from this very moment.

(8) 这项保险为仓至仓保险，从 5 月 15 日起生效。

The cover is to be from warehouse to warehouse and come to effect from May 15th.

Section 3   Dialogues

Dialogue 1

What insurance rate do you suggest we should get?

Mr. Smith is discussing insurance terms with Mr. Fang in the insurance department.

Smith: May I ask you a few questions about insurance?

Fang: Yes.

Smith: Now we've been given a C.I.F. Shanghai price for some steel plates. What insurance rate do you suggest we should get?

Fang: Well, obviously you won't want All Risks coverage.

Smith: Why not?

Fang: Because they aren't delicate goods and are not likely to be damaged on the voyage. F.P.A .will be good enough.

Smith: Then am I right in understanding that F.P.A. does not cover partial loss caused by natural calamities?

Fang: That's right. On the other hand, a W.P.A. policy covers you against partial loss in all cases.

Smith: Are there any other clauses in marine policies?

Fang: Oh, lots of them! For instance, War Risks, TPND and SRCC.

Smith: Well, thank you very much for all that information. Could you give me a quotation for my consignment now?

Fang: Are you going to make an offer today?

Smith: Yes, my customer is in urgent need of the steel plates.

Fang: OK, I'll get the rate right away.

Smith: Thank you.

Fang: Sure.

Dialogue 2

I believe that we have requested an amount twenty-five percent above the invoice value.

Helen: I am calling to discuss the level of insurance coverage you've requested for your order.

Zhang: I believe that we have requested an amount twenty-five percent above the invoice value?

Helen: Yes, that's right. We have no problem in complying with your request, but we think that the amount is a bit excessive.

Zhang: We've had a lot of trouble in the past with damaged goods.

Helen: I can understand your concern. However, the normal coverage for goods of this type is to insure them for the total invoice amount plus ten percent.

Zhang: We would feel more comfortable with the additional protection.

Helen: Unfortunately, if you want to increase the coverage, we will have to charge you extra for the additional cost.

Zhang: But the insurance was supposed to be included in the quotation.

Helen: Yes, but we quoted you normal coverage at regular rates.

Zhang: I see.

Helen: We can, however, arrange the extra coverage. But I suggest you contact your insurance agent there and compare rates.

Zhang: You're right. It might be cheaper on this end.

Helen: Fax me whatever rates you find there and I'll compare them with what we can offer.

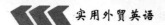

Dialogue 3

It seems that we have a problem with my most recent shipment.

Helen: Good afternoon, Zhang.

Zhang: Well, Helen, it seems that we have a problem with my most recent shipment. As we discussed in March, my consignment was to arrive in two weeks. I have no problem with the timing but I do have a concern with the substantial damage incurred during the shipping. After receiving the shipment, my guys "did the math" and realized that the damage is approximately 40%. Helen, what are we going to do here? I cannot do business this way.

Helen: Well, Zhang, I have no idea about this. I guess your problem is really about the fact that your insurance doesn't cover the total amount of damages. As you know, we are the middleman in this situation so our next step is to contact the insurance company and file a claim.

Zhang: Helen, my concern is that we were advised by your guys. From there, I purchased the insurance but now I am told that breakage is not covered by our policy. And on top of that, the insurance policy is dated to expire in two days so I have no time to adjust my coverage. What am I to do here? Should I take my business elsewhere?

Helen: Indeed this is unfortunate, Zhang. As I am not an expert regarding insurance matters, my goal is to maintain good business relations with you as we have been conducting business for over 10 years now. I believe we can work this out. However we may have to use less conventional means.

Zhang: Oh, what do you have in mind?

Helen: Well, since we are unable to change the wording in the insurance contract, I suppose I could make you an offer that should cover your losses. From my point of view, it is more important to keep you as a customer so I will extend an offer "in good faith". How does that sound to you?

Zhang: Helen, that is why we have been associated for so long. You are a fair person. In the future I will be sure to read the "fine print" and buy the correct insurance coverage.

Notes

1. insurance rate: 保险费率

2. CIF: 成本加保险费加运费(指定目的港)Cost, Insurance and Freight(…named port of destination)

3. F.P.A.: 平安险 Free from Particular Average

4. W.P.A.: 水渍险 With Particular Average

5. delicate goods: 脆的、易碎的货物

6. on the voyage: 在运输途中

7. TPND: 偷窃提货不着险

8. SRCC: 罢工暴动民变险

9. comply with: 服从，遵从

10. insurance agent: 保险代理人

11. file a claim: 提出索赔

12. conventional means: 常规的方法，惯例

13. insurance contract: 保险合同

14. in good faith: 诚心的，诚意的

15. fine print: 契约，证券等含有限制条件、例外等的附属细则

Section 4　Exercises

1. Translate the following sentences into English:

(1)　请为该批货物投保一切险及战争险。

(2)　如果你方需要加保战争险，增加的保费由你方负担。

(3)　我们已为该货物投保水渍险和战争险，保险率 0.8%，投保金额为 50000 美元。

(4)　我们愿代你方投保。

(5)　在未收到客户关于保险的明确指示的情况下，我们一般投保水渍险和战争险。若贵方想投保一切险，请提前告知我们。

(6)　若货物发生损坏，可向贵地保险代理提出索赔，他们将赔偿你方损失。

(7)　现附上上海商检局所签发的检验证明和船公司代理人的报告书，以及保险单原件。

(8)　对于这批货物来说，水渍险的保险范围太窄了，请增加提货不着险。

2. Translate the following sentences into Chinese:

(1)　In compliance with your request, we have covered All Risks for 110% of the invoice value with PICC.

(2)　Insurance should be effected by the seller for 110% of invoice value covering All Risks and War Risks as per CIC of PICC dated 01/01/1981.

(3)　We note that you require the coverage to include War Risk, but our quotation of CIF price includes WPA only.

(4)　We know that according to your usual practice, you insure the goods only for 10% above invoice value; therefore, the extra premium will be for our account.

(5) Please let us know the rate of premium at which leakage is covered by the insurers on your side.

(6) In the absence of your definite instructions regarding insurance, we covered your ordered goods against All Risks for 110% of the invoice value according to our usual practice.

(7) An insurance claim should be submitted to the insurance company or its agents within 30 days after the arrival of the consignment at the port of destination.

(8) The insurance company declined to pay the claim, not for that the Breakage Risk was uncovered, but that the risk was insured with 10% franchise.

3. Translate the following letter into English:

×××先生：

我们想请您参阅关于 500 台电视机的 998 号订单，您一定会注意到该订单以 CFR 术语为基础。

如我们在电话中所说，我们很希望由你方代办保险。若你方能为该批货物按发票金额的 110%(即总金额 2200000 美元)投保一切险，我方将不胜感激。

一收到你方索款通知书，我方即会偿还你方代付保险费。如你方愿意，也可以开具即期汇票。

真诚希望上述请求能得到你方同意。

······谨上

4. Translate the following letter into Chinese:

Dear Mr. …,

In reply to your letter of May 4 asking us to effect insurance on Order No. 998, we are pleased to inform you that we have covered All Risk with the People's Insurance Company of China for USD2,200,000 at a premium of 0.30 %.

The policy is being prepared accordingly and the debit note for the premium will be presented to you in a week.

Yours faithfully,

5. Compose a dialogue based on the following situation:

Mr. Brown is discussing insurance terms with Mr. Yang.

As a matter of routine, the seller may insure the goods only for 10% above invoice value against F.P.A. But Mr. Brown wants to cover the goods he ordered against W.P.A. for 120% of the invoice value.

Section 5   Solution to Problem

1. "I" in "CIF" or "CIP"

Coverage of FPA/WPA/ALL RISKS

The clear distinction among the clauses F.P.A., W.P.A. and All Risks is of great practical significance. It may help exporters choose the right coverage. Products should be insured in the appropriate category. The following chart is especially simple and easy to use.

	F.P.A.	W.P.A.	All Risks
Natural Calamities	T.L.√ P.L.X	T.L.√ P.L.√	T.L.√ P.L.√
Fortuitous Accidents	T.L.√ P.L.√	T.L.√ P.L.√	T.L.√ P.L.√
General Extraneous Risks	T.L.X P.L.X	T.L.X P.L.X	T.L.√ P.L.√
Special Extraneous Risks	T.L.X P.L.X	T.L.X P.L.X	T.L.X P.L.X

Horizontal headings: insurance coverage

Vertical headings: risks

Body: losses covered

Option of proper coverage depends on nature of commodity, possibility of the risk becoming loss and damage, premium of insurance and so on.

Glassware is easily broken, we would better cover glassware against breakage, steel plate is perhaps unnecessary to be covered by this insurance.

Somalia pirates are rampant in Gulf of Aden recently, if Gulf of Aden is on the route of the carriage of your cargo, you would better consider effecting insurance against robbery.

In respect to coverage for glassware, if the premium of all risks isn't obvious higher than that of W.P.A. plus Breakage, all risks maybe are taken in account by you.

2. Are the following risks covered by a W.P.A policy? Why?

loss

robbery

soilage (dirt, pollution)

bending (distortion)

breakage

riot

earthquake	theft
war	hook breakage
oxidation	seawater damage
rust	looting (robbery)
strike	sabotage (damage, injury)
wetness	damages from other cargo

As per ocean marine cargo clauses of P.I.C.C. dated Jan.1,1981, soilage, oxidation, rust, wetness, bending, breakage, theft, hook breakage, looting, and damages from other cargo are general extraneous risks, riot, war and strike as well as aggressive robbery are special extraneous risks, they are not in the coverage of W.P.A.

While, in a sense, loss and sabotage are not any risks.

Earthquake is natural calamity and seawater damage probably resulted from earthquake and (or) tsunami.

Only earthquake and seawater damage are covered by a W.P.A. policy.

Unit 9

Packing and Inspection

Section 1   Introduction

1. Packing (包装)

Whatever mode of transport is used, most products will require packing. Packing has become more and more important in competing for overseas markets. One of its basic purposes is to protect the product. One of its basic purposes is to protect the product. The second purpose of packaging is to make the product look appealing to the buyer.

不论以何种方式运输，多数产品都需要包装，包装是出口贸易的一部分。在争夺国外市场的过程中，包装变得越来越重要。包装的基本作用之一是保护产品；第二个作用是使产品的外观能取悦买家。

(1)　Kinds of Packing (包装的种类)

①　Nude Cargo, Cargo in Bulk/Bulk Cargo and Packed Cargo (裸装、散装及包装货)

Packing is a part of export business. The kinds of cargoes are various in international trade, from the view point of whether they need packing, they fall into three kinds:

贸易中的货物是多种多样的，根据包装的不同可以分为以下三种：

A. Nude Cargo (裸装货)

Nude cargoes or nude packed commodities refer to those kinds of cargoes whose qualities are more stable and to be shipped without any packages or in simple bundles. They are not easy to be influenced by outside circumstances and they become single pieces of their own. They are difficult to be packed or do not need any packing, such as steel products, lead ingot, timber, rubber, automobile, etc.

所谓裸装货是指有些商品的品质比较稳定，只要将商品略加捆扎或以其自身进行捆扎的货物。裸装方式适用于一些形态上自然成件，能抵抗外界影响，或品质稳定，难以包装的货物，如钢材、铅锭、木材、橡胶、车辆等。

B. Cargo in Bulk/Bulk Cargo (散装货)

Cargo in bulk refers to goods which are shipped or even sold without packages on the conveyance in bulk, such as oil, ore, grain, coal, etc.

所谓散装货是指未加任何包装、直接付运直至销售的货物，通常适用于不需要包装即可直接进入流通领域，或不容易包装或不值得包装的货物，例如石油、煤炭、矿砂、粮食等。

C. Packed Cargo (包装货)

Most of commodities in international trade need certain degree of packing during the shipping, storing and sales process. Packed cargoes refer to those which need shipping packing, marketing packing or both.

大多数国际贸易货物都需要某种程度的包装以便于运输、仓储和销售。所谓包装货是指需要运输包装、销售包装或两者都需要的货物。

② Transport/Shipping Packing and Sales /Marketing Packing (运输包装和销售包装)

In international trade, according to the functions of the goods in the process of circulating and the packing materials and methods, packing can be divided into transport packing (also called outer packing) and sales packing (also called inner packing). A third kind of packing, neutral packing is also often used in international trade.

在国际贸易中，根据商品包装在流通过程中作用的不同、包装材料和包装方法的不同，包装可分为运输包装(又称外包装)和销售包装(内包装)。另一种包装——中性包装，也经常在国际贸易中使用。

A. Transport/Shipping (Outer Packing) (运输包装)

Transport/Shipping is also called big packing or outside packing, or outer packing or giant packing. It is used mainly to keep the goods safe and sound during transportation.

The methods of shipping packing usually fall into two kinds:

运输包装又称外包装或大包装，它的作用主要在于保护运输途中的商品，同时，并使之便于防盗、运输、装卸、储存和分配。

运输包装通常分为两种：

a. Single Piece Packing (单件运输包装)

The cargoes are packed as a single unit, i.e., a measuring unit, in the transportation process, which includes cases, drums, bags, bales, bundles, etc.

单件运输包装是指货物在运输过程中作为一个计件单位的包装，包括箱、桶、袋、包、瓶罐、捆等。

b. Collective Packing (集合运输包装)

Collective packing is also called group shipping packing by which a certain number of single pieces are grouped together to form a big packing or are packed in a big container. Collective packing can be classified into container, pallet, flexible container, etc.

集合运输包装是指在单件运输包装的基础上，为了适应运输、装卸作业现代化的要求，将若干单件包装组合成一件大包装。目前常见的组合包装包括集装箱、托盘、集装包和集装袋。

B. Sales/Marketing Packing (销售包装)

Sales packing (also called inner packing, small packing or immediate packing) is not only adopted as a form of protection to reduce the risks of goods being damaged in transit and prevent pilferage, but mainly with the purpose of promoting sales. It can be realized in various forms and with different materials as long as it is nice to look at, easy to handle and helpful to the sales.

销售包装又称内包装、小包装或直接包装。它除了保护商品免受损坏和防盗以外，主要起促销的作用。只要美观，便于操作和有利于销售，销售包装可采用各种形式和材料。

(2)　Marking of Package (包装标志)

Packing mark or recognition mark refers to different diagrams, words and figures which are written, printed, or brushed on the outside of the shipping packing in order that it is easy and convenient for goods' loading, unloading, store, inspection and discharge. According to the uses of the packing mark, it can be divided into:

包装标志是指在商品配包装上书写、压印、刷制各种有关的标志，如图形、文字、数字等，以便识别货物，有利于装卸、运输、仓储、检验和交接工作的顺利进行。根据包装标志的用途可分为：

①　Shipping Marks (运输标志)

Shipping marks are marks of simple designs, some letters, numbers and simple words on packages, often stenciled, that serve as identification of the consignment to which they belong. It is one of the most important elements which are agreed on by the exporter and the importer in a sales contract. The shipping mark consists of(See Fig. 9-1 Shipping Marks):

运输标志是用模板印刷在包装上的标记，由一些简单的几何图形和一些字母、数字及简单的文字组成，用来辨识货物。它是进出口商在销售合同里必须达成一致的几个最重要的事项之一。运输标志由以下几个方面构成(如图 9-1 所示为运输标志)：

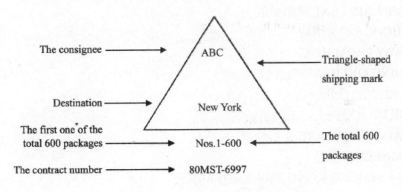

图 9-1　Shipping Marks(运输标志)

A. Name or code of destination (目的地的名称或代号)

Generally, abbreviated forms or codes are not used to show the destination in order to avoid ambiguity.

一般来说，表示目的港的标识都不用缩写，以避免引起歧义。

B. Code of consignee or consignor (收货人和发货人的代号)

The consignee's or consignor's code are usually indicated by different geometrical diagrams, such as triangles, diamonds, circles, square, etc. with letters inside them as the main marks.

一般为自己设计的图形代号，如三角形、菱形、圆形或方形，里面刷有主要标识。

C. Piece number, serial number, contract number or license number (件号、批号、合同号或许可证号)

Below the name of the destination is usually placed the package number. Packages may be numbered consecutively or marked merely with a total number.

件号标志一般放在目的港下面。件号数字可以是从 1 到最后总数这样一个连贯的数字，也可以是最后的一个总数。

② Indicative Marks (指示性标志)

We usually make use of the simple, noticeable design, remarkable diagrams and simple words on the packages to remain the relative workers of the items for attention when they load, unload, carry and store the goods, such as: HANDLE WITH CARE, THIS SIDE UP, etc. which printed in black color generally.

人们通常会在包装上使用简单、醒目的图形和文字标出，货物在运输装卸、搬运、保管过程中应注意的事项，如 "小心轻放" "此端朝上" 等。指示标志一般应印成黑色。

The following are some common markings and phrases.

以下是一些常见的标志和用语。

DO NOT DROP 切勿乱摔

NOT TO BE LAID FLAT 切勿平放

USE NO HOOKS 请勿用钩

STOW AWAY FROM HEAT 切勿受热

NO TURNING OVER 切勿倒置

OPEN HERE 此处打开

THIS SIDE UP 此端向上

PORCELAIN, WITH CARE 小心瓷器

INFLAMMABLE 易燃品

CANADA VIA HONG KONG 经香港运往加拿大

CENTER OF GRAVITY 重心点

LIQUID 液体

NO DUMPING 切勿投掷

DO NOT CRUSH 切勿挤压

HANDLE WITH CARE 小心轻放

PERISHABLE GOODS 易腐物品

FRAGILE 易碎物品

GUARD AGAINST DAMP 防潮

KEEP FLAT 必须平放

SLIDING HERE 从此处吊起

KEEP IN DARK PLACE 暗处存放

KEEP DRY 保持干燥

③ Warning Mark (警告性标志)

The warning mark is also called dangerous cargo mark or shipping mark for dangerous commodities, which is brushed/printed clearly and definitely on the shipping packing of the inflammable, explosive, poisonous, corrosive or radioactive goods, so as to give warnings to the workers/dockers/crew.

Warning marks are usually made up of simple geometrical diagrams, word descriptions and particular pictures, as to which, every country usually has its own stipulation.

警告性标志又称危险货物包装标志，是指凡在运输包装内装有爆炸品、易燃物品、有毒物品、腐蚀物品、氧化剂和放射性物质等危险货物时，都必须在运输包装上标明用于各种危险品的标志，以示警告，使装卸、运输和保管人员按货物特性采取相应的防护措施，以保护物资和人身的安全。

警告性标志是由文字和特定的图案所组成的，各国或地区都有自己的规定。

(3) Neutral Packing and Brand Designated by the Buyer (中性包装和定牌)

① Neutral packing (中性包装)

The neutral packing means that there is neither a name of the origin, nor a name and address of the factory/manufacturer, nor a trade mark, a brand, or even any words on the (outer or inner) the factory/manufacturer, nor a trade mark, a brand, or even any words on the (outer or inner) packing of the commodity and the commodity itself. The purpose of using neutral packing by exporters is to break down the tariff and non-tariff barriers of some countries or regions, or meet the special demand of the transaction (such as entrepot). It may also help the manufacturers in exporting countries to increase the competitiveness of their products, expand the exports and profitably in the importing countries.

中性包装是一种既不标明生产国、厂商的地名和名称，也不标明商标和牌子的包装。出口商采用中性包装的目的是打破某些进口国家和地区的关税或非关税壁垒，或适应交易的特殊需要(如转口销售)。它还能帮助生产厂商提高产品的竞争能力，对进口国扩大出口并赚取外汇。

② Brands designated by the buyer (定牌)

Brands designated by the buyer refer to the packing that the goods should be packed according to the trade marks and brands by the buyer. As to the goods to be ordered regularly in large quantities for a long time by foreign customers, in order to expand sales, we can accept trade marks designated by buyers with indicating the mark of the manufacturing country, that is, the neutral packing with brands designated by the buyers.

Sometimes we may accept trade marks or brands designated by buyers from foreign countries, but under the trade marks and brands, we indicate "Made in China". In some other cases, we may accept the designated trade marks or brands and at the same time, under the trade marks or brands we indicate that the goods are made by a factory in the buyer's country, i.e., trade marks or brands and origins designated by the buyers.

定牌是指按买方要求在出口国商品和包装上使用买方指定的商标或牌名的做法。为了扩大销售的需要，对于那些长期大量订购的外国客户，我方常按买方要求接受对方指定的商标，并根据对方要求不加注生产国别标志，即定牌中性。

有时接受客户指定的商标，但在商标、牌名下标明"中国制造"字样，有时定牌可以用"××公司进口""××公司经销""××公司特制"等字样。

2. Inspection (检验)

Inspection is a very necessary process in international trade. Only by this means can the dealer be sure whether the commodities provided are in accordance with the stipulations in the contract or not. Inspection is performed by the commodity inspection authorities, covering quality, specifications, quantity, weight, packing and the requirements for safety, based upon the inspection standards agreed upon in the foreign trade contracts. If the dealer has any objections to the results of inspection presented by relevant commodity inspection agencies, he may apply to the original commodity inspection agencies or such agencies at higher level, up to the state commodity inspection authority for reinspection.

在国际贸易中商品检验是一个非常必要的过程。只有通过这种方式才能确保交易商提供的商品是否符合合同的规定。检验是由商检机构依据对外贸易合同约定的检验标准检验质量、规格、数量、重量、包装和安全性要求。如果交易商对相关商检机构出具的检验结果有异议，他可以向原商检机构或更高级别的商检机构，甚至向国家商检机关申请复检。

(1) Inspection Stipulated by Law(法律规定的检验)

Import and export commodity inspection is divided into legal inspection and authentic attesting business. Legal inspection refers to the authorized agencies inspect the commodity which must be inspected according to laws and legal inspection procedures, issue the inspection certificate after pass inspection, and permit the import and export of the goods.

The Commodity Inspection Law of China stipulates that the China Entry-Exit Inspection and Quarantine Bureau (CEEIQB) or Commodity Inspection Bureau of China (C.I.B.C.) is the competent authority which supervises the work of inspection of the whole nation. In international trade, inspection institutions must usually examine the quality, quantity, packing, etc. of the goods delivered by the seller to make sure whether the goods are in conformity with the stipulations of the contract and letter of credit, or inspect safety and sanitation conditions, environmental and labour protection conditions as to the goods, or quarantine plants and animalsin accordance with the relative laws and decrees of the country.

进出口商品的检验分为法定检验和公证鉴定业务。法定检验是指依照国家法律，由授权的检验机构对法律规定必须检验的商品，按法律规定的程序进行检验，经检验合格并签发证明书后，才允许商品进口和出口。

我国商检法(《中华人民共和国进出口商品检验法》)明确规定了中国出入境检验检疫局和中华人民共和国商品检验局为全国商品检验的监督管理机构。在国际贸易中，检验机构通常要检验卖方交付的货物质量、数量、包装等是否符合合同和信用证的规定，或检查货物的安全性能和卫生条件、环境和劳动保护条件，或依照国家的相关法律、法规进行动植物检疫。

(2)   Time and Place of Inspection (检验的时间和地点)

There are three ways to stipulate the time and place of inspection:

有三种规定检验时间和地点的方法：

①   To make inspection before shipment, i.e., to make inspection in the export country. (规定装船前检验，也就是规定在出口国检验)

e.g. To make inspection at the factory;

To make inspection at the port of shipment (It also stipulate that "to take shipping or shipped quality or quantity as final").

例如：规定在工厂检验；

规定在装运港检验（"以离岸品质或离岸数量为准"）。

②   To make inspection after the goods have been discharged, i.e., to make inspection in the import country. (规定货物已经运抵后再检验，也就是规定在进口国检验)

e.g. To make inspection at the port of destination (It also stipulate that "to take landing or landed quality or quantity as final");

To make inspection at the user's residence or the location of end user (Such as sealed packing goods, heavy machinery or precision instruments).

例如：规定在目的港检验(通常也规定了"以到岸品质或到岸数量为准")

规定在买方营业处所或最终用户所在地检验(例如不便打开包装的货物、重型机械或精密仪器)。

③   To make inspection in the export country and make reinspection in the import country. (规定出口国检验，进口国复验)

The main advantage of this method is that the inspection certificate provided by the seller is regarded as one of the effective documents to be presented for negotiation, and gives the buyer the right to make reinspection after the goods arrive at the port of destination as well.

采用这种方式的优点就是卖方取得的检验证书可以作为提交议付的有效单据之一，同时买方在货物运抵目的港后也有权进行复验。

(3) Inspection Clauses in Contract (合同中的检验条款)

It should specify clearly the provisions of the right of inspection, inspection time and place, inspection institution and inspection certificate, inspection standards and methods, etc. in the inspection clauses of contract. For example:

It is mutually agreed that the Certificate of Quality and Weight (Quantity) issued by the Entry-Exit Inspection and Quarantine Bureau of the People's Republic of China (CIQ) at the port of shipment shall be part of the documents to be presented for negotiation under the relevant L/C. The Buyer shall have the right to re-inspect the quality and weight (quantity) of the cargo. The re-inspection fee shall be borne by the Buyer. Should the quality and weight (quantity) be found not in conformity with that of the contract, the Buyer are entitled to lodge with the Seller a claim which should be supported by survey reports issued by a recognized surveyor approved by the Seller. The claim, if any, shall be lodged within ____ days after arrival of the cargo at the port of destination.

应在合同中的检验条款中规定清楚检验权、检验时间和地点、检验机构、检验证书、检验标准与方法等项内容。举例如下：

买卖双方同意以装运港中华人民共和国出入境检验检疫局签发的品质和重量(数量)检验证书作为信用证项下议付所提交单据的一部分，买方有权对货物的品质和数量进行复验，复验费由买方负担。但若发现品质和数量(重量)与合同规定不符时，买方有权向卖方索赔，并提供经卖方同意的公证机构出具的检验报告。索赔期限为货物到达目的港后____天内。

(4) Inspection Certificate (商检证书)

The Inspection certificate or survey report is a written document issued by the commodity inspection institution, bearing witness to the result of inspection, which shows the quality or quantity or other elements of the goods (See Fig. 9-2 Quantity Certificate). It mainly performs two functions: Firstly, as a document of quality or quantity, it can decide whether the quality or quantity of the goods shipped by the seller is in conformity with that stipulated in the contract. It is an important proof at the time of refusing payment, lodging or settling a claim. Secondly, it is one of the shipping documents used at the time of negotiating payment.

检验证书是商检机构出具的证明检验结果的书面文件。检验证书或检查报告是表明货物的数量、质量或其他因素的单证(见图 9-2 数量检验证书)。它主要有两方面的作用：第一，作为质量和数量的单证，它可确定所运货物是否与合同中的规定相一致。它是在拒绝付款、索赔或理赔时的一个重要证明。第二，它是议付货款的货运单证之一。

中华人民共和国出入境检验检疫

ENTRY-EXIT INSPECTION AND QUARANTINE OF THE PEOPLE'S REPUBLIC OF CHINA

数量检验证书

QUANTITY CERTIFICAT

编号
No.:

发货人：

Consignor

收货人：

Consignee

品名：

Description of Goods

标记及号码

Mark & No.

报检数量/重量：

Quantity/Weight Declared

包装种类及数量：

Number and Type of Packages

运输工具：

Means of Conveyance

检验结果：

RESULTS OF INSPECTION

　　我们已尽所知最大能力实施上述试验，不能因我们签发本证书而免除卖方或其他方面根据合同和法律所承担的产品质量责任和其他责任。

　　All inspections are carried out conscientiously to the best of our knowledge and ability. This certificate does not in any respect absolve the seller and other related parties from his contractual and legal obligations especially when product quality is concerned.

印章　　　　签证地点＿＿＿＿＿＿　　　签证日期＿＿＿＿＿＿＿　　　签名＿＿＿＿＿

Stamp　　　Place of Issue　　　　　　　Date of Issue　　　　　　　Signature

Official

图 9-2　Quantity Certificate(数量检验证书)

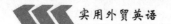
Section 2　Correspondence

1. Sample Letters

Letter 1 (Packing Requirement)

Dear Sirs,

S/C No. 90 SP-24975

We acknowledge receipt of your letter dated the 3rd March enclosing the above sales contract in duplicate but wish to state that after going through the contract we find that the packing clause[1] in it is not clear enough. The relative clause reads as follows:

Packing: Seaworthy export packing, suitable for long distance ocean transportation.

In order to eliminate possible future trouble, we would like to make clear beforehand our packing requirements as follows:

The tea under the captioned contract should be packed in international standard tea boxes, 24 boxes on a pallet[2], 10 pallets in an FCL[3]. On the outer packing, please mark our initials SCC in a diamond, under which the port of destination and our order number should be stenciled. In attention, warning marks[4] like KEEP DRY[5], USE NO HOOK[6], etc. should also be indicated.

We have made a footnote on the contract to that effect and are returning herein one copy of the contract after duly countersigning it. We hope you will find it in order and pay special attention to the packing.

We look forward to receiving your shipping advice and thank you in advance.

Yours faithfully,

Letter 2 (Packing Instruction)

Dear Sirs,

It gives us much pleasure to advise you that the 500 dozen Shirts under Order No. HAC-86 packed in cartons were shipped on board s.s. "Fengqing" on the 25th July to be transshipped at Antwerp[7]. We shall appreciate it if you will inform us of the condition of packing as soon as the consignment arrives at your end.

In regard to packing the goods in question[8] in cartons, we wish to give you our comments as follows:

(1)　Packing in cartons prevents skillful pilferage[9]. As the trace of pilferage will be more in evidence, the insurance company may be made to pay the necessary compensation for such losses.

(2) Cartons are quite fit for ocean transportation, and they are extensively used in our shipments to other ports to the entire satisfaction of our clients. Such packing has also been accepted by our insurance company for WPA and TPND[10].

(3) These cartons are well protected against moisture[11] by plastic lining. The very fact that they are made of paperboard induces special attention in handling and storage. Thus shirts packed in such cartons are not as susceptible to damage by moisture as those packed in wooden cases.

(4) Since cartons are comparatively light and compact, they are more convenient to handle in loading and unloading. Besides, they are not likely to be mixed with wooden cases while in transport or storage, so that the rate of breakage is lower than that of wooden cases. In view of the above reason, it is believed that your clients will find packing in cartons satisfactory and their fears unwarranted. We are awaiting your further comments.

Sincerely,

Letter 3 (Shipping Marks)

Dear Sirs,

After studying your quotation for "Portable Typewriter" dated October 16, 2014, we have decided to finalize[12] this initial transaction with you. We think, however, it is necessary to inform you of our requirements on shipping marks as in the following:

Correct and distinct marks on the containers are absolutely necessary to ensure safe delivery of the merchandise. They should be brushed or stenciled on the containers with indelible[13] ink or paint that will not run off or blur[14] because of dampness or rubbing.

Please let us have your comments by cable.

Yours faithfully,

Letter 4 (Inspection)

Dear Sirs,

Re: Electric Saws

We are pleased by your prompt reply to our inquiry of Dec. 1st, 2014 about the captioned commodity and now wish to order from you as per our Purchase Order enclosed.

It's understood that in case the quality , quantity of the goods be found not in conformity with those stipulated in our Contract after reinspection by the China Commodity Inspection Bureau [15] within 60 days after arrival of the goods at the port of destination, the Buyer shall return the goods to or lodge claims against the Seller for compensation of losses upon the strength of Inspection Certificate[16] issued by the said Bureau, with the exception of those claims for which the insurers or owners of the carrying vessel are liable. All expenses (including inspection fees) and losses arising from the return of the goods or claims should be borne by the Seller. In such case, the Buyer may, if so requested, send a sample of the goods in question to the Seller, provided that sampling is feasible.

We wish to thank you for your cooperation and hope that this transaction will pave the way for further development of business between us.

Yours faithfully,

2. Notes to Text

(1) packing clause 包装条款

packing instructions 包装要求；包装须知

packing charges 包装费用

packing list 装箱单

export packing 出口包装

inner packing 内包装； outer packing 外包装

neutral packing 中性包装

部分常用的包装容器名称：

bag 包；袋；gunny bag 麻袋；polybag 塑料袋；bale 包，布包；barrel 琵琶桶；box 盒，箱；bundle 捆；carton 纸板箱；case 箱；wooden case 木箱；cask 木桶；crate 板条箱； drum 铁皮圆桶；keg 小圆桶；tin (英) = can(美)听，罐头；

部分常见的包装表示法：

① in…用某种容器包装

Walnuts are packed in double gunny bags. 核桃用双层麻袋包装。

② in…of…each 用某种容器包装，每件若干

Men's shirts are packed in wooden cases of 10 dozen each. 男士衬衫用木箱装，每箱 10 打。

③ in…, each containing… 用某种容器包装，每件内装若干

Nylon Socks are packed in wooden cases, each containing 50 dozen. 尼龙袜用木箱包装，每箱装 50 打。

④ …to… 若干件装于一件某容器

Folding chairs are packed 2 pieces to a carton. 折叠椅两把装一个纸板箱。

⑤ each…in…and…to… 每单位装某种容器，若干单位装另一种较大的容器

Each pair of Nylon Socks is packed in a polybag and 12 pairs to a box. 每双尼龙袜装一个塑料袋，12 双装一盒。

⑥ …to…and…to… 若干单位装某种容器，若干此种容器装另一种较大的容器

Pens are packed 12 pieces to a box and 200 boxes to a wooden case. 钢笔 12 支装一盒，200 盒装一木箱。

(2) pallet 托盘，小货盘

(3) FCL = Full Container Load 一整集装箱

(4) warning marks 警告性标记

(5) KEEP DRY 保持干燥

(6) USE NO HOOK 切勿用钩

(7) Antwerp 比利时的安特卫普港

(8) in question 所谈的问题

We hope to arrive at a convergence of opinion on the matter in question.我们希望对所谈问题取得一致的意见。

(9) pilferage 盗窃

(10) WPA 水渍险   TPND 偷窃，提货不着险

(11) moisture 潮湿

These cartons are well protected against moisture by plastic lining. 由于箱内有塑料衬里，防潮性能良好。

(12) finalize 把(计划等)最后定下来

(13) indelible 擦不掉的

(14) blur 涂污，使(轮廓或形状)模糊不清

(15) China Commodity Inspection Bureau 中国商检局

(16) Inspection Certificate 商检证书

3. Useful expressions

(1) 通常涂料每桶净重 10 千克，每箱装 4 桶。

The paint is usually supplied in tins of 10 kilos net, four tins to a crate.

(2) 为预防起见，请在外包装上注明"易碎"和"小心轻放"的字样。

In view of precaution, please mark "Fragile" and "Handle with care" on the outer packing.

(3) 商品必须用塑料袋包装之后再装入纸箱，这是最为重要的。

The goods must be packed in plastic bags before they are put into the cartons. This is of primary importance.

(4) 包装应该符合当地市场偏好。

The packing should be in line with local market preference.

(5) 为预防起见，纸箱必须金属带捆绑确保安全。

For the sake of precaution, the cartons must be secured with metal bands.

(6) 请用防水材料作容器里衬，以免货物受潮。

Please line the containers with waterproof material so that the goods can be protected against moisture.

(7) 纸箱分量较轻，更便于货物的装卸。

Cartons are comparatively light in weight, they are much easier to handle in the course of loading and unloading.

(8) 用国际标准粮食袋装，每集装箱装 20 袋。

In international standard grain sacks, 20 sacks in a container.

(9) 将书装入两个箱子，每箱重 100 公斤。

The consignment of books is packed into two cases, each weighing about 100 kg.

(10) 我们必须采取措施加固包装，使其能够承受野蛮装卸。

We must take measures to reinforce the packing so that it can be strong enough to withstand rough handling.

(11) 自来水钢笔 10 支装一盒，300 盒装一木箱。

Fountain pens are packed 10 pieces to a box and 300 boxes to a wooden case.

(12) 运动款夹克衫先装入塑料袋中再用纸箱装，每箱 10 件。

Sports jackets in polybags are packed in cartons of 10 pieces each.

(13) 我方建议这批货物改用中性包装希望同意。

We propose neutral packing instead for these goods, and expect your acceptance.

(14) 可否在包装上做些改进？这是我们的包装设计，供参考，它可能有助于推销商品。

Can you make some improvement in the packing? This is our design of the packing for your reference. It will probably help push the sales.

(15) 由于包装不良，致使部分货物到达时毁坏严重，我们不得不大幅削价处理。

Owing to faulty packing, several of them arrived in a bad order so that we were compelled to dispose of them at greatly reduced prices.

(16) 双方同意以制造厂出具之品质及数量或重量检验证明书作为卖方向付款银行议付货款单据之一。但货物的品质及数量或重量的检验应按合同规定办理。

It is mutually agreed that the certificates of quality and quantity or weight issued by the manufacturer shall be part of the documents to be presented to the paying bank for negotiation of payment. However, the inspection of quality and quantity or weight shall be made in accordance with the contract.

Section 3　Dialogues

Dialogue 1

What kind of packing do you plan to use for goods?

Miao: What kind of packing do you plan to use for goods?

Owen: Cartons.

Miao: Wouldn't it be better to use wooden cases?

Owen: We used to pack our goods in wooden cases, but after several trial shipments in carton packing, we found our cartons just as seaworthy as wooden cases. Besides, cartons are less expensive, lighter to carry and cost lower freight, so nowadays more and more clients prefer carton packing to wooden case packing.

Miao: You know, the goods are to be transshipped at Hong Kong, I'm concerned about the possible jolting, and squeezing and banging around that may take place when they are moved about.

Owen: That has been taken into account. All the cartons are lined with shockproof corrugated cardboard and are wrapped up with damp proof polythene sheets. So they are seaworthy and can stand rough handling on the docks.

Miao: Your comments sound reasonable.

Owen: We always pay a lot attention to the safety of packing, especially for those fragile commodities, as I said, cartons are good enough for goods like this. However, if you insist, we surely use wooden case, but the charge will be much higher.

Miao: No, let stick with cartons. OK, now, I'd like to know how the goods will be in the cartons, please tell me in detail.

Owen: The goods will be packed one per box, 20 boxes to the carton.

Miao: What are the dimensions of the carton?

Owen: 30.5 cm high, 42.5 cm wide and 49 cm long.

Miao: And the weight?

Owen: The gross weight is 12.5 kg, the net weight is 11 kg. You see, the tare is 1.5 kg only.

Miao: Another question is about labeling; I require three languages on the labels: English, French and Chinese.

Owen: Usually we use two languages: English and Chinese, but we will take your point to add the French language to the labels.

Miao: Thanks.

Owen: Any other requirements?

Miao: Yes, one more thing. Indicative marks "Keep Dry" and "Fragile" should be stenciled on the cartons.

Owen: All right. Your suggestions for labeling and marking will be included in the contract.

Miao: Thank you very much.

Dialogue 2

The exported goods should be inspected before shipment,
and the imported goods should be reinspected after their arrival.

Mr. Feng is going to negotiate the matter of inspection with Mr. Clay.

Clay: Well, it's our turn to the matter of inspection, isn't it?

Feng: Yes. Let's go down to the issue now. Careful and proper inspection is an indispensible part to ensure the quality of the goods to be purchased.

Clay: Right. Shall we first specify the inspection right?

Feng: All right. What are your inspection stipulations for your exports and imports then?

Clay: According to the inspection clauses, inspection must be conducted before shipment by recognized surveyors, who then issue certificates concerning the quality, quantity and other things. These certificates may be taken as the basis for negotiating payment. Upon arrival of the imported goods, the Administration for Quality Supervision and Inspection and Quarantine at the port of destination should reinspect the goods, Should the quality, specifications, quantity or weight found not in conformity with the stipulation of the order, due to causes other than those for which insurance company, shipping company, airlines or post office are liable, the buyer should have the right to lodge a claim against the seller on the strength of the survey report or inspection certificate issued by the Administration for Quality Supervision and Inspection and Quarantine at the port of destination. Such a survey report shall be final and shall serve as the basis for filing a claim.

Feng: What you mean is that the exported goods should be inspected before shipment, and the imported the goods should be reinspected after their arrival, is that right?

Clay: You are right. It is quite common in international trade today.

Feng: Very reasonable. The interests of both the buyer and seller are taken into account.

Clay: It's true.

Notes

(1)　inner packing 内包装，又称单个包装、销售包装或小包装。直接与产品接触的包装。起直接保护商品的作用。在包装外表面上多数印有商品名称、商标、商品性能和保管使用方法等说明，用以宣传商品、指导消费和赢得市场。

(2)　packing for transportation 运输包装，又称外包装，其主要作用在于保护商品，防止在储运过程中发生货损货差，并最大限度地避免运输途中各种外界条件对商品可能产生的影响，方便检验、计数和分拨。

(3)　Let's go down to the issue now. 我们继续吧。To go down to sth.：“延续，继续……”

(4)　Upon arrival of the imported goods, the Administration for Quality Supervision and Inspection and Quarantine at the port of destination should reinspect the goods. 进口商品在到达以后，目的港国家质量监督检疫总局会对商品进行复检。Administration for Quality Supervision and Inspection and Quarantine 意为"质量监督检疫总局"，世界各国基本都设有类似的对进出口商品检验的机构。这一机构的英文全称为 Genera Administration of Quality Supervision , Inspection and Quarantine of the People's Republic of China (AQSIQ).

(5)　Should the quality, specification, quantity or weight found not in conformity with the stipulation of the order, due to cause other than those for which insurance company, shipping company, airlines or post office are liable, the buyer should　have the right to lodge a claim against the seller on the strength of the survey report or inspection certificate issued by the Administration for Quality Supervision and Inspection and Quarantine at the port of destination. 如果发现货品的质量、规格、数量或者重量与订单不符，而原因又不在保险公司、运输公司、航空公司或邮局的话，那么卖方有权按照目的港国家质量监督检疫总局颁发的检验报告或证书样卖方提出索赔。

Section 4　Exercises

1. Translate the following sentences into English:

(1)　我们可以满足你方对包装的特殊要求，但是额外增加的费用需由你方承担。

(2)　纸箱长 40cm，宽 20cm，高 30cm，容积 0.024 立方米，毛重 25 千克，净重 24 千克。

(3)　每件装一个塑料袋，12 件装一个出口纸箱，每个纸箱内混色混码装。出口纸箱必须牢固。

(4)　主唛须用黑色油墨印在纸箱正面，包括 AAA，购货合同号，目的港以及箱号。

(5)　等进一步检验每箱的损坏情况之后，即将寄详细的检验报告给你们。

(6) 这些纸箱和里面的货物，均已检验，保险公司的检验员确认该货的损坏是由于包装不当所致。

(7) 尽管货物在装运前已被检验，买方有权在货物抵达后复验。

2. Translate the following sentences into Chinese:

(1) 20 pieces of blanket are packed in one export standard carton, same color and size in a carton.

(2) The recycle mark must be printed in black ink on all polybags and outer cartons.

(3) The cartons are well protected against moisture by polythene sheet lining.

(4) If necessary we will ask you to send another set of samples to the laboratory in Hong Kong for initial testing, please wait for our instructions.

(5) The goods will be inspected by China Commodity Inspection Bureau and their quality certificate shall be taken as final.

(6) We enclose a copy of the Inspection Certificate issued by the Shanghai Commodity Inspection Bureau. Please settle the case immediately.

3. Translate the following letter into English:

布朗先生：

感谢你方 5 月 18 日来函，以及随附的 998 号售货合同。但是我们发现合同中于包装条款不够清晰。为了避免可能出现的问题，我们希望先对包装要求作如下说明：

(1) 上述合同项下的家具应用木箱包装，一套一箱。同时箱子内要求垫有塑料泡沫以免货物受压。

(2) 外包装上要印刷本公司的名称缩写 AF，缩写下面印刷目的港和订单号。此外，请标明"保持干燥""勿压"等指示性用语。

我们已在合同中就上述内容处做了脚注，并返还贵方一份我方已签署的合同。希望你方对包装特别留意。

……谨上

4. Translate the following letter into Chinese:

Dear Mr. …,

We have received your letter of April 20 inquiring information about the commodity inspection. As a usual practice, all exports are subject to inspection by an inspection organization in that country, which issues a survey report after inspection.

In order to benefit both the buyer and the seller, the buyer is entitled to reinspect within the contracted time limit. That is, the buyer shall have the right to apply to the surveying agent for inspection at the port of destination. The reinspection certificates shall be final and serve as the basis for making a claim if any discrepancy should be found not in agreement with the contract.

We hope the above information will be helpful to you.

Yours faithfully,

5. Compose a dialogue based on the following situation:

Mr. Smith found the goods received less than the weight stipulated in the contract, so he calls Mr. Li, manager of the seller, to discuss about inspection certificate.

Section 5   Solution to Problem

1. What is appropriate and proper packing?

Let's analyze the following letter which is from your count part.

Letter:

Our Order for 10,000 doz. Gent's Shirts

We dispatched to you this order as per yesterday's cable:

"1000DOZ MENSSHIRTS HAIDABRAND MAYSHIPMENT DIRECT STEAMER PLSCONFIRM"

Particular care should be taken about the quality and the packing of the goods to be delivered in this first order. It is the usual practice here that 10 shirts are packed to a carton and 10 cartons to a strong seaworthy wooden case. There will be a flow orders if this initial order proves to be satisfactory.

We are enclosing our Confirmation of Purchase in duplicate. Please sign one copy and return it to us for our records. As soon as we receive your confirmation, a letter of credit will be opened through Barclay's Bank of London.

We trust this order will be the first of a series of deals between us.

Analysis and solution:

It is likely ponderous overkill for shirts packing, cartons as outer packing lined with shockproof corrugated cardboard and wrapped up with damp proof polythene sheets are as seaworthy as wooden cases and can stand rough handling, besides, cartons are less expensive and lighter to carry. Anyway, if your counter part insists on using wooden cases, you may also meet his demand and ask him to pay extra charges.

2. Is AQSIQ (General Administration of Quality Supervision, Inspection and Quarantine of the People's Republic of China) always involved in each foreign deal traded by Chinese importer or exporter?

Remark: Previous name of AQSIQ is the State Administration of Commodity Inspection.

Let's refer to Regulations for the Implementation of the Law of the People's Republic of China on Import and Export Commodity Inspection

Article 4

In the light of the need in the development of foreign trade, the State Administration of Commodity Inspection shall work out, adjust and publish a "List of Import and Export Commodities" for those commodities which involve public interest.

Article 5

The compulsory inspection on imports and exports by the commodity inspection authorities or inspections agencies designated by the State Administration of Commodity Inspection or commodity inspection authorities covers:

(1)   inspection of import and export commodities included in the List of Commodities;

(2)   sanitary inspection on the foods for export;

(3)   testing and inspection on the performance and employment of the packages and containers for the outbound dangerous goods;

(4)   suitability inspection on the vessels' holds, containers and other means of transportation for carrying the outbound perishable foods and frozen goods;

(5)   inspection of imports and exports to be conducted by the commodity inspection authorities according to relevant international treaties; and

(6)   inspection of imports and exports to be carried out by the commodity inspection authorities as stipulated in other laws and administrative rules and regulations.

Generally speaking, commodities included in the "List of Import and Export Commodities" are subject to compulsory inspection enforced by the commodity Inspection authorities, AQSIQ is involved in. Anyway, if contract or letter of credit stipulates inspection by AQSIQ, concerned party needs to apply AQSIQ for inspection.

 Unit 10

Complaints, Claims and Arbitration

Section 1   Introduction

1. Complaints (投诉)

Complaint refers to a statement that a situation is un satisfactory or unacceptable or that someone has done something wrong. In business activities, no matter how perfect an organization may be, complaints from the customers are certain to arise.

投诉是指对令人不满意或不可接受的情况，或对某人做错事的陈述或声明。在商业活动中，无论一个公司是多么完美，肯定会有来自客户的投诉。

(1)   The Purpose of Making Complaints (投诉的目的)

The party making complaints aims at either the improvement of current products /services of their business partner, e.g. a supplier or a carrier, or the compensation for the losses caused by the wrongdoings of the business partner. Sometimes the two goals are combined when the party receiving complaints not only accepts the compensation request but also promises to deliver a better job in the future.

Of course, the one who makes complaints does not always have reasonable grounds and sometimes will exaggerate the seriousness of a minor problem. Therefore the one who faces complaints needs to analyze the legitimacy of the charges using rational thinking of both business and ethics, and then respond in an appropriate manner.

投诉方旨在改善其商业伙伴(如供应商或承运人)现有的产品/服务，或索赔由于商业伙伴的违约行为所造成的损失。当受投诉的一方不仅接受了赔偿请求，也承诺在将来会做得更好时，这两个目的就合二为一了。

当然，投诉者并不总是有合理的理由，有时会夸大一个小问题的严重性。因此面对投诉，当事方需要运用商业和伦理的理性思维分析控诉的合理性，然后用适当的方式回复。

(2)   Kinds of Complaints (投诉的种类)

The complaints can be divided into two kinds(投诉可以分为两种):

①   The genuine complaint, which arises from one of the following situations:

A. The wrong goods may have been sent.

B. The quality may not be satisfactory.

C. The goods may have delivered damaged or late.

D. The prices charged may be excessive, or not as agreed.

真实投诉，这来自下列情形之一：

A. 发送了错误的货物。

B. 质量令人不满意。

C. 交付的货物损坏或迟延。

D. 计价过高，或与约定不符。

② The complaint used as an excuses. There is complaint made by buyers who find fault with the goods as an excuse to escape from their contracts, either because they have found that they can get them cheaper elsewhere.

当作借口的投诉。发现货物有瑕疵的买方，将投诉作为借口以逃避合同，或者因为他们发现可以从他处按更便宜的价格获得货物。

2. Claims (索赔)

Claim means that in international trade, one party breaks the contract and causes losses to the other party directly or indirectly, the party suffering the losses may ask for compensation for the losses. In contract, the two parties often stipulate clauses on settlement of claim as well as inspection and claim clauses.

所谓索赔，就是指争议发生后，遭受损害的一方向违约方提出赔偿的要求。买卖双方通常都会在合同中写明索赔的办法以及有关商检和索赔的条款。

(1) Types of Claims and Objects of Claims (索赔的类型与索赔对象)

Breach of contract means the refusal or failure by a party to a contract to fulfill an obligation imposed on him under that contract. In practice, it is not infrequent that the exporter or the importer neglects or fails to perform any of his obligations, thus giving rise to breach of contract and various trade disputes, which, subsequently, leads to claim. According to the objects of claims, the claims can be divided into the following four types:

违反合同的意思是合同的一方拒绝或未能完成合同中所规定的义务。在实践中经常会发生出口商和进口商忽略或不能履行他们的义务的情况，由此会产生违反合同和各种各样的贸易纠纷，进而会导致索赔。根据索赔对象的不同，索赔可分为以下四种类型：

① Claims Filed by the Buyer against the Seller (买方向卖方提出索赔)

A claim may be filed by the buyer against the seller where the seller fails to make timely delivery or refuses to make delivery; where the goods delivered by the seller is not in accordance with the contracted quantity, quality, specifications; and the goods are damaged due to improper packing, etc.

如卖方未按期交货或拒不交货或其所交货物的数量、品质、规格与合同规定不符；包装不良而使货物受损，那么买方将会向卖方提出索赔。

② Claims Filed by the Seller against the Buyer (卖方向买方提出索赔)

A claim may be filed by the seller against the buyer where the buyer does not open an L/C or in time; where he rejects the goods unreasonably; where, under FOB, he fails to dispatch a vessel to carry the goods or advise the carrier and name of vessel in time, etc.

如买方拒不开证或未按时开立信用证；无理拒收货物；在 FOB 条件下，未及时派船接运货物或未及时通知承运人和货船船名等，那么卖方将会向买方提出索赔。

③ Claims against the Carrier (向承运人索赔)

It is also called transportation claim. For ocean transportation, it means claims against the shipping company which carries the goods. The shipping company is responsible for the relevant losses or damages where shipping company is responsible for circumstances such as: the quantity of the goods is less than that stated in the relevant B/L; the goods have traces of damages under a clean B/L, etc.

向承运人索赔也被称为运输索赔。就海运货物来说，向承运人索赔是指向承运货物的船公司索赔。如货物数量少于提单所载的数量；提单是清洁提单，而货物有残损情况等情形下货物的相关灭失或损坏，承运船方应承担责任。

④ Claims against the Insurance Company (向保险公司索赔)

It is so-called insurance claim. Goods in transit incur losses or damages that are caused by natural calamities, accidents and other events, which are within the coverage of insurance, then the insurance company shall be responsible for the losses and damages.

向保险公司索赔及所谓的保险索赔。由于自然灾害、意外事故或运输中其他事故的发生而使货物受损，并且属于承保范围内的，那么应由保险公司赔偿损失。

(2) Claim Clauses (索赔条款)

In international trade contract, claim clause is also called discrepancy and claim clause. It also include, besides stipulating that if any party breaches a contract, the other party is entitled to lodge claim against the party in breach, other aspects in respect of proofs presented when lodging a claim and effective period for filing a claim, etc.

在国际贸易合同中，索赔条款经常被称为异议与索赔条款。它的内容除规定一方如违反合同，另一方有权索赔外，还包括索赔期限和赔付的金额等。

① Proofs (索赔依据)

Clause in this respect stipulates the relevant proofs to be presented and the relevant authority competent for issuing the certificate. Proofs include legal proof which refers to the sales contract and the relevant governing laws and regulations and fact proof which refers to the facts and the relevant written evidence in respect of the breach.

主要规定索赔必须具备的证据和出具证明的机构。索赔依据主要包括法律依据和事实依据两个方面。前者是指相关贸易合同和适用的有关法律法规，后者是指违约的事实真相及其书面证明。

② Period for Claim (索赔期限)

Period for claim refers to the effective period in which the claimant can make a claim against the party in breach. Claims beyond the agreed effective period can be refused by the party in breach. In addition, a detailed stipulation in respect of the starting date for making a claim should also be included in the clause.

索赔期限是指索赔方向违约方提出的有效时限，逾期索赔，违约方可以不予受理。在规定索赔期限时还应该对索赔期限的起算时间做出具体规定。

③ Claim Amount (索赔金额)

Claim amount should include invoice value of a contract and incidental damages such as inspection fees, loading and unloading expenses, bank charges, storage charges and interest, etc.

索赔金额除合同规定的商品价值外，还可以提出有关的费用索赔。比如商品检验费、装卸费、银行手续费、仓租、利息等。

④ Penalty (罚金条款)

Clause in respect of penalty in a contract should stipulate that "any party who fails to perform the contract shall pay an agreed amount as penalty for compensating the other party for the damages". Penalty clause is fixed where the seller fails to make timely delivery; the buyer fails to open the relevant L/C or the buyer fails to take delivery on time, and the penalty ceiling is also included in the contract.

合同规定，当一方未履行合同义务时，应向另一方支付合同约定的金额，以补偿对方的损失。罚金条款一般适用于卖方延期交货，或买方延迟开立信用证或延期接货的情况下。合同一般还规定罚金的最高限额。

The example of claim clause (索赔条款实例):

In case of quality discrepancy, claims should be filed by the buyer within 30 days after the arrival of the goods at port of destination, while for quantity discrepancy, claims should be filed by the Buyer within 15 days after the arrival of the goods at port of destination. In all case, claims must be accompanied by survey reports of recognized public surveyors agreed to by the Seller. If the goods have already been processed, the Buyer shall thereupon lose the right to claim. Should the responsibility of the subject under claim be found to rest on the part of the Seller, the Seller should, within 20 days after receipt of the claim, send his reply to the Buyer together with suggestion for settlement. Claims in respect of matters within responsibility of insurance company, shipping company or other organization will not be considered or entertained by the Seller.

Should the Seller fail to make delivery on time as stipulated in the contract, the Buyer shall agree to postpone the delivery on the condition that the Seller agree to pay a penalty which shall be deducted by the paying bank from the payment under negotiation, or by the Buyer direct at the time of payment. The rate of penalty is charged at 0.5% of the total value of the goods whose delivery has been delayed for every 7 days, odd days less than seven days should be counted as 7 days. But the total amount of penalty, however, shall not exceed 5% of the total value of the goods involved in the late delivery. In case the Seller fails to make delivery ten weeks later than the time of shipment stipulated in the contract, the Buyer shall have the right to cancel the contract and the Seller in spite of the cancellation, shall still pay the aforesaid penalty to the Buyer without delay.

品质异议须于货到目的港之日起 30 天内提出，数量异议须于货到目的港之日起 15 天内提出，并均须提供经卖方同意的公证行的检验证明。如果货物已经过加工处理，买方即丧失索赔权利。如责任属于卖方，卖方收到异议 20 天内答复买方并提出处理意见。对于属于保险公司、船公司或者其他运输机构责任范围内的索赔，卖方不予受理。

若卖方不能按合同规定如期交货，在卖方同意由付款行在议付货款中扣除罚金或由买方于支付货款时直接扣除罚金的条件下，买方应同意延期交货。罚金率按海 7 天收取延期交货部分金额的 0.5%，不足 7 天者按 7 天计算。但罚金不得超过延期交货部分总金额的 5%。若卖方延期交货超过合同规定期限 10 周时，买方有权撤销合同，但卖方仍应不延迟地按上述规定向买方支付罚金。

3. Arbitration (仲裁)

In international trade practice, in case of disputes, the two parties should try to settle the disputes through amicable negotiations. In case no settlement can be reached through negotiation, the case shall then be settled through conciliation, arbitration or even litigation. Nowadays, arbitration is a widely used method to settling disputes in international trade.

在国际贸易中，买卖双方发生了贸易纠纷，应当采用友好的协商办法来解决纠纷。但当双方当事人不能经协商解决问题时，就不得不采用调解、仲裁甚至诉讼解决问题。目前，在国际贸易中广泛使用的一种解决争议的方法就是仲裁。

(1) The Definition of Arbitration (仲裁的定义)

Arbitration means that the two parties, before or after the disputes arise, reach a written agreement that they will submit the disputes which cannot be settled through amicable negotiations to the third party for arbitration. Arbitration is of the two parties' own will, in case no agreement can be reached, any party cannot force the other party to submit to arbitration while resorting to judicial proceedings the plaintiff may take a unilateral action against the defendant without agreement between the two parties in advance.

仲裁又称公断，指交易双方在争议发生前或争议发生后达成书面协议，自愿将他们的争议提交双方同意的仲裁机构裁决，以解决争议的一种方式。仲裁是建立在双方自愿的基础上的，当事人通过仲裁解决争议时，必须先签订仲裁协议，仲裁机构只有收到当事人提交的仲裁协议才可受理。

(2)　Characteristics of Arbitration (仲裁的特点)

Compared with over a court trial, arbitration has the following advantages:

同诉讼相比，仲裁有以下几个优点：

①　The parties concerned may choose the arbitrator from the Arbitration Organization, and an arbitrator who is familiar with the technical or social setting of the dispute may be chosen. Normally a board of arbitration consists of three arbitrators. Firstly, the plaintiff and the defendant choose one arbitrator respectively. Then, the two arbitrators so chosen by the plaintiff and defendant choose a third arbitrator.

双方均有在仲裁机构中推选仲裁员的自由，可以选择熟悉争议处理技巧、争议社会背景的仲裁员。通常仲裁庭由三位仲裁员组成。首先，原告和被告各选一位仲裁员，然后由这两位仲裁员再选第三位仲裁员。

②　Compared with trial which may sometimes take several years to get the disputes settled in court, there is less delay in disposing of the dispute through arbitration.

通过仲裁处理争议比较迅速，而法院审理有时则可能要几年才能将争议解决。

③　Since the arbitration procedure is simpler and more informal than in court, the parties may choose not to be represented by lawyers, and the cost of arbitration is cheaper. Arbitration can be handled according to commercial practices, so arbitration is more flexible and permissive.

仲裁程序比诉讼简单，不如诉讼正式，当事人可以不请律师，仲裁费用也较低。仲裁的办理可以按照商业习惯来进行，因而仲裁更具有灵活性和可执行性。

④　The arbitration award is final and has binding force upon the parties concerned.

仲裁裁决一般是终局的，对双方当事人都有约束力。

⑤　Privacy can be maintained in both the arbitration bearing and the award.

仲裁的审理和裁决可以不公开。

(3)　Arbitration Clauses (仲裁条款)

①　Place of Arbitration (仲裁地点)

Since applicable laws concerning arbitration differ from country to country, and different applicable laws differ in their interpretations in respect of the rights and obligations of the parties concerned, therefore parties concerned are always making efforts to choose a arbitration place they trust and know quite well.

仲裁地点不同，适用的法律可能不同，对双方当事人的权利、义务的解释就会有差异。因此，交易双方都会争取在自己比较了解和信任的地方仲裁。

② Arbitration Body (仲裁机构)

Disputes in international trade can be either referred to a permanent arbitration organization for arbitration as can be stipulated in the arbitration agreement by parties concerned or submitted for arbitration to a interim arbitration tribunal as formed by the arbitrators agreed by the two parties. In China, China International Economic and Trade Arbitration Commission and Maritime Arbitration Commission are permanent arbitration organizations.

在国际贸易中，争议可由当事人在仲裁协议中规定在常设仲裁机构进行，也可以由当事人双方共同指定仲裁员组成临时仲裁庭进行仲裁。我国的常设机构是中国国际经济贸易仲裁委员会和海事仲裁委员会。

③ Applicable Arbitration Rules (仲裁规则的适用)

The country where the arbitration is going to be made and the relevant applicable arbitration rules should be made clear in the sales contract. According to the usual international practice of arbitration, the arbitration rules in the arbitration place shall in principle apply, but it is legal for the parties concerned to agree in their contract that the arbitration rules of the arbitration organization in other country (regional), other than the arbitration rules of the county where the arbitration is going to be made, shall apply.

在买卖合同中，应订明进行仲裁的所在国以及适用的仲裁规则。按国际仲裁的一般做法，原则上采用仲裁所在地的仲裁规则，但有的法律上也允许双方当事人在合同中约定，采用仲裁地点以外的其他国家(地区)仲裁机构的仲裁规则进行仲裁。

④ Validity of Arbitral Awards (仲裁裁决的效力)

The arbitral award is usually final. But it is still important to stipulate in the contract that: "The arbitration award is final and shall have binding force upon the two parties."

仲裁的裁决一般是终局的。但仍应规定："仲裁裁决是终局的，对双方有约束力。"

The examples of arbitration clauses (仲裁条款实例):

All disputes arising out of the performance of，or relating to this contract, shall be settled amicably through friendly negotiation. In case no settlement can be reached through negotiation, the case shall then be submitted for arbitration. The location of arbitration shall be in the country of the domicile of the defendant. If in China, the arbitration shall be conducted by the China International Economic and Trade Arbitration Commission, Beijing, in accordance with its Rules of Arbitration. If in ×××, the arbitration shall be conducted by ×× in accordance with its rules of arbitration. The arbitral award is final and binding upon both parties.

凡因执行本合同所发生的或与本合同有关的一切争议，双方应通过友好协商解决。如果协商不能解决，应提交仲裁。仲裁在被诉方所在国进行。如果在中国，由中国国际经济贸易仲裁委员会根据其仲裁规则进行仲裁。如果在×××国，则由×××(对方所在国仲裁机构名称)根据其仲裁规则进行仲裁。仲裁裁决是终局的，对双方都有约束力。

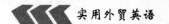

Section 2　Correspondence

1.　Sample Letters

Letter 1 (Complaint)

(1)　Complaint for Delay in Shipment

Dear Sirs,

Referring to our previous letters and cables in respect of our order of January 22 for 1,000 metric tons of Zinc Sheets[1], we have to call your attention to the fact that so far we have not had any definite information from you as to when we may expect[2] delivery, although these goods were contracted to be shipped before the end of June.

Needless to say, we have been put to[3] no little inconvenience through the delay. It is therefore imperative that you inform us by cable immediately of the earliest possible shipment for our consideration, without prejudice to our right to cancel the order and/or lodge claims[4] for losses thus sustained.

Please look the matter up[5] at once and let us have your cable reply by the earliest opportunity.

Yours faithfully,

(2)　Complaint of Wrong Goods Delivered

Dear Sirs,

Our Order No. 145

We duly received the documents and took delivery of the goods on arrival of the s/s "Lucky" at Shanghai.

We are much obliged to[6] you for the prompt execution of this order, everything appears to be correct and in good condition except in case No. 1-92. Unfortunately when we opened this case we found it contained completely different articles, and we can only presume that a mistake was made and the contents of this case were for another order.

As we need the articles we ordered to complete deliveries to our own customers, we must ask you to arrange for the dispatch of replacements at once. We attach[7] a list of the contents of case No. 1-92, and shall be glad if you will check this with our order and the copy of your invoice.

In the meantime, we are holding the above-mentioned case at your disposal[8]. Please let us know what you wish us to do with it.

Yours faithfully,

(Reply)

Dear Sirs,

Your Order No. 145 per s/s "Lucky"

Thank you for your letter of ... we were glad to know that the consignment was delivered promptly, but it was with great regret that we hear case No. 1-92 did not contain the goods you ordered.

On going into the matter[9] we find that a mistake was indeed made in packing, through a confusion of number, and we have arranged for the right goods to be dispatched to you at once. Relative documents will be mailed as soon as they are ready.

We will appreciate it if you will keep case No. 1-92 and contents until called for by the local agents of World Transport Ltd., our forwarding agents[10], whom we have instructed accordingly[11]. Please accept our many apologies for the trouble caused to you by the error.

Yours faithfully,

Letter 2 (Claim)

(1) Claim for Inferior Quality

Dear Sirs,

Re: Claim[12] for 10 pcs of valves

We are enclosing a copy of the Inspection Certificate No. 204 issued by the Shanghai Commodity Inspection Bureau[13]. The certificate proved that the above goods we received on May 5 are much inferior in quality to your previous samples. As this lot of goods is of no use at all to us, we require you refund[14] the invoice amount and inspection fee of the goods amounting to US$...

We trust you will promptly settle this claim. As soon as the settlement is accomplished, we will send the goods back to you. All the expenses will be for your account.

Yours faithfully,

(2) Claim for Poor Packing

Dear Sirs,

We regret having to inform you that the Cotton Goods covered by our Order No. 6013 and shipped per s.s. "PEACE" arrived in such an unsatisfactory condition that we can not but lodge a complaint against you. It was found, upon examination, that nearly 20% of the packages had been broken, obviously attributed to improper packing. Our only resource, in consequence, was to have them repacked before delivering to our customers, which inevitably resulted in extra expenses amounting to US$650. We expect compensation from you for this, and should like to take this opportunity to suggest that special care be taken in your future deliveries as prospective customers are apt to misjudge the quality of your goods by the faulty packing.

Yours faithfully,

Letter 3 (Replying to Complaint About…)
Dear Sirs,

We regret to say that our representative has found through inspection deterioration of a very small part of the first lot of the wheat, delivered on July 14, under the Purchase Contract No. 156. Please accept our apologies for the inconvenience caused to you.

Nevertheless, as you know quite well, such deterioration can hardly be avoided at the stage of storage. So we hope that you will not take this case as a breach of the contract and refrain from making any claim since the loss is quite negligible.

About the last two lots of the wheat, besides we shall make careful inspections, we will take other urgent measures to ensure that nothing like that will happen.

We rely upon your confidence in us.

Sincerely,

Letter 4 (Rejecting a Complaint)
Dear Sirs,

Re: Your Complaint About Quality and Weight of Caustic Soda[15] ex s.s. "Great Wall"

Referring to our letter of November 22 on the above subject, we wish to inform you that the shipment in question was carefully examined by our experts at the time of shipment and was found to be in strict conformity with the provision in the contract as regards both quality and weight.

Under such circumstances we regret that we are not in a position to entertain your claim and trust that you will clearly see the way to treat the matter properly.

Yours faithfully,

Letter 5 (Proposing Arbitration)

Dear Sirs,

We are surprised to note from your letter dated September 9, that you are not prepared to consider our offer of 15% discount to compensate you for the defects in the goods supplied according to S/C No. 112.

Though we consider our offer adequate, and even very generous, we are prepared to admit that our views may not be all justified. At the same time, we regard with disfavor your threat to suspend business connection if we do not entertain your claim. We suggest that the dispute be settled by arbitration.

We shall be pleased to discuss with you where and how the arbitration is to take place.

Yours faithfully,

2. Notes to Text

(1)　Zinc Sheets 锌皮

(2)　expect 期望，预期

(3)　be put to 使遭受

(4)　to lodge/make/file/raise a claim against (on, with)… 向……提出索赔

This guarantee shall be valid only for claims lodged with this bank on or before September 30, 2014. 本担保在 2014 年 9 月 30 日或之前向银行提出索赔有效。

The goods are short-landed by 1,000 kilos; therefore we raise a claim against you. 货物到达时短缺 1000 千克，因此我们向你方提出索赔。

(5)　look up 查询；(价格)上涨；(情况好转)

The prevailing opinion is that price is looking up. 当前人们普遍认为价格看涨。

(6)　be obliged to 感激

(7)　attach 附加，随附

attachment 附件

(8)　disposal 处理，处置

at sb.'s disposal 由某人做主，听某人之便，由某人支配

put (or leave) sth. at sb.'s disposal 把某事交某人自由处理

We will leave the case No. 1-19 at your disposal. 我们将把 1～19 号箱的货交你方自行处理。

(9)　on going into the matter 经调查此事

(10) forwarding agent 运输代理

　　　forwarding order 托运单　　　forwarder 运输商

(11) accordingly 照着(办、做等)；相应地

Our contract stipulates that the goods should be packed in seaworthy packing, so you must act accordingly. 我方合同规定货物包装应为适于海运的包装，你方必须照办。

(12) claim 索赔，赔偿要求

  表示索赔的原因 claim for

  表示索赔的金额 claim for

  表示对某批货物索赔 claim on

  表示向某人索赔 claim against

  为某事向某人索赔若干金额 to claim (a compensation of)… from sb. for sth.

We should claim US＄1,500.00 from you for the loss caused by improper packing. 我们必须为由于不良包装所造成的损失向你方索赔 1500 美元。

(13) the Shanghai Commodity Inspection Bureau 上海商品检验局

(14) refund 归还，偿还

(15) caustic soda = sodium hydroxide 苛性钠，氢氧化钠

3. Useful expressions

(1) 从你方 5 月 8 日的来函中获知我方发错了玩具，对此我方深感抱歉。

We are very sorry to have learned from your letter of May 8th that we sent you the wrong toy.

(2) 非常遗憾地通知你方，发运给我方的货物没有达到规定的标准。

We are sorry to inform you that the goods forwarded to us are not up to the standard prescribed.

(3) 你方按我方第 352 号订单供应的折叠椅至今尚未到货，我方深表遗憾。

We very much regret that the folded chairs supplied by you under Order No. 352 have not yet reached us up to now.

(4) 贵方 6 月 6 日来函收到，并获悉有我方承运的木箱包装的货物中发现有几件破损，我方对此感到遗憾。

We are sorry to learn from your letter dated 6 June that several pieces packed in the wooden cases carried by us have found greatly damaged.

(5) 我们歉难接受今天收到的货物，因为货物到达我处时已经完全粉碎。

We are unable to accept the shipment which we received from you today, as they had been completely smashed when they reached us.

(6) 这并非第一次延误交货，而且此类情况的发生有增无减。这迫使我方感到，除非你方有所改进，否则我们难以与你方继续长久的贸易往来。

This is not the first time to delay delivery, and the frequency of the occurrence is on the increase. That compels us to feel difficult to continue our business for long unless the cooperation is improved from you.

(7)　"宁波"号货轮于 5 月 24 日抵达本港，由于运来的童鞋数量短缺，特向贵方提出索赔。

Claim is filed for shortage of Kid Shoes shipped on board s.s. "Ningbo" which arrived here on May 24th.

(8)　我方因你方发货短缺 400 公斤而提出索赔。

We have to lodge a claim against you for a short delivery of 400 kg.

(9)　经检验，你方所发运的我方第 14 号订单的货物短重 1500 千克，因此，我们提出 600 美元的索赔，另加检验费。

After inspecting your shipment of our order No. 14, we found them short in weight by 1,500 kg. Therefore we raise a claim amounting to US\$ 600 plus inspection charges.

(10)　我方现汇去 550 美元，以赔偿由此事你方遭受的损失。

We shall remit to you an amount of US\$ 550 in compensation for the loss you suffered from the incident.

(11)　为最终全部了结此次索赔，随函寄上我方支票，金额为 2500 美元。

We enclose our check in amount of US\$ 2,500 in final and complete settlement of this claim.

(12)　我们即刻发货更换那些受损茶具。

We are immediately sending replacements of those damaged tea sets.

(13)　请在本周末寄来那些计算机，因我们的顾客急等需要。

Please have the computers sent to us by the end of this week, because our customers are very eager to have them.

(14)　由于我们的装运单据能确认货物离开此地时完整无损，显然是货物在运输途中受损，因此，我们不能对你方的索赔予以考虑。

As our shipping documents can confirm that the goods were in perfect condition when they left here, and that evidently show they were damaged in transportation. Therefore, we cannot give our consideration to your claim.

(15)　我们相信你方会全力以赴立即澄清这一问题。

We believe that you will spare no efforts to straighten this matter out immediately.

(16)　由于给你们带来了不便，我们冒昧地多寄去了一打免费的棉枕套，作为一点补偿。

We are taking the liberty of sending you an extra dozen of cotton pillowcase, at no cost, as small compensation for your inconvenience.

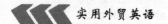

Section 3   Dialogues

Dialogue 1

I hope we can settle the problem in a pleasant way.

Feng is complaining to Morgan.

Feng: Good morning, Mr. Morgan. I guess you may know why I come here today.

Morgan: Yes, I've read your email. You complained that the last shipment of fertilizer arrived in a very bad condition and nearly 200 bags were seriously broken.

Feng: Yes. That's true.

Morgan: I hope we can settle the problem in a pleasant way.

Feng: Obviously it was due to inadequate packing.

Morgan: Our company has always been careful in its packing, and never before has such a thing occurred. Perhaps this damage took place en route to the buyer?

Feng: I don't think the shipping company is responsible for the claim. It is stipulated in the contract that new gunny bags are used in packing, but to our regret, you used 200 second-hand bags. It was reported that poor packing caused the breakage and no other person.

Morgan: This is really unbelievable. If so, we'll settle the problem in accordance with the contract and help you out of your trouble.

Feng: I'm glad to hear that. We expect a compensation of RMB 3,500 of repacking fees.

Morgan: Please send us a letter of confirmation and a copy of your survey report. It'll be solved soon if your claim is well grounded.

Feng: OK. We'll send you the report and the confirmation letter as soon as possible.

Dialogue 2

If negotiation fails, then what ?

Liu Yun explains the arbitration clause to his new customer from Toronto, Canada.

Moore: Since it's first time I'm doing business with you, I'm afraid I'm not quite clear on the arbitration clause.

Liu: Anything particular you want to know.

Moore: Please explain it in general, Mr. Liu.

Liu: All right. Generally speaking, we hold all disputes can be settled amicably by negotiation.

Moore: If negotiation fails, then what ?

Liu: The case may be submitted for arbitration.

Moore: Do you permit arbitration in a third country?

Liu: Yes, we do. Traditionally, our contracts did not contain provision for third country arbitration. Only in recent years, our contract clauses permit arbitration in third countries.

Moore: Third countries like…

Liu: Switzerland and Sweden are most common, but Canada, Singapore, and others have also been used.

Moore: If in China?

Liu: In China, the Arbitration Commission of the CCPIT will execute the arbitration.

Moore: I see.

Liu: The decision of the arbitration shall be accepted as final and binding upon both parties.

Moore: Of course.

Liu: We prefer to resolve disputes by amicable, nonbinding conciliation between the two parties.

Moore: Do you think amicable discussions are sometimes rather time consuming?

Liu: Yes, but it's still best to attempt to settle disputes without invoking arbitration.

Moore: I agree.

Liu: When you've a long-term relationship with us, it's also usually easier to settle the dispute through adjustments to future contracts.

Moore: Is that so? Interesting! Perhaps we'll have no formal, legal dispute.

Liu: I hope not.

Moore: Well, thank you for your time.

Liu: No problem.

Notes

(1) It'll be solved soon if your claim is well grounded. 如果你方索赔要求合理, 问题很快会得到解决。

(2) amicably: friendly in feeling; showing good will, peaceable

(3) provision: a clause in a legal document, agreement, etc.

(4) The Arbitration commission of the CCPIT 中国国际贸易促进会仲裁委员会

(5) binding: that holds one to the agreement

(6) time consuming 花费时间

(7) without invoking arbitration 不实行仲裁

Section 4　Exercises

1. Translate the following sentences into English:

(1)　写此邮件的目的是想投诉盒子上我公司的商标印错了。

(2)　请放心我们会立即调查此事。有了结果我们会尽快通知您。

(3)　对所装货物的任何异议若属于保险公司，轮船公司及其他运输机构责任的，我方不负任何责任。

(4)　我方可以妥协，但是赔偿金额不能超过 500 美元，否则我只能将此案提交仲裁。

(5)　考虑到我们长久以来的良好贸易关系，我方同意汇给你方 500 美元作为对你方损失的赔偿。

(6)　由于你方一再延迟交货，我方只能撤销 109 号订单。

(7)　在任何情况下，索赔均须提供经卖方同意的公证行的检验证明。

2. Translate the following sentences into Chinese:

(1)　In case of quality discrepancy, claim should be lodged within 30 days after the arrival of the goods at the port of destination, while for quantity discrepancy, claim should be lodged within 15 days after the arrival of the goods at the port of destination.

(2)　Should the responsibility of the subject under claim be found to rest on the part of our company, we shall send our reply to the you together with suggestion for settlement within 20 days after receipt of your claim.

(3)　We shall not hold liable for non-delivery or delay in delivery of the entire lot or a portion of the goods hereunder by reason of natural disasters, war or other causes of Force Majeure.

(4)　Although the quality of the consignment is inferior to that of the sample, we might accept them if you reduce the price by 15 percent.

(5)　As the cartons are in good shape and do not appear to have been opened in transit, we surmise that you must have short-shipped.

(6)　We have suffered a serious setback due to your poor quality, and the claim was at least USD1,000.

(7)　Because your claim expense list of this claim is not clear enough, we won't pay for this charge.

3. Translate the following letter or terms into English:

(1)　史密斯先生：

286 号订单项下 300 箱床单已收到。但是我们很遗憾通知你方，我们发现质量并不令人满意。由上海商品检验局出具的检验报告证明，你方所交货物质量达不到样品的标准。质量太差无法适合市场需要。

因为整批货物对我们毫无用处，我们不得不退回这些货物并提出索赔，索赔金额为5000美元。

期待你方早日解决。

……谨上

(2) 一切因执行本合同或与本合同有关之争议，都应通过协商解决。如果协商不能解决，则应提交中国国际经济贸易仲裁委员会按照其仲裁规则进行仲裁。仲裁应在上海举行。仲裁裁决是终局的，对双方都有约束力。

4. Translate the following letter or terms into Chinese:

(1)

Dear Mr. ×××,

We have received your claim for late delivery time. However, we should explain that there are several reasons for this result.

Firstly, we received the L/C 30 days after the signing of the contract. And we could do nothing but waiting for your L/C opening.

Secondly, improving quality according to your request takes about a week for your confirmation. We couldn't do the mass production before getting your final approval.

In some respects, we are also partially to blame. We could inform you some more days ago before shipment.

I'm sure that we'll keep strengthening communication and avoid any potential danger for our business.

Yours faithfully,

(2)

LATE DELIVERY AND PENALTY:

In case of late delivery, the buyer shall have the right to cancel this contract, reject the goods and lodge a claim against the seller. Except for Force Majeure, if late delivery occurs, the Seller must pay a penalty. The rate of penalty is charged at 0.5% for every 7 days, days less than 7 days must be regarded as one 7 days , the penalty should be deducted by the paying bank or the buyer from the payment.

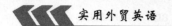

5. Compose a dialogue based on the following situation:

Because 1/4 of the goods ordered were seriously damaged, Mr. Brown, a clerk of the import company, is lodging a claim against the seller.

Mr. Zhou, sales manager of the export company, is trying to convince Mr. Brown that the goods were damaged during transit. So the claim should be lodged against Shipping Company.

Section 5   Solution to Problem

1. If you were the recipient of the following letter, what would you answer?

Letter:

Re: Claim on Tea

We are holders of Policy No. 54321 issued by your agents on 1,000 cases of tea valued at Stg. 25,500. The ship encountered heavy weather, and 252 cases were damaged by sea wager. We are enclosing the certificate of survey, also the Policy, which is against F.P.A.

Answer:

Re: Your claim on tea

We have got your letter of claim on tea with thanks.

Regret to say, because the loss you suffer is partial loss, heavy weather is one kind of natural calamities, you cover the goods against F.P.A, F.P.A. does not cover partial loss caused by natural calamities, we are unable to compensate for the loss. We are sorry.

Yours faithfully,

×××

2. What are extraordinary circumstances? Are they stipulated in S/C?

Letter:

We have received your letter of 15th July, informing us that the sewing machines we shipped to you arrived damaged on account of imperfectness of our packing.

Upon receipt of your letter, we have given this matter our immediate attention. We have studied your surveyor's report very carefully.

We are convinced that the present damage was due to extraordinary circumstances under which they are transported to you. We are therefore not responsible for the damage; but as we do not think that it would be fair to have you bear the loss alone, we suggest that the loss be divided between both of us, to which we hope you will agree.

Analysis and solution:

"Extraordinary Circumstances" mentioned in above letter, in a sense, is force majeure, the key to this problem lies in that so called "Extraordinary Circumstances" is stipulated exactly in the contract, if so, the writer of above letter is not responsible for the loss, otherwise, it may caused disputes between two parties.

In order to clarify what the term of force majeure covers under a particular contract, different ways have been adopted.

(1) Stipulate the Force Majeure Clause in a General Way

If the shipment of the contract goods is prevented or delayed in whole or in part <u>due to force majeure</u>, the seller shall not be liable for non-shipment or late shipment to the goods of this contract. However, the seller shall notify the buyer by cable or telex and furnish the latter within 15 days by registered airmail with a certificate issued by the China Council for the promotion of International trade attesting such event of events.

(2) Stipulate the Force Majeure Clause in a Way to List the Contents

If the shipment of the contract goods is prevented or delayed in whole or in part <u>by reason of war, earthquake, flood, fire, storm, heavy snow,</u> the seller shall not be liable for non-shipment or late shipment to the goods of this contract...

(3) Stipulate the Force Majeure Clause in a Way to Colligation

The seller shall not be held responsible for failure or delay to perform all or any part of this contract <u>due to war, earthquake, flood, fire, storm, heavy snow</u> **or other cause of force majeure**...

Among these three ways, the last one is the best, because it is of some flexibility. If the contingency not stipulated in the contract occur, the way will be useful and helpful for the parties in question to solve the problems. It is better use the way in the contract.

3. Option of consultation (negotiation), conciliation (mediation or intermediation), arbitration and litigation (legal action)

In international trade, disputes often arise between the two parties when one party thinks that the other fails to carry out the duties stipulated in the contract wholly or partially.

Dispute commonly to be settled by 4 ways:

Consultation (Negotiation)

Conciliation (Mediation or Intermediation)

Arbitration

Litigation (Legal Action)

In case of disputes, the two parties would better try to settle the disputes by themselves through amicable consultation firstly.

In case no settlement can be reached through negotiation, the case shall then be settled through conciliation (mediation or intermediation), arbitration and litigation (legal action).

Sometimes having a competent third party such as skilled attorneys to speak as a mediator is more effective than speaking for oneself. The mediator often tries first to communicate the position of the parties to each other, and then usually proposes a basis or several based for settlement. A conciliation merely facilitates consultation, no award or opinion or the merits of the disputes are given. It is especially useful in situations where the parties have some continuing relationship, because it allows them to compromise and to reach a solution themselves.

Arbitration is an important way of settling a dispute through the medium of a third party who is not partial to either of the parties to the dispute and whose award on the dispute is final and binding. Once it is made, an arbitral award has the force of law and there is no need to register and keep it in a law court. Compared with litigation, arbitration is more flexible, less expensive and much quicker in handling the case, therefore, arbitration has become the most popular method to resolve disputes. Arbitration is of the two parties' own will, an arbitration clause is usually made in the contract well before a dispute arises.

Litigation has jurisdiction, and resorting to judicial proceedings the plaintiff may take a unilateral action against the defendant without agreement between the two parties in advance.

Unit 11

Telegrams and Telex

Section 1   Introduction

Telegrams and telexes can send messages and data directly between two parties, and make transaction in international business efficient and convenient. Since time element means a great deal to the buyers and sellers. Telegrams and telexes are used to transmit urgent messages of all kinds. Nowadays, with the development of communication, telegrams are rarely used, but the language used is still having effects on business documents.

电报和电传可以在双方当事人之间直接发送消息和数据，并使国际商务交易具有效率和方便。因为时间对买方和卖方来说意义重大，电报和电传就用于传输各种紧急信息。如今，随着通信的发展，电报已很少使用，但其使用的语言对商务单据仍有影响。

1. Telegrams (电报)

Once, transactions in international business are discussed in detail through airmails. When telegram was introduced, it quickly took over the job of airmails. Actually, telegrams are letters in a highly compressed form, so the abbreviations and the compounding are used to serve the purpose.

以前，国际商务中的交易细节都是通过航空信函进行商讨。当电报被引入后，其迅速接替了航空信函的工作。实际上，电报是高度压缩格式的信件，所以使用缩写字和复合字以满足其目的。

1)   Characteristics of Telegrams (电报的特点)

(1)   Combinations, abbreviations and transformations are often used to reduce words in message of telegrams.

在电报报文中通常使用复合字、缩写字及替换字以减少电文字数。

① Combinations (复合字)

ASSOONAS   as soon as

BANKRATE   bank rate

② Abbreviations (缩写字)

A/C   account

ACPT	accept
S/C	sales confirmation
D/P	documents against payment
ETA	estimated time of arrival
ETD	estimated time of departure
FOBST	free on board, stowed and trimmed
RYI.	refer to your letter
ROT	refer to our telegram
RCVD	received
TKS	thanks

③ Transformations (替换字)

LETTER FOLLOWS —WRITING

HURRY UP—RUSH, EXPEDITE

AS SOON AS—SOONEST

PLEASE AMEND L/C—PLSAMENDL/C

(2) No punctuation marks or symbols are used in the message of telegrams, we usually use natural words to replace or explain them. For example:

在电报报文中不使用标点符号或记号，通常用自然字来代替或说明。例如：

,	COMMA
.	STOP
&	AND
?	QUESTION MARK
" "	QUOTE...UNQUOTE
£	STERLING (STG)
$	DOLLAR (S), USD
&	AND
#	NUMBER
"	INCH, SECOND
'	FOOT, MINUTE
180°	DEGREES
@	AT
=	IS EQUAL TO, EQUALS
+	PLUS
ABC	ABC UNDERLINED
△	A IN TRIANGLE

(3)　Some words, such as the first personal pronouns, the verb "be", the particle "to", the articles "a", "an", "the", some auxiliary verbs and most prepositions are often omitted. The nouns, numerals, action verbs and other notional words are emphatically used in the message of telegrams.

一些单词，如第一人称代词，动词"be"，小品词"to"，冠词"a""an""the"，一些辅助动词和介词常常省略。电文中着重使用名词、数词、行为动词等实词。

(4)　Present participles and past participles are used to show the future tense and the finished actions respectively. For example:

现在分词和过去分词是分别用来表示将来时态和完成的行为。例如：

a. SSEASTWIND SAILING DIRECT YOURPORT MIDAUGUST (= The steamship "East wind" will sail directly to your port in mid August.)

b. SHIPPING SPACE BOOKED (= We have booked the shipping space.)

2)　Kinds of Telegrams (电报的种类)

Generally speaking, telegrams can be divided into two kinds: Plain Language Telegrams and Code Language Telegrams.

The code language telegrams are written in commercial codes, and now they are only used by a few traders who are accustomed to use it.

The plain language telegrams may be classified into three types: ordinary, urgent (UGT) and letter telegrams. However, since January 1, 1980, letter telegrams have not been accepted in most countries and areas. So, only the ordinary and urgent telegrams are widely used in the world.

An ordinary telegram can be sent to the receiver within 3-4 hours, while an urgent telegram can reach the destination even quicker with an even more expensive charge.

一般而言，电报可分为两种：明语电报和电码电报。

电码电报用商业代码书写，现在仅是少数习惯于使用它的贸易商还在使用。

明语电报可以分为三种类型：普通电、加急电(电文标志为"UGT")和书信电。然而，自1980年1月1日起，大多数国家和地区已经不接受书信电。所以，只有普通电和加急电在世界上广泛使用。

普通电可以3～4小时内送达收电人，而加急电可以更快地到达目的地，但需更昂贵的费用。

3)　Charge of Telegrams (电报的计费)

Telegrams are charged by the number of words transmitted, the class of telegrams sent, and the localities destined for. Telegrams in international business adopt the charging method of "ten letters as a word". Natural words (e.g., meeting, conference, invoice), abbreviations (e.g.: ABV, INFO, EXRATE) and compoundings (e.g., BESTOFFER, CABLEREPLY TWODOZENOF) are all "words" in telegrams, every ten letters can be counted as a "word". If the number of letters in a word is more than ten, but less than twenty, it must be counted as two "words" in the telegrams, for example, "SEWINGMACHINES" can be counted as two words.

电报是按发报的字数、发报的种类、发报的目的地计费。国际商业电报实行"十码作一"的计费方法。普通字(如：会谈、会议、发票)、缩写字(如：在……之上、情报、EXCHR)和复合字(如：最低报售价、电复、两打)都是电报中的"字"，每 10 个字母计作一个"电报字"。如果一个单词中字母个数超过 10 个，但不到 20 个，在电报中它必须计作 2 个"电报字"，例如，"SEWINGMACHINES"应计作 2 个电报字。

2. Telex (电传)

Telex is the short form of "Teletypewriter" and "Exchange", compared with telegram, which is more effective and economical. The telex equipment is installed in the subscriber's office. Through teleprinter set, messages can be directly sent to or received from foreign countries. Due to the quick and convenient service, telex has been widely used in the international business in recent years.

电传是"电传打字机"和"交换"的缩写，与电报相比，电传更有效和经济。电传设备安装在用户办公室，通过电传打字机组直接对外收、发电报。由于快捷、方便的服务，近年来电传已广泛应用于国际业务中。

(1) Characteristics of Telexes (电传的特点)

① Telex can make the calling and the called parties practically "talk on paper". Moreover, since the telex equipment works automatically, it can receive messages with the machine left unattended, and the messages received at night may be first dealt with the next morning.

电传可以使打电话和通话方几乎"在纸上交谈"。此外，由于电传设备自动工作，在机器无人看管下也可以接收信息，并且晚上接收到的信息在第二天早上就能首先处理。

② Abbreviation, ellipsis and transformation are used to simplify words and phrases in the message of telexes, but combinations are generally not used, each word is separated by a space.

在电传信息中使用缩写字、省略字和变形字来简化单词和短语，但不常用复合字，每个字之间用一个空格来分隔。

③ In the message of telexes, either punctuation marks (except ";") or symbols (except "$", "%", "@" and "°") or words "COMMA", "STOP", "ETC." can be used, but using punctuation marks is more common.

在电传信息中，可以使用标点符号("；"除外)、符号("$""%""@""。"除外)或"逗点""句点""等等"字词语，但使用标点符号更常见。

④ In the message of telexes, several matters can be stated either one after another preceded by AAA (or 111 or A, or 1), BBB (or 222 or B, or 2) etc., or passage without any preceding signals.

在电传信息中，可以将事项一一罗列出来，并在事项前面标注顺序号 AAA(或 111，或 A，或 1)、BBB(或 222，或 B，或 2)等，或段落前没有任何序号。

(2) Kinds of Telexes (电传的种类)

Telexes can be divided into two kinds, one is written in natural words as a short letter, and the other is rather brief somewhat like a telegram in simplified words.

电传可以分为两种：一种是用普通字写的作为短信的电传，另一种是用简化字写的更简短的类似于电报的电传。

(3) Charge of Telexes (电传的计费)

Telex is charged by the time engaged in transmission. The minimum charge for a telex is fixed on the basis of three minutes. Any odd minutes less than three minutes shall be deemed to three minutes for calculation. In case of more than three minutes, the additional charge is fixed on the unit of one minute. About 400 letters can be transmitted every minute.

电传是按用于传输的时间计费。电传计费以三分钟起算，不足三分钟，也按三分钟计算。超过三分钟，以一分钟为单位算增收费用，每分钟约可发 400 个字码。

Section 2 Correspondence

1. Sample Letters

Letter 1

Letter

We have received your cable offer of April 25 and have the pleasure of confirming our acceptance of 500 sets of "Butterfly" brand Sewing Machines offered by you. For your information, we are arranging with our bank to issue the relative L/C and will have you informed of its establishment.

Telegram

YC25 SEWING MACHINES ACCEPTED L/COPENING

Letter 2

Letter

Thanks for your shipping advice regarding the shipment of goods under our Order No. 305. Please send us a cheque to cover our 5% commission just as you did in the past for our previous orders. Best regards.

Telex

TKS FR SHIPG ADV RE GOODS UNDR ORDR 305. PLS SEND US A CHEQUE TO

COVER OUR 5 PCT COMM JUST AS U DID FR PREVIOUS ONES. RGDS

Letter 3

Letter

We have received your letter of 9th December and have submitted to our customer the velvet, of which you sent us samples.

We have obtained an order for 700 pieces on condition that a trade discount of 5% must be given. We are most anxious to build up our export connections and hope you will assist us in this respect.

Your reply by return will be appreciated.

Telex

YL9/12 HV OBTAINED AN ORD FR 700 PCS VELVET SUBJ TO 5 PCT DISC ANXIOUS TO BUILD UP EXP CONNECTNS HOPE TO HV YR ASSISTANCE RGDS

2. Commonly Used Abbreviations of Telegrams and Telexes

A

abbreviation	ABBR
above	ABV
about	ABT
abstract statement	ABS
accept	ACPT
acceptance	ACPTC
accepted	ACPTD
account	A/C(AC, ACCT)
account curren	A/C
account of	A/O
account paid	A/P
account sales	A/S
acknowledge	ACK
actual weight	A/W
addition	ADD, ADDN, ADDTN
additional	ADDL, ADDNL
additional premium	A/P
address	ADR
addressee	ADRSEE
adjustment	ADJ
advertisement	AD, ADV
advise	ADV, ADVS
after date	A/D
after sight	A/S
again	AGN
against all risks	AAR
agreed	OK
a good brand	AGB
airfreight	AIRFRT
airmail	AIR
airmailed	AIRD
airmailing	AIRG
airway bill	AWB
all after	AA
all correct	OK
all risks	AR
amount	AMT
ampere	AMP
Anno Domini	AD
answer	ANS

answered	ANS	barrel (s)	BBL (S), BL (S)
a number-one	A-1	before Christ	BC
any good brand	AGB	beginning	BEG
apartment	APT	bill book	BB
April	APR	bill of entry	B/E
approximate	APPROX	bill of exchange	B/E
approximately	APPROX	bill of health	B/H
army post office	APO	bill of lading	B/L ,BL.
Arizona	ARIZ	bill of parcels	BP
Arkansas	ARK	bill of payment	B/P
arrival	ARVL	bill of sale	B/S, BS
arrive	AR, ARV	bill receivable	B/R (BR)
arrived	ARVD	bills payable	B/P, BP
assignment	ASSMT	Birmingham Gauge	BG
assistant	ASST	Birmingham Wire Gauge	BWG
association	ASSN	bonded warehouse	BW
assortment	ASSMT	book value	BV
atmosphere	ATM	British thermal units	BTU
attention	ATTN(ATT, ATTEN)	brokerage	BRKGE
		brought down	B /D
auction	AUCT	brought forward	B/F
August	AUG	brought over	B/O
authorize	AUTH	budding	BLDG
avenue	AVE	Bureau Veritas	BV
average	AVG, AVRG	business	BIZ, BUS
awaiting	AWTG		

B

C

bag	BG	cable	CBL
balance	BAL, BALCE	cash against documents	CAD
balance sheet	B/S, BS	California	CALIF
bale(s)	BL(S)	cancel	CCEL
bank	BK	canceled	CANC
bank draft	B/D	cancellation	CANC
bank post bill	BPB	candle power	CP
		cannot	CANT

capital account	C/A	consignment	CONSGT
captain	CAPT	constructive total loss	CTL
carbon copy	CC	Consular invoice	CON INV
care of	C/O	container	CNR, CNTR, CONT,
carriage	CARR		COTR, CTNR
carried forward	C/F	container freight station	CFS
carried over	C/O	container load	CL
cash before delivery	CBD	container yard	CY
cash book	CB	contract	CONTR
cash on delivery	COD	corporation	CORP
cash on shipment	COS	cost and insurance	CI
cash order	C/O	cost and freight	CAF, CANDF, CF
cash with order	CWO	cost and freight commission	CAFC, CANDFC,
cast iron	CI		CFC
catalogue	CAT	cost, freight and exchange	CFANDE
cent	CTS	charter party	C/P
centimeter	CM	cost, insurance and freight	CIF
certificate	CERT	cost, insurance, freight and commission	
certificate of origin	C/O		CIFANDC, CIFC
certified	CERT	cost, insurance, freight and interest	CIFANDI
check	CHQ	cost, insurance, freight, commission and	
cheque	CHQ	interest	CIFCI
Christmas	XMAS	cost, freight and insurance	CFANDI, CFI
collation	COL	could	CUD
collect on delivery	COD	credit note	C/N
Colorado	COLO	cubic	CU, CUB
commission	COMM	cubic feet	CFT
company	CO		
compare (confer)	CF		

D

concerning	CONC	day after acceptance	D/A
condition	CONDI	days after date	D/D, DD
confirm	CFM	days after delivery	D/D, DD
confirmation	CFMTN	day's date	D/D, DD
confirmed	CFMD	days' sight	D/S
Connecticut	CONN	dead weight	D/W

debenture	DEB	estimated time of departure (start)	ETD(ETS)
debit note	D/N	et cetra	ETC
debtor	DR	exchange	EXCH
December	DEC	ex coupon	XC
Delaware	DEL	ex dividend	XD
deliver	DLVR	exempli gratia	EG
delivery	DELY, DLVRY	ex interest	XIN
delivery order	D/O	export	EXP
demand draft	D/D	export licence	E/L, EL
department	DEPT		
deposit account	D/A		
deposit receipt	DR		
discharge afloat	D/A		
discount	DIS		
dishonored	DISHD		
destination	DEST, DESTN		
ditto	DO		
dividend	DIV		
dock warrant	D/W		
document	DOC		
documents against acceptance	D/A		
documents against payment	D/P		
dollars	DIGS, (DLRS)		
double	DBLE		
down	DWN		
dozen(s)	DOZ		
drawing	DRG, DRWG		

F

facsimile	FAC
Fahrenheit	F
fair average quality	FAQ
fair average quality of the season	FAQS
favor	FAV
February	FEB
Federal Maritime Commission	FMC
Federal Reserve Bank	FRB
feet	FT
fiberglass reinforced plastic	FRP
figure	FIG
financial statement	FIN STAT
firm offer	FO
first open water	FOW
flight	FLT
floating policy	FP
Florida	FLA
following	FOLG(FLWG)
foot	FT
foot pound	FT-LB
foreign bill of exchange	FBE
for instance	FI
forward delivery	F/D
for your guidance	FYG

E

effective horsepower	EHP
electric horsepower	EHP
enclosure	ENCL
errors excepted	EE
esquire	ESQ
estimated time of arrival	ETA

for your information	FYI	gold bonds	GB
for your reference	FYR	good bye	GB
free alongside ship	FAS	good till cancelled	GTC
free at quay	FAQ	government	GOV, GOVT
free from alongside	FFA	government issue	GI
free from particular average	FPA	grain	GR
free in and out	FIO	gram	GR
free in harbor	FIH	Greenwich mean time	GMT
free of all average	FAA	gross ton	GT
free of capture and seizure	FCS	gross weight	GR WT
free of charge	FOC	group	GP
free of damage	FOD	guineas	GS
free of general average	FGA		
free on board	FOB		

H

free on car	FOC	Hamburg	HAM
free on rail	FOR	head office	HO
freight	FRT	high pressure	HP
freight list	F/L	His or Her Imperial Highness	HIH
Friday	FRI	Hong Kong	HK
from	FM	Hong Kong dollar	HKD
fuel oil	FO	horsepower	HP
full address	FULL ADR	hundredweight	CWT
fully good fair	FGF		
fully paid	FP		

G

gallon	GALL	id est (that is)	IE
galvanized iron	GI	Illinois	ILL
galvanized iron sheet	GIS	immediate	IMMD
general	GEN	immediately	IMMDLY
general average	G/A	import	IMP
general average quality	GAQ	import licence	I/L, IL
general post office	GPO	inch	IN
Georgia	GA	include	INCL, INCLD
Germanischer Lloyd	GL	included	INCLDD
		Indiana	IND
		inform	INFM, IFM (INFO)

I

information	IFMN, INFMTN
insolvency	INSOL
installment	INST
instead of	I/O
institution	INSTN
instruction	INSTRCTN (INSTN)
in transit	IN TRANS
invoice	INV, IVO
invoice book	IB
I owe you	IOU

J

January	JAN
Japan Industrial Standard	JIS
Japanese Agricultural Standard	JAS
Japanese standard time	JST
Japan External Trade Organization	JETRO
joint account	J/A
journal	JL
July	JUL
June	JUN
junior	JR

K

Kabushiki Kaisha	KK
Kansas	KANSA
Kentucky	KY
kilogram	KG
kiloliter	KL
kilometer	KM
kilovolt	KV
kilovolt ampere	KVA
kilowatt	KW
kilowatt hour	KWH

L

large paper	LP
leave	LV
less than carload lot	LCL
less than container load	LCL
letter	L, LET, LTR
letter of advice	LA
letter of authority	L/A
letter of credit	L/C, LC
letter of guarantee	L/G
lift on/lift off	LO/LO
limited	LTD
liter	L, LTR
load water plane	LWP
local mean time	LMT
local standard time	LST
London	LN, (LDN)
long-distance telephone	LDTEL
long ton	L/T, LT, LTON
Los Angeles	LA
loss and damage	LANDD
loss and gain	L/G
Louisiana	LA

M

madame	MME
mail steamer	MS
manager	MGR
manifest	M/F
manufacture	MANUF
manufacturing	MFG
manuscripts	MSS
March	MAR
marine insurance policy	MIP
marked capacity	MC

market	MKT, MRKT	New Mexico	NMEX
mate's receipt	MR	New York	NY
Massachusetts	MASS	nickel steel	NS
maximum	MAX	Nippon Kaiji Kyokai	NK
meantime	MNTIME	Nippon Kaiji Kentei Kyokai	NKKK
Member of Parliament	MP	no account	N/A
memorandum	MEMO	no advice	N/A
merchandise	MDSE	no fund	NF
message	MSG	no mark	N/M
messieurs	MESSRS	nonacceptance	N/A
metric ton	M/T, MT, MTON	no orders	N/O
middle	MID	no reduction	NORED
military police	MP	no risk	NR
milliampere	MA	North Dakota	ND, NDAK
millimeter	MM	nota bene(note well)	NB
minimum	MIN	not enough	N/E
minutes	MINS, MNS	noted	NTD
Minnesota	MINN	not specified	NS
Monday	MON	November	NOV
money order	MO	number	NO, NR(NBR)
months after date	M/D		
months after sight	M/S, MS		

O

months date	M/D	October	OCT
motor ship	M/S, MS	Oklahoma	OKLA
motor vessel	MV	official receiver	OR
my account	M/A	old measurement	OM
		omissions excepted	OE

N

		on account of	O/A
negotiate	NEGO	on demand	O/D
net proceeds	N/P	on sale	O/S
net ton	NT	on the job training	OJT
net weight	NTWT(NWT)	open charter	OC
new bond	NB	open policy	OP
New Hampshire	NH	operation research	OR
New Jersey	NJ	order number	O/NO

Oregon	OREG	piece(s)	PC(S)
ounce	OZ	please	PLS(PSE)
our account	O/A	please turn over	PTO
out of print	OP	policy proof of interest	PPI
out of stock	O/S	port of call	POC
overcharge	O/C	possible	POSSBL
overdraft	OD	postal money order	PMO
over voltage	OV	postal order	PO
owner's risk	OR	postcard	PC
owner's risk of breakage	ORB	postmaster	PM
owner's risk of fire	ORF	post meridiem	PM
P		post office	PO
		post office box	POB
packed weight	PW	postscript	PS
packing	PKG	pound(s)	LB(S)
page	P	power of attorney	P/A, PA
paragraph	PARA	Preference share	PREF SHR
parcel post	PP	Prime-Minister	PM
part	PT	premium	PM
partial loss	PL	prices current	P/C
particular average	P/A, PA, P/AV	private account	P/A
parts per million	PPM	profit and loss	PANDL
patent	PAT	promissory note	PN
payable on receipt	POR	proximo	PROX
payment	PAYT	public relations	PR
pay on delivery	POD	**Q**	
pence	P		
Pennsylvania	PA	quality	QLTY
per annum	PA	quantity	QNTY, QT
percent	PC, PCT	quart	QT
percent perannum	PPA	quartermaster	QM
percent permillion	PPM	quay	QY
per procuration	PERPRO	quiet	QT
petty cash	P/C	quotation	QTN, QUTN
petty cash book	PCB	quote	QOT, QTE

R

receipt	RCPT
receive	RCV
received	RCVD, RECD, RECVD
received payment	RCVD PAYT
reference	REF (RE)
reference our cable	ROC
referring to our letter	ROL
referring to our telegram	ROT
referring to your letter	RYL
referring to your telegram(telex)	RYT
referring to (reference)	RE(REF)
refer to acceptor	R/A
refer to drawer	R/D
refrigerated	REF
refrigerated container	REFCON
refrigerating	REFRIG
registered	REGD
remark	REM
remittance	REM
repeat	RPT
request	REQST, RQ
requirement	REQMNT
reserve	RES, RESV
Rhode Island	RI
roll on/roll off	RO/RO
revolutions per minute	RPM
rural free delivery	RFD

S

San Francisco	SF
sales book	SB
salvage loss	SL
save our ship or souls	SOS(通称)
savings bank	SB
Saturday	SAT
schedule	SCDUL SCHDL
sea damaged	S/D
section	SECT
September	SEPT
set up in carloads	SUCL
shilling	S
shipment	SHIPMT, SHIPT
shipped	SHIPD, SIPD
shipper and carrier	SANDC
shipping	SHPG
shipping order	SO
short ton	S/T, ST, STON
signature	SIG, SIGN
Singapore	SPORE
sized and calendered	SANDC
South Carolina	SC
South Dakota	SDAK
specification	SPEC
specific gravity	SPGR
Standard Wire Gauge	SWG
standing operating procedure	SOP
steamship	SS
statement of billing	S/B
sterling	STG, STLG
Sterling Pound	STGL
stop	STP
subject	SUBJ
subject to particular average	SPA
Sunday	SUN
surveyor	SURV

T

tare	T
telegram	TEL, TLG(T)
telegraph	TEL, TLG
telegraphic address	TA
telegraphic transfer	TT
telegraph money order	TMO
telephone	TEL
teleprinter	TPR
telex	T, TLX
telex conversation	TELECON
temperature	TEMP
Tennessee	TENN
text	TXT
thanks	TKS
through	THRU
Thursday	THUR
through bill of lading	THROB/L
ton	T
time deposit	T/D
time loan	T/L
total loss only	TLO
transfer	TFR
trust receipt	T/R
Tuesday	TUES

U

ullage	ULL
underwriter	U/W
Union of Soviet Socialist Republics	CCCP(USSR)
United Kingdom	UK
United States of America	USA
United States Standard Gauge	USG

unquote	UNQTE
unreceived	UNRCVD
uranium Y	UY
U.S. dollars	USD, USDOL

V

very important person	VIP
vessel	VSL
vice-chairman	VC
videlicet	VIZ
visible supply	VS
volt	V
volts per meter	V/M
voltmeter	VM
volume	VOL

W

waiting order	WO
warehouse book	WB
warehouse warrant	W/W
war risk	WR
Washington	WASH
water ballast	WB
watt-hour	WH
waybill	W/B, WB
Wednesday	WED
weight	WT
westbound	WB
wire gauge	WG
with average	WA
without charge	WC
without prejudice	W/P
with particular average	WPA
working group	WG

would	WUD	yours	YRS
		yesterday	YSTDY
Y			
yard(s)	YD	**Z**	
you	U	zinc	ZN
your	UR, YR(Y)	zum Beispiel (for example)	ZB

Section 3   Exercises

1. Translate the following telegrams into English:

(1) 合同第 889 号项下台灯备妥待运请速开信用证。

(2) 感谢你方 6 月 20 日询价。毛毯有现货。

(3) 你方 5 月 4 日电悉承兑交单歉难接受建议即期付款交单请电告接受。

(4) 你方 3 月 8 日发盘电视机价格可接受条件是 4 月底装运请电复。

(5) 第 998 号合同交货期已过请于 8 月 1 日前速运否则取消订单并保留索赔权。

(6) 兹报实盘 5000 件裙子每件 40 美元 CIF 纽约限 1 月 31 日前复有效。

2. Translate the following telegrams/telexes into Chinese:

(1) L/C656 DIRECT STEAMER UNAVAILABLE PLSAMEND ALLOWING TRANSHIPMT

(2) STEELPRICE RISING SUGGEST IMMEDIATE ACCEPTANCE

(3) SC109 FOREVERBIKES SHIPD 15APR SSDONGFENG ETAENDAPR

(4) PLSCABLE FORMOFFER 1000MT GREENBEANS CIFNY INDICATING TERMS PAYMT EARLIEST SHIPMT

(5) YC15/APR 5000SETS COMPUTERS ACCEPTTED L/COPENING

(6) RE YT5/JUL PLS DISCNT 20PCT AS SIMLR PRODTS SOLD HERE ABT 20DOLRS LOWER THAN YRS WILLORDER 5000MT IF ABV DISCNT GIVEN

3. Convert the following letter into telegram:

Dear …,

We have received your Letter of Credit No.577 and thank you for your prompt establishment.

But we regret to find that the amount of L/C is USD60,000, but actually the amount of our contract is USD65,000. Please amend the above L/C as soon as possible, so that we can catch S/S

"DONGFENG" sailing on June 8, 2014.

Your prompt attention to this matter will be appreciated.

Yours faithfully,

4. Convert the following letter into telex in English:

×××先生：

第 356 号销售合同项下货号 909 的 5000 件床单已到货。但我方很遗憾地发现，该批货物与合同中注明的样品的尺寸和颜色均不相符，我方客户无法接受。鉴于这种情况，我方须索赔 20000 美元以弥补损失。

期待你方电传答复。

…… 谨上

Section 4 Solution to Problem

Do we need to learn this lesson yet?

Yes. Although more advanced means of correspondence than telegram and telex are more frequently and widely used in business circle nowadays, some young business persons even have never seen telex machine.

Actually, as traditional even a bit old means of correspondence, it seems that telegram and telex will retire, but they are still useful, at least some business persons like using telegram and telex short words and abbreviations in their letters, faxes and e-mails, students majoring in foreign trade and economics should command those telegram and telex short words and abbreviations.

Appendix 1

Business Letter Writing

1. 英文商务信函的组成

英文商务信函通常由七个基本部分组成：信头(Letterhead)、日期(Dateline)、信内地址(Inside Address)、称呼(Salutation)、正文(Body of the Letter)、结尾套语(Complimentary Close)、签名(Signature)。适当之时，英文商务信函还可以包括一些选择性项目，如经办人姓名(Attention Line)、事由或标题(Subject or Re Line)、署名(Initials)、附件(Enclosures)、抄送(Carbon Copy Notation)、附言(Postscript)等。

Letterhead	**TEXTILES** Zhejiang Textiles Imp. & Exp. Corp. 100 Tianmu Road Hangzhou 310006, China Tel: 86-571-85179999 Fax: 86-571-8517888
Date line	May 25, 2008
Inside address	Sigma Trading Company 405 112nd Ave. Miami, Fl, USA 33186-4816
Salutation Body of the letter	Dear Sirs, We have obtained you name and address form············ ···················
Complimentary close	
Signature	Yours Sinerely, *Wang Xiaohua* Wang Xiaohua Marketing Manager

(1)　信头(Letterhead)

外贸公司对信笺的信头及信封需经特殊设计和印刷,以示公司的形象。

信头通常包括公司的名称和地址、邮编、电话号码、电传号码、传真号码、电子邮件地址,有时可用一个简练的短语来说明公司的经营范围。

如果信笺上没有印刷信头,应在信笺上端按照格式打上公司名称、通信地址、电话号码、电子邮件地址等。

(2)　日期(Dateline)

每封商务信函都必须标有准确的日期。日期的位置应根据信头的设计和所使用的书信格式来确定。可打在信头的日期线上,也可打在信头以下空两行处。

各国日期的写法习惯不尽相同,例如,美式写法为月/日/年,英式写法为日/月/年,而日式写法为年/月/日。因此,月份最好不要用数字来代表,以免引起误解。

(3)　信内地址(Inside Address)

信内地址包括收信公司名称或收信人姓名、通信地址及邮政编码等。

收信人的姓名应使用全名,前面加上适当的头衔,如 Dr.,Prof. 等,或一般称呼语,如 Mr.,Ms.,Mrs.等。如果公司名称较长时,可分为两行,第二行缩进两格。

(4)　称呼 Salutation

称呼是信函开头的礼貌问候。它位于信内地址之后空一行的位置,左边对齐。

如已知收信人姓名,则男性以 Mr. 称呼,女性一般以 Ms.称呼,除非对方要求以 Mrs. (已婚)或 Miss. (未婚)称呼。如不知收信人姓名,则常用 Dear Sirs,Dear Sir or Madam,Gentleman等。注意,没有 Dear Gentleman 的说法。

称呼中的第一个单词和其他所有名词的第一个字母均须大写。因此,Dear Sir 和 Dear Captain Lau 这两种写法是正确的,而 My Dear Mr. Saito 是错误的(因为 dear 不是名词)。

(5)　正文(Body of the Letter)

正文是信函的核心部分,它包括你要向收信人传达的信息。现代商业信函中的文字趋向于口语化,总的要求是内容清晰、扼要,措辞要有礼貌,段落宜短不宜长。

正文的第一行应在称呼或事由以下空一行的位置开始打,段落之间空一行。

(6)　结束语(Complimentary Close)

结束语是书信结束时的客套用语,放在正文最后一行空一行的位置。常见的结束语有Sincerely,Yours sincerely,Sincerely Yours,Yours truly,Truly yours,Very truly yours,Yours faithfully,Faithfully yours。

(7)　签名(Signature)

书信中签字以钢笔亲自手签为准。为了便于辨认,常常在手写签名下方再打印签字人的姓名,也有将其职位头衔一起打出的。

女性签名时,为便于回信人正确使用称呼,一般会在打字的姓名前加注 Ms.。

(8) 经办人姓名(Attention Line)

经办人姓名表示写信人希望信件达到公司时能够直接交给某个具体人或具体部门亲启办理，但由于信内地址的首行可以写明收信人的姓名，此向现已不常用。经办人姓名一般放在信内地址下两行或称呼上端两行的位置。例如：

Zhengjiang Textiles Imp. & Exp. Corp.

100 Tianmu Road

Hangzhou 310006, China

Attention: Export Dept.

(9) 事由或标题(Subject or Re Line)

事由或标题是为了便于收信人迅速了解信的主要内容。Subject 可缩写为 Subj.，Re 为拉丁语，作 Regarding 解。此项一般放在称呼上或下两行处，居左或居中，字体常用大写，亦可下加横线。例如：

Subj.: Our Sales Confirmation No. T123

Re: Our Sales Confirmation No. T123

OUR SALES CONFIRMATION NO. T123

(10) 署名(Initials)

署名又为 reference initials 或 identification initials。指的是发信人和打字员/速记员姓名的首字母，亦可称责任字母，目的是备日后查考。例如：

JS:MS   JS/MS   JS-MS   JS:ms   JS/ms   JS-ms

(11) 附件(Enclosure)

如果商务信函附有其他文件，如宣传册、产品目录、价格表等，就应该在信中加注附件提示。附件通常位于署名之后两行的位置，其写法如下：

Enclosure(s):

Encl(s):

Enc(s):

(12) 抄送(Carbon Copy Notation)

此项是为了让收信人知道信文还抄送其他人或公司，放在附件以下两行处，常用 cc (carbon copy(ies))表示。"cc" 之后可以加冒号，也可不加，"cc" 还可大写。

(13) 附言(Postscript)

附言放在信中最后空两行处，从左边开始打，可以是打印的，也可以是手写的。加封信封之前，如果发现信中内容有遗漏，可以在 P.S.附言中补上遗漏的事情，然后再简单签名。不过，应该尽量避免使用 P.S.，因为它表示你在写信或口述信件之前没有周密考虑。

2. 英文商务信函的格式

常见的英文商务信函格式有 4 种，第一种最正式，最后一种最不正式。

(1)　缩进式(indented style)

缩进式是传统的英式信函书写格式，信头居中，日期位于右上方，结束语和签名置中间偏右下方。缩进式的商务信函每段起始行首需缩进 4～5 个字母。

(2)　混合式(modified style)

混合式即在缩进式的基础上段落首行不缩进。

(3)　齐头式(blocked style)

齐头式信中每一行均从左边开始并且左对齐。

(4)　简化式(simplified style)

简化式与齐头式相似，但删去了称呼和结束语，而事由则为书信中不可缺少的组成部分。

信头		信头	
信内地址　　　　日期		信内地址　　　　日期	
称呼		称呼	
正文		正文	
结束语		结束语	
签名		签名	
附件		附件	

附录图 3-1　缩进式　　　　　　　　　　　　附录图 3-2　混合式

信头 日期 信内地址 称呼 正文 结束语 签名	信头 日期 信内地址 事由或标题 正文 签名 附件
附录图 3-3　齐头式	附录图 3-4　简化式

3. 信封书写方法

在信封上，发信人的地、名称一般是在左上角打印好的；收信人的地址、名称一般放在中间偏右。地址最好用大写字体，采用齐头式、单行打，门牌号要与街道号同一行，然后隔行打上城市、州/省和邮政编码。"航空邮寄"或其他的付邮方式应在信封的左下方。例如：

Registered Mail　挂号信

Via Air Mail Registered　航空挂号信

Urgent (Immediate)　急件

Express　快件

Confidential　机密

Top Secret　绝密

Printed Matters　印刷品

Personal　亲收

Private　私信

Photographs: Please Do Not Bend　照片，请勿折叠

下面是一个典型的信封格式。

写信人地址

PRICE REALTORS INC.

9001 INDIANAPOLIS BOULEVARD

HIGHLAND, IN 46322

Stamp

收信人地址

SALES MANAGER

CARPET DEPARTMENT

ZHEJIANG NATIVE PRODUCE &

ANIMAL BY-PRODUCTS I/E CORP.

102, FENGQI RD., HANGZHOU 310006

P.R. OF CHINA

Appendix 2

Important Ports

1. Algeria 阿尔及利亚

ALGIERS 阿尔及尔
ANNABA 安纳巴
ORAN 奥兰
SKIKDA 斯基克达

2. American 美国

BALTIMORE 巴尔的摩
CHARLESTON 查尔斯敦
HOUSTON 休斯敦
JACKSONVILLE 杰克逊维尔
MIAMI 迈阿密
NEW ORLEANS 新奥尔良
NEW YORK 纽约
NORFOLK 诺福克
PORT EVERGLADES 埃佛格雷兹
SAVANNAH 萨凡纳
SEATTLE 西雅图
Washington 华盛顿
WILMINGTON 威尔明顿
LONG BEACH 长滩
LOS ANGELES 洛杉矶
OAKLAND 奥克兰
PORTLAND 波特兰
SAN FRANCISCO 三藩市

3. Angola 安哥拉

CABINDA 卡宾达

LUANDA 罗安达
LOBITO 洛比托

4. Arabia and the United Arab Emirates 阿拉伯联合酋长国

SHARJAH 沙迦

5. Argentina 阿根廷

BUENOS AIRES 布宜诺斯艾利斯

6. Australia 澳大利亚

ADELAIDE 阿德莱德
BRISBANE 布里斯班
DARWIN 达尔文
FREMANTLE 弗里曼特尔
MELBOURNE 墨尔本
SYDNEY 悉尼

7. Bangladesh 孟加拉

DHAKA 达卡
JUDDAH 吉达港

8. Belgium 比利时

ANTWERP 安特卫普
ZEEBRUGGE 泽布赫

9. Benin 贝宁

COTOUNOU 科托努

10. Brazil 巴西

ITAGUA 伊塔瓜伊港
ITAJAI 伊塔雅伊
MANAUS 玛瑙斯
PARANAGUA 巴拉那瓜
RIO DE JENERIO 里约热内卢
RIO GRANDA 里奥格兰德
SANTOS 桑托斯
SAO FRANCISCO DO SUL 孟弗朗西斯特
SEPETIBA 塞佩提巴

11. Britain 英国

FELIXSTOWE 费里克斯托
GRANGEMOUTH 格兰厅茅斯
LIVERPOOL 利物浦
IMMINGHAM 伊明赫姆船坞
SOUTHAMPTON 南安普敦
THAMESPORT 泰晤士港

12. Bulgaria 保加利亚

VARNA 瓦尔纳

13. Burma 缅甸

YANGON 仰光

14. Cameroon 喀麦隆

DOUALA 杜阿拉

15. Canada 加拿大

CALGARY 卡尔加里
EDMONTON 埃德蒙顿
HALIFAX 哈利法克斯
MONTREAL 蒙特利尔
TORONTO 多伦多
VANCOUVER 温哥华
WINNIPEG 温尼伯

16. Chile 智利

IQUIQUE 伊基克
LIRQUEN 利尔昆
MEJILLONES 梅希约内斯
SAN ANTONIO 圣安东尼奥
SAN VICENTE 圣文森特
VALPARAISO 瓦尔帕莱索

17. Columbia 哥伦比亚

BARRANQUILLA 巴兰基亚
BUENAVETURA 布埃纳文图拉
CARTAGO 卡塔哥
CATAGENA 卡塔赫纳

18. Congo 刚果

POINT NOIRE 黑角

19. Costa Rica 哥斯达黎加

PUERTO LIMON 利蒙港
PUERTO CALDERA 卡尔德拉港
SAN JOSE 圣何塞

20. Croatia 克罗地亚

RIJEKA 里耶卡

21. Cyprus 塞浦路斯

LIMASSOL 利马索尔

22. Dominican Republic 多米尼加共和国

CAUCEDO 考塞多
RIO HAINA 艾纳
SANTO DOMINGO 圣多明哥

23. Dubai 迪拜

ABU DHABI 阿布扎比
AJMAN 阿扎曼
JEBEL ALI 杰贝阿里
PORT RASHID 拉希德港

24. East Timor 东帝汶

DILI 第利

25. Ecuador 厄瓜多尔

BARRANQUILLA 巴亚基尔
GUAYAQUIL 瓜亚基尔

26. Egypt 埃及

ALEXANDRIA 亚历山大
DAMIETTA 达米埃塔
PORT SAID 塞得港
SOKNA 苏克纳

27. France 法国

DUNKERQUE 敦刻尔克
FOS 福斯
LE HAVRE 勒阿弗尔

28. Garner 加纳

TEMA 特马

29. Germany 德国

BREMERHAVE 不莱梅港
HAMBURG 汉堡

30. Greece 希腊

PIRAEUS 比雷埃夫斯
THESSALONIKI 塞萨洛尼基

31. Guatemala 危地马拉

GUATMALA CITY 危地马拉城

PUERTO QUETZAL 圣何塞

32. Guinea 内亚

BISSAU 比索
CONAKRY 利纳克里

33. Haiti 海地

PORT PRINCE 太子港

34. Holland 荷兰

AMSTERDAM 阿姆斯特丹
ROTTERDAM 鹿特丹

35. India 印度

BANGALORE 班加罗尔
CALCUTTA 加尔各答
CHENNAI 清奈
CHITTAGONG 吉大
COCHIN 科钦
HALDIA 霍尔迪亚
KANDLA 根德拉
MADRAS 马德拉斯
MULUND 默伦达
MUNDRA 蒙德拉
NEW DELHI 新德里
NHAVA SHEVA 那瓦夏瓦
TUTICORIN 杜蒂戈林

36. Indonesia 印尼

BELAWAN 勿拉湾
JAKARTA 雅加达
MERAK 孔雀港
SAMARANG 三堡垄
SURABAYA 泗水

37. Iran 伊朗

BANDAR ABBAS 阿巴斯港

38. Iraq 伊拉克

UMM QASR 乌木盖兹

39. Israel 以色列

ASHDOD 阿什杜德
海法(HAIFA)

40. Italy 意大利

ANCONA 安科纳
CAGLIARI 卡里亚里
GENOA 热内亚
GIOIA TAURO 热亚陶罗
LAS PEIZIA 拉斯佩齐亚
LEGHORN 来航
LIVORNO 利禾奴
NAPLES 那不勒斯
TRIESTE 的里雅斯特
TARANTO 塔蓝托
VENICE 威尼斯

41. Jamaica 牙买加

KINGSTON 金斯敦

42. Japan 日本

CHIBA 千叶
HAKATA 伯方
KOBE 神户
MATSUYAMA 松山
MOJI 门司
NAGOYA 名古屋
NIIGATA 新鸿
OSAKA 大阪
SHIMIZU 清水
TOKUYAMA 德山
TOKYO 东京
TOMAKOMAI 沾小牧

YOKKAICHI 四日市
YOKOHAMA 横滨

43. Jordan 约旦

AQABA 亚喀巴

44. Kampuchea 柬埔寨

PHNOM PENH 金边
SIHANOUKVILLE 西哈努克

45. Kenya 肯尼亚

MOMBASA 蒙巴萨

46. Korea 韩国

BUSAN 釜山
FANGCHENG 防城
INCHON 仁川
KWANGYANG 光阳
NAOETSU 直江津
OITA 大分
PYEONGTAEK 平泽
SAKATA 酒田
ULSAN 惠山

47. Lebanon 黎巴嫩

BEIRUT 贝鲁特

48. Libya 利比亚

BENGHAZI 班加西
KHOMS 克胡姆斯
MISURATA 米苏拉塔
TRIPOLI 的黎波理

49. Madagascar 马达加斯加

TAMATAVE 塔马塔夫

50. Malaysia 马来西亚

JOHORE 柔佛州
PASIR GUDANG 巴西古单
PENANG 槟城
PORT KLANG(N/W) 巴生(西/北港)

51. Malta 马基他

MALTA 马基他

52. Mauritius 毛里求斯

PORT LOUIS 路易港

53. Mexico 墨西哥

ALTAMIRA 亚尔塔米拉
ENSENADA 恩塞纳达
GUADALA JARA 瓜达拉哈拉
LAZARO CARDENAS 拉萨罗，卡德纳斯
MANZANILLO 曼萨尼约
MAZATLAN 马萨特兰
MEXICO CITY 墨西哥城
MONTERREY 蒙特雷
PROGRESO 普罗格雷索
PUERTO MORELOS 莫雷洛斯港
TAMPICA 坦皮科
VERA CRUZ 韦拉克鲁斯

54. Mo sang Columbia 莫桑比亚

BEIRA 贝拉
MAPUTO 马普托
NACALA 纳卡拉

55. Namibia 纳米比亚

WALVIS BAY 鲸湾港

56. New Zealand 新西兰

AUCKLAND 奥克兰
BLUFF 布拉夫
CHRISTCHURCH 克赖斯特彻
HAMILTON 哈密尔顿
NAPIER 内皮尔
NELSON 纳尔逊
NEW PLYMOUTH 新普利茅斯
PORT CHALMERS 查默斯港
TIMARU 蒂马鲁
TAURANGA 陶朗加
WELLINGTON 威灵顿

57. Nicaragua 尼加拉瓜

CORINTO 科林托
MANAGUA 马拉瓜

58. Nigeria 尼日利亚

LAGOS/APAPA 拉各斯/阿帕帕

59. Oman 阿曼

MUSCAT 马斯喀特
SALALAH 塞拉莱

60. Pakistan 巴基斯坦

KARACHI 卡拉奇
PORT QASIM 昆新港

61. Panama 巴拿马

BALGOA 巴尔博亚
CRISTOBAL 克里斯托瓦尔
COLON 科隆
PANAMA 巴拿马

62. Peru 秘鲁

CALLAO 卡亚俄

ILO 伊洛

63. Philippines 菲律宾

MANILA(S/N)马尼拉(南/北港)

64. Puerto Rico 波多黎各

SAN JUA 圣胡安

65. Qatar 卡塔尔

DOHA 多哈

66. Romania 罗马尼亚

CONSTANZA 康斯坦察

67. Russia 俄罗斯

NOVOROSSIYSK 新西伯利亚

68. Salvatore 萨尔瓦多

ACAJUTLA 阿卡胡特拉
SAN SALVADOR 圣萨尔瓦多

69. Saudi Arabia 沙特阿拉伯

DAMMAN 达曼
JEDDAH 吉达
RIYADH 利雅德

70. Senegal 塞内加尔

DAKAR 达喀尔

71. Singapore 新加坡

SINGAPORE 新加坡

72. Slovenia 斯洛文尼亚

KOPER 科佩尔

73. South Africa 南非

CAPE TOWN 开普敦
DURBAN 德班
PORT ELIZABETH 伊丽莎白港

74. Spain 西班牙

ALGECIRAS 阿尔赫西拉斯
BARCELONA 巴塞罗那
BILBAO 毕尔巴鄂
VALENCIA 瓦伦西亚

75. Sri Lanka 斯里兰卡

COLOMBO 科伦坡

76. Sultan 苏丹

PORT SUDAN 苏丹

77. Syria 叙利亚

LATTAKIA 拉塔基亚

78. China Taiwan 中国台湾

KAOHSIUNG 高雄
KEELUNG 基隆
TAICHUNG 台中

79. Tanzania 坦桑尼亚

DAR ES SALAAM 达累斯萨拉姆
TANGA 坦噶

80. Thailand 泰国

BANGKOK 曼谷
LAEM CHABANG 林查班
LAT KRABANG 拉各拉邦

81. The Bahamas 巴哈马

FREEPORT 弗里波特
NASSAU 拿骚

82. The Persian Gulf 波斯湾

BAHRAIN 巴林
KUWAIT 科威特

83. Trinidad Island 特立尼达岛

POINT LISAS 特立尼达
PORT OF SPAIN 西班牙港

84. Togo 多哥

LOME 洛美

85. Tunisia 突尼斯

TUNISA 突尼斯

86. Turkey 土耳其

GEMLIK 盖姆利克
ISTANBUL 伊斯坦布尔
IZMIR 伊兹密尔
MERSIN 梅尔辛

87. Ukraine 乌克兰

ODESSA 敖德萨
ILLICHEVSK 伊利乔夫斯基
ILYICHEVSK 伊利伊雷夫斯基

88. Uruguay 乌拉圭

MONTEVIDEO 蒙特维的亚

89. Venezuela 委内瑞拉

LA GUAIRA 拉瓜伊拉
PRERTO CABELLO 卡贝略

90. Vietnam 越南

HAIPHONG 海防
HANOI 河内
PANANG 岘港
VICT/CAT LAI/NEW PORT 胡志明

91. Yemen 也门

ADEN 亚丁
HODEIDAH 荷台达

92. Zaire 扎伊尔

MATADI 马塔迪

Appendix 3

Commonly Used Vocabulary

A

abandonment 委付，废弃，放弃货载

abandonment charge 废弃费用

ability to pay 偿付能力

absorption 吸收

abstracts 摘要

accept an order 接受订货

acceptance 验收，承兑，承诺，认付，已认付的期票

acceptance 承兑票据

acceptance commission 承兑手续费

acceptance fee 认付费

acceptance for honour 参加承兑

acceptance house 期票承兑行

accepted 照票，验票

acceptor 承付人，验收入

acceptor for honor 参加承兑人

accepting bank 承兑银行

accepting charge 承兑费

accident beyond control 不可抗力事故

accommodation 调节，通融，贷款，空头票据

account 账，账户，账目，会计科目，计算书，账单

accountant 会计，会计人员

account bill 账单

account book 账簿，会计簿册

account payable 应付账，应付未付账

account purchase 赊买

account receivable 应收账款，应收未收账

account sales 销货账，销货清单，分户账

account of goods sold 账目单，销货账目

account of receipts and payments 收支表

account year 会计年度

accounting statement 会计报表(告)

accounting unit 会计单位

accrued expense 应计费用

accrued item 应计项目，前期债务

accumulation of capital 资本累积

acknowledgement 回单，收悉，回报，承认收悉

acknowledgement of orders 处理订货

acquisition 获利，赢利

act of God 天灾

acting manager 代理经理

active demand 畅销

actual cost 实际成本

actual liabilities 实际负债

actual price 实际价

addendum 追加条款

additional expenses 追加费用

additional order 加订订货

additional premium 加保费

address 地址

addressee 抬头人(信用证书的)，收信人

adjustment 理赔，调整

advalorem duty 从价税

advance 预付，垫款，预支，贷出款项

advance in price 涨价

advance payment 预付款

advance price 增价

advance sample 先发样本(品)

advance settlement of exchange 预缴外汇

advance surrender of export exchange 预缴出口外汇

advice 通知书，汇票票根

advice of arrival 货物运到通知

advice of shipment 船运通知，装船通知

advising bank (notifying bank)通知银行

advertise 登广告，广告

advertisement matter 广告邮件

advertising 广告法(学)

advertising agency 广告公司，广告社

advertising expense 广告费

advertising media 广告媒介物

affiliated company 联营公司，附属公司

after charge 附加费率

after date…日期，……日后，发票后，票据记日后

after sight 票据照票后，见票后照付

affidavit of export 输出宣誓书

A grade 甲级(指货品)

against All risks 保全险

agency 代理

agency agreement 代理约定书

agency contract 代理契约

agent 代理人，代理商，掮客，经理人

agent service 代理业务

agreed upon 同意，商定

agreement 契约，契约书，约定书

agricultural products 农产品

air freight 航空运费

air-mail 航空信件

air-mail service 航空运奇

air-tight 不透空气，密封

air transportation insurance 空运保险

airway bill 航空提单

all risk 一切险(全险)

all round price 包括一切费用价格

all sorts of goods in stock 各种货色齐备

allied company 联号

allocation 分配

alongside delivery 船边交货

allowance 扣除，津贴，折让，减免，货币之公差

allowance on sales 销货折让

alter an agreement 变约

amendment 修正书，修改

amicable allowance 友好让价

amicable settlement 友好解决

amount 总数，合计，共计

amount insured 保险金额

amount of exports 输出额

amount of imports 输入额

analysis certificate 化验证书

analysis report 化验报告

announcement 通告，布告，公告

announcing removal 迁移通知

annual 年报，年鉴，年刊

annual income 岁入经费

annual interest 年息，年利

annual production 每年生产

annual report 年报，决算书，年度财务报告

anticipated buying 预期购买

anti-dumping 反倾销

apartments 公寓住宅，房地产

applicant 申请人

applicant for the credit 信用状申请人

application 申请，求职信，申请书

application fee 申请费

application for Conversion 折换申请书

application for export permit 输出许可证申请书

application for import of foreign goods 外货进口报单

application for importation of controlled commodities 管制物资输入申请书

application for letter of credit 开发信用状申请书

application for negotiation of draft under letter of credit 出口押汇申请书

application for outward remittance for Conversion 汇出汇款或折换申请书

application for space 舱位申请书

application for transfer 信用状转让申请书

application to pass goods through the customs (notice，report) 报关单

apply at the following address 向下列地址询问

apply by letter 函向，通信申请

apply in person 亲自询问，亲自申请

apply for a position(job) 谋职

apply for information 探向消息

apply for remittance 托汇

appointed store 特约商店，指定商店

appraisal 估价，鉴定

apprentice 学徒

appreciation of money 货币增值

appropriation 拨款，科目，挪用，指定用途，法定支用

approval 核准

arbitrage 套汇买卖

arbitrage of exchange 套汇

arbitrator 公断人(仲裁人)

arbitration clause 公断条款

arbitration of exchange 汇兑率比例，汇兑率的裁定

area 面积

army supplies 军需品

arrival at port 入港

arrival notice 抵埠通知

article 商品，条款

articles made to order 训制品

articles of luxury 奢侈品

artificial flower 人造花

as agreed (contracted) 按照合同，照约定

ask the price of 询价

assets 资产，财产

assigned 过户，转让

assignee 受让人

assignment 让与(委托)证书

assignment Claus 转让条款

assignment of policy 保险单之转让

assignor 转让人，让与人

assistant 店员，会计，助理

assistant manager 副经理，协理

association 公会，协会，公司，社团

as soon as possible shipment 迅速装船

assortment 花色，各色俱备

assurance 保证，担保，保险，财产转

让书

assured 被保险人，被保证者

assurer 保险人，保证者

at a discount 无销路，票面价格以下(股票等跌至)，折扣

at a premium 超过票面以上的价格(股票)

at a profit 赚钱，获利

at sight 见票即付，即期

at the market 照市价

auction 拍卖，竞卖

auction market 公开标售市场

audit 查账单计，决算，会计检查

auditor 会计检察官，查账员，合计员

auditing 查账

authority to purchase 委托购买证

authority to pay 委托付款证

authorization 授权

average 平均数，海损

average bond 共同海损保证书

average cost 平均成本

average tare 平均皮重

average unit cost 平均单位成本

average unit price 平均单价

average weight 平均重量

award 授予，赔款，决标，公断书，公断赔偿

award of bid 决标

B

background 背景

back to back L/C 化一抵一之转开信用状

bag 袋

bagging 盛装费

bailee 受托人

bailee clause 受托人条款

bailling 大包

bakery 面包厂

balance 差额，条数，尾数，决策，平衡

balance in our favour 我方受益(应收)

balance in your favour 你方受益

balance of payment 收支差额

balance of trade 贸易差额

balance sheet 资产负债表

balance sheet analysis 资产负债表分析，分析平衡表

bale 包，捆包

bale breaking 松包

ball 粒，球

bank acceptance 银行承兑

bank balance 银行(存款)余额，银行差额

bank bill 纸币，钞票(美)，银行票据

bank's buying rate 银行购买汇率

bank charges 银行手续费

bank commission 银行佣金，银行酬劳金

bank draft 银行汇票

bank holiday 银行假日

bank hours 银行营业时间

bargain offer 廉价优待

bargain sale 大廉价

barratry 船长船员之恶意行为(或故意损害行为)

barrel 大桶

barrier 关卡

barter 交换，以货换货，物物交换，用货换货，实物交易

barter arrangement 易货协定

barter system 物物交换制，以货易货制，易货方式

basic price 基价，底价，基本价格

basket 篮

be booked up 预订一空

be booked for 购买往……去的飞机(车、船)票

be engaged in export 做出口

bank notes 钞票，银行兑换票

Bank of China 中国银行

bank of commerce 商业银行

Bank of communications 交通银行

Bank of Taiwan 台湾银行

bank rate 银行贴现率，银行日息

bank reference 银行备咨

bank's buying rate 银行购入汇率

bankrupt 破产

bankruptcy 破产，倒闭

banking 银行事务，银行业

banker 银行业者，银行家

banker's acceptance 银行承兑，银行信用状

banker's credit 银行承兑汇票

bar 条，棒

bargain 交易，契约，合同，廉价品

be held responsible for 应负赔偿之责

be in default 不履行(契约)

be in demand 销路好，有需要

be in vogue 正流行中

be kept upright 保持正值

bear (short)空头，拉跌卖方

bear a loss 负担损失

bearer 持票人

bearish 看跌的，起跌风的(股)

bearish market 市场疲跌

become (or fall) due 期满

bedrock price 最低的价目

beneficiary 收款人，受益人，享受保险赔偿的人

benefit 保险给付

berth terms 定期船条件

best in quality 品质优良

best seller 畅销品，畅销书

be out of vogue 已经不流行了

beware of fire 小心火烛

B grade 乙级(指货品)

bid 出价，标价，竞买，投标买卖

bid bond 投标押金

bid price 标价，已还之价

bidder 投标人，出价者，竞买人，投标商

bilateral contract 双边契约

bilateral trade 双边贸易

bill 账单，清单，招贴，告白，传单，证券，汇票，支票，票据，钞票

bill at sight 见票即付的汇票

bill for collection 托收票据

bill of exchange 汇票，押汇，交换券，国外汇票

bill of lading 运货证书，提单，提货凭单，提货单

bill payable 应付账款

bill purchased 出口押汇

bill receivable 应收票据(账款)

bill undue 票期未到

billing 开发票

black and white advertising 黑白广告

black market exchange 黑市汇兑

blacksmith shop 铁工厂

blank bill 空白票据

blank check 空白支票

blank endorsement 空白背书，不记名背书

blank order forms 空白订单

board of administration 董事会，理事会

board of directors 董事会

board of supervisors 监事会

bona fide 出于善意

bond 公债，证券，债券，保税单，契约，公债证书，保证保险

bonded warehouse 保税仓库

bonded goods 保税货

book 注册，挂号，预订，买票，托运，订(车位)，赌票，支票，记账

boom 利市，畅销，生意兴隆

borrow 借债(账，货)

borrow money 借钱

borrow money from (of) 由……处借钱

bottom price 最低价

box 盒，箱，匣

boycott foreign goods 抵制外货

branch 支店

brand 商票，火印，品种，厂牌

branch office 分店，分公司，分社，分局

brand 商标

breach a contract 负约，违约

breach Of contract 背约，毁约

break an agreement 负约

break bulk 下货，卸货

break even 不赚不赔

break even point 营业损益两平点

breakage 破损

brisk (active；lively) 生意兴隆的

broker 经纪人，掮客

brokerage 经纪，事业，掮客，佣钱，回扣经手费

brought down 移入下页，过次页

brought forward 承上页，前页滚结

budget 预算

bulk 散装，正货

bulk cargo 散装，散装货

bulk sale 大宗卖

bull 多头业者，买方，买空者

bull market 上涨行情

bundle 束，捆，包

burden 负荷，载货重，装载重

burlap 麻布

business 商业，营业，业务，事务

business cards 商业名片

business circles 商业界

business correspondence 商业通信

business English 商业英语

business expenses 营业费

business hours 营业时间

business letters (commercial letters) 商业尺牍

business-like 工作认真，商业化的

business school 实业学校，商业学校

business year 营业年度

buy 买，购，收买

buy at a bargain 购得便宜

buyer 买主，买方，买手，办货员

buyer's market 购买者市场，买主市场

buying agent 买人代理人，进货经纪人

buying and selling on commission 代客买卖

buying contract 买货契约

buying expenses 购买费用

buying price 买价

buying power 购买力

buying rate 银行买价，买人汇率

by mutual consent 双方同意

by parcel post 当包裹寄

by-product 副产品

by the gross 整批，按笔计算

by the hour 按钟点(给工钱等)

by weight 论斤(卖等)

C

cable address (telegraphic address) 电报挂号

cable charge 电报费

cable confirmation 电报确认书

cablegram 海底电报

cable transfer 电汇

calendar year 日历年度

can 罐头

can afford 买得起

cancel (write off)注销，取消

cancel an order 取消订货

cannery 罐头工厂

capacity 容积，最高承受额，承保力量

capital 资本，基金，股款，本钱，劳资

capital account 资本账户(清算)

capital goods 资本财货

capital in trade 本钱

capital market 资本市场

carbon copy 副本

card-board box 纸板盒

care of(c/o)转交

cargo 货物

cargo in bulk 散装货

cargo insurance 货物险

cargo vessel 货轮

carrier 搬夫，运送人，运输行，运输业者，保险业者

carrying charges 置存资产费用，储囤支出(指存货而言)

carrying cost 储囤成本(指存货而言)

carriage 搬运费

carriage forward 运费交货时照付，运费由收货人支付

carriage paid 运费付讫，运费在内，运费预付讫

cartage 搬运费

carton box 硬纸盒

case 箱

casing 装箱费

cash 现金，现款

cash against delivery 交货付款

cash against document 凭单据付款

cash and carry 现金出货

cash before delivery 现金交易，付款后交货

cash on arrival 货到付现

cash on delivery (C.O.D.)货到付现

cash price 现价，现售价目

cash purchase 现金购买

cash receipts 现金收入

cash register 现金记录器，出纳机，现金登记簿

cash with order 订货付款

cashier 收支员

cashier's check 本票

cashing 现金，支票兑现

cask 桶

catalogue 目录，条目，总目

catty 斤(东方通用)

caution mark 小心标志

ceiling 最高限额

ceiling price 限价，最高价格

Central Bank 中央银行

Central Trust Of China 中央信托局

centralized purchasing 集中采购

certificate 签证，证书，牌照

certificate and list of measurement and/or weight 产量证明书

certificate for advance surrender of export exchange 预缴出口外汇证明书

certificate of analysis 化验证明

certificate of inspection 检验合格证书

certificate of insurance 保险证明书

certificate of import license 进口证明，特许进口证明书

certificate of origin 原产地证明书

certificate of shipment 出口证明书

certificate of weight 重量证明书

certify 证明

C grade 丙级(指货品的)

C.F. price 货价及运费价格

chain stores 连锁商店

chairman of the board 董事长

chairman of board of directors 董事长

chamber of commerce 商会

Chang Hua Commercial Bank 彰化商业银行

charges 费用，借项，捐税

charge for remittances 汇费，汇票费

charges paid 各费付讫

charge (a sum) to one's account 记某人账上

charter 特许(成立公司等)，发给特许执照，包租(车、船等)

charter by time 论时计费

charter by voyage 论航次计费

charter-party 租船契约

chartering 雇船，雇飞机等

cheap 廉价的，便宜的

cheap clearance sale 底货贱卖

cheap labor 低廉劳工

cheating 行骗

check，cheque 核对，支票

check mark 注销符，核对符号

check payable to bearer 无记名支票

check to bearer 不记名支票

check to order 记名支票，认人支票

checking account 核对账目，活期存款，用支票账户

chemical works 化学工厂

cheque 支票

chief executive 董事长

China Productivity and Trade Center 中国生产力贸易中心

chop 图章，图记，戳记，官印

circulating 流动

circular 传单，报单

circular letter 宣传信，传单

circular letter of credit 巡回信用状

civil commotion 内乱

claim 赔偿，要求赔偿损失，索赔

claim for damages 要求损失赔偿

claim for proceeds 应得价款之要求

claim letter 要求赔偿书

claimant 索赔人

classified advertisements 分类广告

clean bill 光票，清洁汇票，信用票据

clean bill of lading 清洁提单，没有附带纠纷的装货证

clean draft 光票(普通汇票)

clean 出货，结关

clear n port 出港

clear a ship 卸货

clearing 票据交换，结算

clearing house 票据交换所

clearance 清运出港证，出港许可，过关手续；纯益，票据交换总额

clearance sales 出清存货，大贱卖，销售底货，放盘

clerical error 记录错误

clerk 店员(美)，伙计，办事员(公司)，职员

client 委托人，顾客，客人

close an account 结账，停止信用，交易(清账后)，停止赊购

close inspection 严格检查

closing 结算，收盘

closing quotation 收盘，股市行情

closing rate 收盘汇率

closing time 关店(打烊)时间，下班时间

C.O.D. cash on delivery 交货收款

code number 标号数码

code telegram 密电

C.O.D. sales 交货收款销售

coil 卷

coin 货币，硬币，金钱

collated telegram 校对电报

collateral 侧面的，附属担保

collector 收买员，收款员，收款人，收账人，收税员

collecting agent 代收人

collecting bank 代收银行

collecting bill 收款汇票

collection 托收，收入款

collection charges 代收票据费

collection expenses 收款费用

collection fees 代收票据费

collection letter 收账信

collection of bills 代收汇票

collision 碰撞

combined offer 联合发价

come (go) into operation 开始工作，开始运转

come into the market 出现于市场，山笼

come into vogue 开始流行

commence business 开始营业

commercial 商业的，贸易的，商业广播，跑生意的，电视商业节目

commercial abbreviations 商业略字

commercial agent 代理商

commercial agreement 商业合约

commercial attache 商业参事，商业专员(帮办)

commercial bank 商业银行

commercial bill 商业汇票，票据

commercial center 商业中心

commercial credit 商业信用，商业信用状

commercial correspondence 商业通信，商业书札

commercial documentary letter of credit 商业跟单信用状

commercial letter of credit 商业信用状

commercial paper 商业票据(文件)

commercial profit 商业利益

commercial relations 商业关系

commission 委托，经纪，佣金

commission agent 代理商，代办人，代理贸易商

commission agency 代理贸易

commission business 经纪业，委托贸易

commission broker 捐客

commission house 抽佣商行

commission merchant 代售商，佣金批发商

commission sale 委托贩卖，代售，寄售，经销，托销

commitments 承约，承受债务

commodity 商品，货物，日用品

commodity price 商品价格

common carrier 运输业者，铁路(轮船)公司，运输费

company 公司，商号，商社

comparative advantage 比较利益

compensate 赔偿，报酬，付工钱(美)

competitive demands 竞争需求

competitive market 竞争市场

competitive price 公开招标价格

competitor 竞争者

compilation 编制

compilation of statistics 编制统计

complaints and claims 抗议与索价

compute (one's loss) 估计(损失)

computer 计算机，电脑

consecutive numbers 连号

conciliation 调解

condition 条件，状况

condition sale 附条件销售

conditional acceptance 附条件认付

conditional endorsement 有条件背书

conditional sales contract 有条件售货契约

conference freight rate 协议运费率，运输同盟运费率

conference tariff 公会议决运价表

confirmed letter of credit 保兑信用状

confirmation 查证，证实询证

confirmation of order 订货承诺书

confirmatory sample 确认样本

confirming bank 保证银行，确认银行

considerable orders 大量订购

consign 托卖，委托，寄售

consignee 收货人，承销人

consigner 发货人，交付者

consignee's address 收货人地址

consigned goods 寄销品

consignment 寄销品，寄销交付，托卖，托卖货

consignment note 寄销通知书

consignor 寄销人

consolidation 合并，统一

constructive total loss 推定全损

consul 领事

consul-general 总领事

consulate 领事馆

consulate invoice 领事签证发票

consular fee 领事签证费

consular invoice 领事发票，领事签证书

consumables 消耗品

consumer 消费者，用户

consumer demand 消费者的要求

consumer goods 消耗品

consumer market 消费者市场

consumption 销路，行销，消耗量，消费

container service 货柜运输

contents 目录，内容

contract 契约，合同，契据，章程；承包

contract for future delivery 订货, 订期货

contract for purchase 承买

contract goods 契约货品

contract of sale 卖契

contribution 捐款, 补助品, 分配, 摊派

control 管制, 管理, 核对, 存根, 底本, 对照簿, 监察

control of foreign exchange 外汇管制

conversion 转换, 兑换

conversion rate 折合率

conversion table 换算表

convey 让与, 转让(财产等)

Co-operative Bank of Taiwan 台湾合作金库

copy 副单, 副本

copy of draft 汇票股本

corner the market 垄断巿场

corporation 股份有限公司, 社团, 公会, 协会

correspondents 顾客, 来往客户, 代商行

correspondent bank 往来银行, 代理银行

corrugated paper box 瓦楞纸盒

cosmetic 化妆品

cost 价格, 成本

cost and freight 货价加运费, 运费在内价

cost insurance and freight 货价及保险运费在内

cost, insurance, freight and commission cost 到岸价值加佣金(包括保险及运费)

cost insurance, freight, commission and interest 到岸价格加佣金及利息

cost insurance freight and exchange 到岸价格加兑换费

cost control 成本的管制

cost free 免费奉送

cost of goods sold 销货成本

cost of labor 劳务成本

cost of living 生活费

cost of living index 生活指数

cost of material 原料成本, 材料成本

cost of maintenance 维持费

cost of manufacture 制造成本

cost of marketing 运销成本

cost of operation 作业成本

cost of production 生产成本

cost of reproduction 复制成本

cost of sales 销货成本

cost of transfer 转移费用

cost of transportation 运费

counter 计算器, 计算者, 筹码; 号码, 伪币, 柜台

counterfeit 伪造的, 假冒的, 仿造的, 伪品

counterfeit note(bill) 伪钞

counterfeit trade-marks 影射商标

counter L/C 对开信用状

countermark 对号(货色等上所附记的), 标签

counter-offer 还价, 还盘

counterpart 副本

counter-sign 副署, 会签, 副签

counter-signature 副署, 副书, 复证

country of origin 原产地, 出产地

counts 支数(纱)

coupon 息票, 利息单, 联票, 股利票(商品中的), 赠券

cover 购入，担保，补进(预先卖出的股票)，抵销(收支)，投保

cover note 承保通知书，保险证明书

coverage 保额，付保险额

covering 补进

covering letter 伴书，详函

craft 手工艺，行业，同行，同业工会

craft, etc. clause 驳船等条款

craftsman 技工，工匠

crate 枝条编制的篮，篓

creation 创造(时装等类)

credit 债权，信用，放账，赊账，贷款，贷方，贷项，信用证书，信任

credit analysis 信用分析

credit card 信用卡，赊购证

credit information 信用报告

credit inquiry 商行信用之调查

credit note 贷方票，付款票

credit sale(business)赊卖，信用买卖

credit side 贷方

creditor 债主，债家，债权人

cross out(off)注销，删去，取消

cross rate 套价，套汇汇率，裁定外汇行情

cubic 立方

cubic foot 立方尺

cubic inch 立方寸

cubic meter 立方米

cubic yard 立方码

cubic measure 容量，体积

currency 货币，通货，流通，时价，市价，行情，流通期间

currency areas 货币区域

current deposit 活期存款

current information 现行消息(资料)

current price 时价，市价，买盘

current price on market 行市，市场价

current rate 现价，当日汇率，成交价

current year 本年度

custom 光顾，顾客，主客

custom made 定制

customs 海关

customs barrier 关卡

customs broker 报关行

customs clearing charges 报关费

customs duties 关税

customs entry 海关手续

customs invoice 海关发票

customs warehouse 海关仓库

customary discount 常例折扣,习惯折扣

customary tare 习惯皮重，按习惯皮重

customer 买主，顾客

customers' account 客户账户

cut down ones' expenditures 节省开支

cut down the price 减价

D

daily expenses 每日费用

daily interest 每日利息

daily necessity 日用品

daily pay 日给工资

daily reports 日报

damage 损害，赔偿金，赔偿损失

damaged goods 水渍货，毁坏物品

dangerous goods 危险货物

data 资料

date due 到期日

date of contract 签约日期

date of delivery 交货日期

date of draft 发票年月日

day of maturity (due date) 到期日

deadweight cargo 重量货品

deadweight ton 重量吨

deadweight tonnage 载重吨位

deal on credit 赊账买卖商人，贩卖

dealer 交易商

dear 昂贵的，高价的

debit 借，借入；借项，借记，账簿的借方

debit note 发票、账单，借方票，收款票，借项清单

debit side 借方

debit 借款，欠款，债务

debit and credit 借贷

decimal fraction 小数

decimal point 小数点

decimal system 十进法(度量衡等)

deck cargo 甲板货物

deck rate 甲板运费率

declare at the customs 报关

declaration 申报，报单

declaration for exportation 出口报单

declaration for importation 进口报单

decline 下落(物价的)

decreasing 递减

decreasing cost 递减成本

deduct money 扣钱

deductible 减得，可减的

deduction 减除数，扣除额，折扣额，折扣，扣除

default 违约，拖延(欠款等)，不履行条款

defer 递延，延期；扣存，定存

deferred payment 延十；十货款

deficit 亏空(额)，赤字，调头寸

deflation 通货紧缩

delay 延期

delay in payment 延期支付

delay shipment 延期装船

del credere 买主资力的保证，买主资力保证费

delcredere agents 保证买主资力的代理商

decline an order 谢绝订货

deliver the goods 送交物品，履行契约，如期交货

delivery 交货，交付，交割期，交货条交

delivery note 货证书，交货单

delivery order 提货单

demand 销路，需求，请求

demand an indemnity 要求赔款

demand bill 即期汇票

demand draft (bill) 票汇，即期汇票

demand price 需求价格

demurrage 延搁卸载，延期费

deposit 存款，保证金

deposit account 存款账户

deposit at bank 银行存款

deposit certificate 银行存款单

depositor 存款人

depressed market 市面清淡

depression 不景气，营业萧条

depreciation 价值低落，跌价，贬值，折旧

deputy manager 剧经理

description 说明书；种类，详单，表记，货物名称

description of goods 货物摘要

design of products 产品设计

design paper 打样纸，图案纸

despatch money 快递费

destination 口的地，指定地

detained goods 扣留货物

detainment 扣禁

deterioration 耗损，变质，降低(品质等)

detour 改道，改航

devaluate 减价，减低币值

devaluation 贬值

developed countries 已开发国家

development bank 开发银行

development cost 开发成本

development expenses 发展费用

deviation 误差(统计上的)，越出航道(船只)

difference 差额，余额

direct mail advertising 直接邮件广告

direct price 直接价格

direct quotation 直接估价

direct sales 直接销售

direct trade 直接贸易

director 董事

director board 董事会

directory 商品目录，工商人名录，工商宝鉴(指南)

directory of importers and exporters 贸易商名录

dirty bill of lading 有债务提单

disburse 支付

discharge 卸货，解雇，清偿(债务等)

discharging expenses 卸货费用

disclosure 直述

discount 折扣，贴现，贴现息，减价

discount a bill 扣减期票

discount rate 贴现率

discrepancy 不符，差异

dishonour 拒绝付款，拒付，拒收(票据等)

dishonoured check 差头支票，不兑现支票

dishonoured bill 退票

display 陈列品，展览品

disposal 处理方法(转让或出售处理权)

distribute 配给，分配，分销

distribution 分配，配给品，分销，配给方法

distributor 配给者，经销商

district bank 地方银行

diversification 分散(资金分散等)，危险的分散

divisible L/C 可分割信用状

division of labour 分工

division of work 分工

dock 船坞

dockage 船坞费

documents 证券，单据，文件

document against acceptance 承兑交单，汇票承兑后交付提单

documents against payment 付款交单，付款后交付运货单据

document of shipping 装货单据

documentary acceptance bill 承兑汇单，照票

documentary bill (draft) 押汇，跟单汇票

documentary credit 押汇信用状

dollar countries 美元国家

dollar loan 美金借款

dollar shortage 美金缺乏

domestic bill 国内汇票

domestic communication 国内交通

domestic economy 家庭经济

domestic letter of credit 国内信用状

domestic market 国内市场

domestic products 土货，国货，土产

domestic telegrams 国内电报

do not drop 不可抛掷

do not turn over 不可倒置

down payment 分期付款之定金，第一期付款

dozen 一打(12 个)

draft 汇款兑付通知单，付款通知单，汇票，支票

draft for remittance 汇票

draft on demand 即付汇票

draft or note payable to bearer 凭票即付

draw 开给(支票等)，提款，取款，借款

draw a bill 出票

draw up a contract 拟合同

drawee 付款人，受票人

drawer 出票人，开票人

drawings 提款，提存

drum 鼓形桶

dry goods 绸缎呢绒类货品

dual-use packaging 双重用途的包装

due 期满，付款日期

dues 会费，税，手续费

due date 到期日，满期日(票据的)

dull market 市面冷淡

dull sale 滞销，销路不好的

dumping 倾销

duplicate 复本，副本，底本

duplicate copy 副本，第一副本

duplicate invoice 副联

duplicate of draft 汇票复本

duplicate sample 复样

dutiable 应征税的

dutiable goods 应完税货品

duties (taxes) 税捐(税饷)

duty free (to exempt from taxes) 免税

duty free goods 免税品

duty paid 关税已付

duty paid Keelung 基隆交货进门税完纳价

duty paid terms 通过海关后交货条件

duty unpaid 关税未付

E

each 每，各

earmark 明白指定(资金的)用途

card 赚得，挣得

earning 赚钱，收入，薪水，赚得，挣得数

earning power 收益力(资本的)，赚钱能力

econometrics 计量经济学

economics 经济状态(国家的)

economic growth 经济成长

economic policy 经济政策

ecomomic take-off 经济起飞

economy 经济

eight-hour system of labour 八小时工作制

elastic demand 弹性需求

electric appliances shop 电器行

electric power cost 电力成本

electronic computer 电子计算机，电脑

elimination 消除，除去，淘汰

embargo 封锁，禁止(船只进出口，通商)，扣留，输出，没收(货物)

embargo on the export of gold 禁止黄金出口

emission 发行(纸币等的)发行额

employed 雇用

employee 雇员

employer 雇主，主人

employment 职业，雇用，职工招聘

empty forms 空白式样

enclosure 附件

endorse 背书(支票的)，背署，保证，担保

endorsed in blank 空白背书

endorsee 被背书的人，承受背书票据的人

endorser 背书人

endorsement in blank 无记名签批

endorsement in full 完全(记名)背书

endorsement to order 指派式背书

engineer 工程师

enlarge 扩充

ensure 保险，担保，保证

enter 报进口

enter into an agreement 订约

enter into (make) a contract with 与……订约

enterprise 企业，事业心

entrance 入口，会费，入会费，入港手续

entrance fee 会费，入场费

entry 报关手续，报单，登记，入场

equalization 平衡

equilibrium；balancing 平衡

equilibrium price 平衡价格

equipment 设备

equivalent 同价，等于

establish a business 创业

establishment 公司，商店

estate 财产，遗产，所有权

estimate 预算额(书)，估价单

estimate price 估价

estimated cost 预算费用，计算成本

estimated market value 估计市价

estimated revenue 岁入预算

estimated statement 估计表

European Common Market 欧洲共同市场

evaluation 估价，估计

evidence 证明书，凭证

evidence of debt 借据

ex(fret，out of)交货(船边，码头)，(红利)

exact interest 抽息

exact quantity 确数

examination 验后放行

examine goods 验货

examined 验讫

examiner 查核员

ex bond 关仓交货价

ex buyer's godown 买方仓库交货价

excess 过量，超出额

exchange 兑换，交易，汇兑行情，兑换率，贴水，交易所

exchange hank 汇兑银行

exchange clause 汇兑条款

exchange control 汇兑管制

exchange fluctuations 汇兑的变动

exchange fund 汇兑资金

exchange of commodity 商品交易

exchange rate 汇率，外汇汇率

ex dock 码头交货价

execute an order 接受订货

execute one's promises 履行契约

executive 总经理(美，商)，董事，社长

exempt from taxation 免税

exemption 豁免，免除

ex factory 工厂交货价

ex godown 仓库交货价

exhibit 正表，主要表，附件

exhibition 陈列品，展览会

exit 出口，退席

ex lighter 驳船交货

ex mill 工厂交货价

exorbitant prices 非法价格，价格过高

expansion project 扩建计划

expenditure 费用，消费，开销，支出，支出额，消费额

expense 开支，花费，损耗费用，业务费用

expenses 费用

expensive 高价的，昂贵的

ex pier(wharf)码头交货价

expiration notice 满期通知书

expiring date 到期日

expiry date 有效期限

ex plane 空运飞机上交货价

ex plantation 农场交货

expo 展览会(美)，义卖市场

export 输出，出口货

export agent 出口代理商

export bill 出口单，出口汇票

export bill for collection a/c 托收出口汇票科目

export bill of lading 输出提货单

export credit insurance 输出信用保险

export declaration 出口申报书

export duties 输出税，出口税

export insurance 输出险

export licence 出口证

export loan 输出贷款

export merchant 输出商

export order 出口订单

export packing 出口包装

export permit 输出许可证(书)

export processing 加工出口

export quotas 输出限额

export Sales 外销

export trade 外销，出口贸易

exportation 出口(货)

exporter 出品商人，输出者

exports 输出额，出口签证

express 捷运公司(美)

express fee 快递费

express mail 快信

ex quay 码头交货价

ex rail 铁路旁交货价

ex ship 船上交货价

ex store 仓库交货，店铺交货价

ex store terms 店铺交货条件

extend 调期，展期

extensions 展期，扩充，延期

extensive order 大批订货

external trade 对外贸易

extinguish 价清(法)，消灭

extra 额外津贴，赠品

extra charge 额外费用

extra discount 额外折扣

extra expense 额外费用

extra work 加班，加工

extra premium 额外保险费

extra vagent price 过高的价格

ex works 工厂交货价

ex works terms 工厂交货条件

ex warehouse 仓库交货价

ex warehouse terms 仓库交货条件

ex wharf 码头交货价

F

fabric 工厂，纤维品，织品

face 票面价格，票面金额

face value 面值，面额，票面

facility 设施

factor 代理商，中间商人，成本中心

factory 工厂，代理店，在外商店

factory expenses 制造费用

factory planning 工厂计划

factory report 工厂报告

factory supplies 工厂供应品

facsimiles of authorized signatures 有权签字员样本

failed bank 破产银行

fair 定期市集(赶场)，义卖市场，物产赛会

fair average quality 中等品质,良好平均品质

fair average sample 平均中等样品

fair market value 公平市价

fair price 平价

fair trade 合法贸易，互惠贸易，公平交易

fake 骗人货，假冒物

fall (or become) due 到期(支票)，期满

falling price 跌价

family size 家庭用特大号

fancy goods 杂货，花色货

fare 运费(车船等)，车费，船费

farm 农场

farmer 农民

farm produce 农产品

fashion 时髦，时兴货

favourable balance 有利差额

favorable trade balance 出超

fee 费，费用，手续费，入场费，会费，小账

feed 加工原料,附属在大公司下的运输公司

feeling 预感(市场行情的)

field service 就地服务

figures 价格，金额，数字，计算

filing 档案

fill your order 供应订货

firm offer 稳固发价

financial 财政的，金融的

financial analysis 财务分析

financial ability 财力

financial circle(world)金融界，财经界

financial condition (situation) 财务状态

financial expense 财务费用

financial investigation 财务调查

financial position 财务状况

financial report 财务报告

financial statements 决算表，资产负债表，借贷对照表，财政报告

finance 财务，财政，金融，财力，财源，财政学

fine gold 纯金

finished goods 成品，加工品，精制品，制成品

finished product 制成品

firm 商号，商行，字号

firm order 定期订货

firm price 固定价目

fire risk 火险

fire policy 火灾保单

fireproof 防火

fiscal year 会计年度

First Commercial Bank OF Taiwan 台湾第一商业银行

Citibank, N.A 美国花旗银行

first quality 上等品质

fixed cost 固定成本

fixed prices 不二价，标价

fixed rate 固定率

floating policy 流动保单，预定保险

floor price 底价，最低价

flour mill 麦粉厂

fluctuation 物价波动，涨落，摇动

fluctuating market 变动行市

fur account of 在(某人)账上

for sale 廉让，出售

force majeure 不可抗力

forecasting 预测(商场价格等)

foreign capital 外国资本

foreign currency 外币

foreign department 国外部

foreign exchange 外汇

foreign exchange control 外汇管制

foreign exchange market 外汇市场

foreign exchange quotation 外汇价目表

foreign exchange reserve 外汇准缶

foreign mail 外国邮件

foreign trade 对外贸易

formal contract 正式合同

formal notice 正式通知

form of application 申请书格式

forward 转递，预约，送达，期货

forward agent 运送经纪人

forward business 期货交易

forward exchange 远期汇兑

forward exchange transaction 远期外汇，买卖

forwarding agency 运输业

forwarding agent 运输商，运输行

forwarding business 运输业

foul bill of lading 不洁提单，不完全提单，有债务的提单

fragile 当心破碎

franco 全部费用在内价

franchise 专利，特权，特许代理权，免赔额，免赔限度

free alongside ship 船边交货价

free enterprise 自由企业

free foreign exchange 自由外汇

free goods 免税品

free in 包括装船费在内之运费

free in and out 包括装卸费在内之运费

free of all average 全损赔偿，担保全损条件

free of capture & seizure clause 扣押免责条款，掳获夺取不赔条款

free of charge 免费

free of cost 免费奉送

free of expense 免费，无偿

freight paid to...terms 运费预付至……条件

free of particular average 单独海损不赔

free of particular average clause 单独海损不赔条款

free of strikes riots and civil commotions clause 罢工，暴动，内乱，不赔条款

free of tax 免税

free on board (F.O.B.)船上交货价

free on board shipping point 起运点交货

free on board destination 目的地交货

free on rail 火车上交货价

free on truck 卡车上交货价

free overside 输入港船上交货价格

freightage 货运，运费，船费

freighter 装货人，货主，承运人，货船

freight 运费，水脚，货运，水上运输

freight broker 运货经纪人，运货掮客

freight boat 货船

freight charges 运费

freight forward 运费待收，运费由提货人支付

freight paid 运费付讫

freight payable on delivery 货到付运费

freight prepaid 运费先付

freight to be collected 运费(水脚)待收

freight to collect 运到收费

freight ton 装载吨

freight train (美)运货列车=<英>goods train

freight to be paid after discharge at destination 货物到埠运费卸载时付给

frozen foods 冷冻食物

fruit ship 水果船

fulfil 履行(契约)，满期

fulfil the terms 履行条款

full service 完全服务

full state trading 完全国有贸易

fumigation(船)烟熏消毒

functional expense 业务费用

futures 期货，期货契约

future market 未来市场

G

gainer 获利者

gain profit 得利益，利润

gallon 加仑(即四 quart)

gamble 孤注一掷，冒险

garage 汽车行

general affairs 总务

general agents 总代理，总代理人，一般代理人

General Agreement on trade and Tariffs 贸易及关税总协定

general average 共同海损，总平均

general cargo 普通货

general cargo rate 一般货物运费率

general letter of hypothecation 押汇质押书，一般押汇质押书

general merchandise 杂货

general offer 一般发价

general terms and conditions 一般交易条件

gift coupons 赠券(商品中积有相当数可换赠品)，出售礼券

gift shop 礼品店

godown 堆栈，仓库，栈房

godown charges 仓租

godown keeper 仓库管理员

godown receipt 仓库收条

godown warrant 仓单

good merchantable quality 标准品，上等可销品质

good-will 诚意，好意，亲切，热心，信誉

goods 货物，商品，物品，财产，所有物 (尤指动产)

goods in bond 在关栈货物，保税税货物

goods in process 在制品，在产品

goods in stock 存货

goods in transit 在运品

goods on consignment 寄销商品

grace 缓期，宽限

grace period 宽限，优惠时间

grade 等级，品级

grading 分级，归类

grand prize 特奖

grand sale 大减价

grand total 总计

gross 总计，笒(即十二打)

gross amount 毛计，概数

gross average 平均毛额

gross imports 进口总数

gross proceeds 总货价收入

gross sales 销货总额

gross weight 总重量，毛量

guarantee 保证，保证人

guarantor 保证人

guaranty 保旺书，担保金

gunny 粗麻袋

gunny sack 麻袋

H

half finished goods 半成品

half&half 对半，各半

half price 半价

half price ticket 半价票

handicraft 手工业，手工

handicraft industry 手工业

hands off 不准手触，不准动手

handle 买卖，经营(美)

handle with care 小心轻放(搬动)

handle with great care 特别当心搬动

handling expense 处理费用

harbour bureau(port office)港务局

harbour dues 港税

hard goods 金属品

head (main) office 总局，总行

health certificate 卫生证明书

heavy weight goods 重量货物

hedge 现买现卖(交易所)

hedging 抛买(卖)，套作交易

high 高价的

high class 高级

high interest rate 高利贷

high price 价昂，高价

highest price 最高价

highest possible price 最高价

hike 加价，加票价

hire 租用，雇用，租金，工钱，薪水

holder 持票人

holding company 控股公司(美)，股权公司

home industries 国内工业

home-made 自制的

home market 国内市场

home products 国产

home trade 国内贸易(内销)

house 商店，伦敦证券交易所(俗)

I

illegal payment 非法付款

illegal profit 不当利益

imitate (forge) a trade-mark 冒牌

imitation brand 冒牌

immediate delivery 即刻交货

immediate payment 即时付款

immediate shipment 迅速装船，随即装船

imported goods 进口货，舶来品

import agent 进口代理商

import bill 进口汇票

import cargoes 吞量，进口货物

import credit 进口信用证书

import commission house 进口佣金商行，进口代理商

import declaration 进口报单，进口声明书

import duty 输入税，进口税

import letter of credit 输入信用状

import licensing system 进口签证许可制

import merchant 进口商

import permit 进口证，进口准单

import price 输入价格

import quota 输入限额

import tariff 输入税单，进口税则

import trade 输入贸易，进口贸易

import without exchange settlement 不结汇进口

imported goods 进口货

importers 进口商

impose a tax upon a person 向某人收税

in bond 在保税仓库中，关栈中交货价

incidental expenses 杂费，零用费，车马费

inclosure 附件

income 定期收入，所得进项，收益

inconvertible 不能交换的，不能兑现的

incorporated company 有限责任公司

incorporation 登记，注册，设立，公司

increasing 递增

increasing cost 递增成本

increasing expense 递增费用

incur losses 蒙受损失

indebtedness 负债

in demand 顾客需要

indemnify for the loss incurred 赔偿所受损失

indemnity 赔偿损失，赔偿金，契约赔偿

indent 双联订货单，购买委托书

indirect cost 间接成本

indirect damage 间接损害

indirect expenses 间接费(地租房租工资等)

indirect labor 间接人工，补助人工

indirect trade 间接贸易

industry 工业，实业

inflate 使(通货)膨胀，使(物价)上涨

inflation 通货膨胀，暴涨(物价)

inflation policy 通货膨胀政策

inflationism 通货膨胀主义

inflationist 通货膨胀论者

in force 有效

informal agreement 非正式(随意)契约

inherent defect 固有瑕疵

inherent vice 固有瑕疵(保险)

inland bill of lading 内陆提单

inland bill of lading clause 内陆提单条款

inquire 询价(向商店查询商品等)

inquirer 询价者

inquiry 询问，询价，调查，审查

inquiry agency 调查所，征信所

inquiry sheet 询价单

insert 插进，登(报)，插页

insist 催逼，坚持

insolvency 倒账，破产，无力支付

inspection 检查，调查

inspection and certificate fee 检验证明费用

inspection report 检验报告书

instalment 分期付款

instalment delivery 分期交货

instant 本月

institute cargo clause 货物附带条款，协会装船货物条款

in stock 有存货

instruction 说明书

insurance 保险，保险费，保险金额

insurance broker 保险掮客(经纪)

insurance business 保险事业

insurance certificate 保险证明书

insurance company 保险公司

insurance expense 保险费

insurance policy 保险费

insurance premium 保险费

insured the 被保险人

insured amount 保险金额

insurer 保险人，保险商，承保人

interest 利息，股份，财产，所有权

interest per annum 年息

interest rate 利率

interested party 有意者

International Chamber of Commerce 国际商会

international market 国际市场

international Monetary Fund 国际货币基金(联合国)

international money orders 国际汇票

international parcel 国际包裹

international relation 国际关系

International Shipping Company 国际航运公司

international trade 国际贸易

international trade organization 国际贸易机构

interview 访问

in transit 业呈装船，业经运出

introductory offer 宣传品(新货色的)，推荐品

invest 投资

investor 投资人

investigate 调查报告，清查

invisible exports 无形出口

invisible trade 无形贸易

invite to tender 招标

invoice 发票，发单，装货清单

invoice amount 发票额

invoice for sales 销售发票

invoice price 发票价目

invoice weight 发票所开重量

inward documentary bills 进口押汇票

iron straps 铁皮条

iron works 铁工厂

irrevocable credit 不可取消信用状

irrevocable letter of credit 不可取消信用状

issue(支票)发行，发行额

issuing bank (opening bank) 开证银行，发行银行

issuing date 发行日期，开证日期

item 项目，细目

items of business 营业项目

J

jettison 抛弃，船货投海

jewellery 珠宝类

job 作买卖股票，批发，包工，散工，赚钱

joint cost 联合成本

joint enterprise 合办事业，共同事业

jump 抬高(物价等)，提高(薪水等)

junk 便宜货，旧货

K

keep cool 放置冷处，保持凉爽

keep dry 勿受潮湿，保持干燥

keep flat 平堆平放，请勿倒放

keep out of the sun 离开阳光,避免阳光

keep upright 竖放

keg 小桶

key currency 主要通货

key industries 基本产业

king-size 大号

L

label 标签

labour (labor)苦工，劳动，工人，劳动阶级

labour force 劳力

labour market 劳工市场

labour movement 劳工运动

labour problems 劳工问题

labour union 工会

landed price 包括起货费用在内价目

landed terms 岸上交货

landing 起货

landing certificate 登陆证，上岸证明书

large order 大批订货

latest market reports 最近市场报告

laydays 装货(卸货)期间

lay-off 停工期间，休息，临时解雇

layout 广告图样，设计

leading article 吸引顾客的东西

leading market 主要市场，大市

leaflet 单张广告印刷品

leakage 漏泄，漏耗

leakage proof 避漏

legal interest 法定利息

legal price 法价

legal rights 法定权利

legal tender 法币，法定债款

legal weight 法定重量

length，capacity and weight 度量衡

less than carload rate 不足一辆货车运费率

letter 信件

letter of advice 发货通知单，汇票通知单

letter of assignment 转让书

letter of authorization 权利书，委托书，委托拨款证

letter of confirmation 证实书，确认书

letter of credit 信用状，信用证书

letter of guarantee 保证书

letter of hypothecation 押汇负责书，押汇质押书

letter of inquiry 询价函件

letter of introduction 介绍信

letter of indemnity 赔偿保证书，赔款执照，保结书

letter of notice 通知单

letter of recommendation 保荐信，介绍书

letter of reference 调查信，保证书

letter reference number 书信备查号数

letter transfer 信汇

letter telegram 书信电报

levy 抽(税)，征收

license 签证，执照，许可证

licensing of export 出口许可

licensing of import 入口许可

licensing system 许可制度

lien 留置权，扣押(财产以待偿债的)权，优先债权

light cargo 轻量货品

lighterage 驳船费

high interest rate 高利率

limit prices 限价

limited liability company 股份有限公司

line 单位，行业，生意，买卖，种类(商品的)

line of business 营业范围

line of credit 信用透支，融通额度

liner 定期航线

liquid goods 液体货物

list 目录表，一览表，价目单

list of award 决标单

list price 定价

loading 装载，货船，额外保险费(人寿保险)

loading charges 装货费

loading expense 装货费用

local L/C 本埠信用状

local products 土产

local retailers 地方零售商

local wholesaler 本地批发商

location 地点

loco (or spot) 当地付货，当场交货价

long(bull)多头，买方

long term 长期

long term agreement 长期合同

long (gross) ton 大吨，英吨，长吨

lose one's interest 对……失掉兴趣

lose one's market 失去买卖的机会

lose (or ruin) ones reputation 失去人的信用

loss 亏本(卖出等)，损失

loss capital 蚀本

lost 遗失(启事)

lost check 遗失支票

lost time 虚耗时间

lot 批，分割(土地)，分堆(售商品)

low 低廉的(价格)

low grade goods 劣货

low in price 低价

low price 廉价的

low priced 低价

low priced goods 下等品，下价货

low quality 下品，品质低劣

lowest bidder 最低价标商

lowest possible price 最低价

lowest quotations 最低价格

luxuries 消耗品，奢侈品

M

machine 机器

machine cost 机器成本

machinery and equipment 机器及设备

machinery and tools 机器及工具

machinery equipment 机器设备

mail 邮寄

mail order 邮购，通信订购

mail remittance 信汇

mail transfer 信汇

mailing list 邮寄名簿

maintenance 维持费，保养，维护

major product 主要产品

make 估计，计算，赚得，制造，定价钱

maker 制造者

make an offer 还价，出价

make a profit on 在……上头赚钱

make a quotation 开价

make compensation 补偿

make money 赚钱，挣钱

make reservations 订位，订房间等，附保留条件(在契约上的)

made to order 定制

manage 经营，管理

managing director 常务董事

management 经营，管理，经营力，经营手腕

manager 经营者，经理(人)，理事

managership 经理人身份

manageress 女经理

manpower 人力

manifest 舱单，货单，船货详单，报关单

manner of packing 包装方式

manual 手册，指南，便览

manufactory 工厂

manufacture 制造，制造品，机器制造

manufactures department 制造部

manufacturer 制造人，生产者，正厂主人，厂商

manufacturer's agent 厂商代理人，工厂代理商

manufacturing cost 制造成本

manufacturing expenses 制造费用

margin 赚头，原价与卖价之差，保证金

margin money 预收保证金

marine risks 水险

maritime transport 海运

mark 商标，唛头，马克(德货币单位)

market price 标明价目

mark down 记账，减价，记录

mark up，涨价，记账，赊账

market 市价，市场，行情市况，食品店(美)

market analysis 市场分析

market day 市集，定期市集，交易口

market demand 市场需要

market feeling 市场人心

market place 市场，商业中心地

market potential 市场潜力

market report 市况报告

market value 市价，时价

marking 刷唛头，支票的承认

marking expenses 销售费用，运销费用

marketing 在市场中买卖，销售，市场学，市场营运

marketing research 市场研究

marketable 销路好的

marketable goods 易销的货物

marine cargo insurance 海上运输保险

marine insurance 海亡保险(费)水险

marine products 水产物，海产物

marine policy 水险保单

marine risks 水险

mass media 大众传播工具

mass production 大量生产

master contract 主约

mate's receipt 收货单(向船主取得收

据），大副收据

materials 原料，材料，必需品

materials shortage 材料缺乏(短少)

material supplies 材料供应

mats 席包

mature 到期(票据等)

maturity 到期(票据等的)

maximum capacity 最高(生产)能量

maximum price 最高价

means 财产，资产，资力，收入

measure 重量，尺寸，尺度，度量法

measurement 尺寸

measurement cargo 轻量货品

measurement goods 容积货物

measurement tons 容积吨

measurement ton method 容积吨计运费法

mediator 中间人，居间人，调解人

medium quality 中等货

meet 偿还，偿付

meet one's liabilities 偿还债务

member 会员

member rate 会员运费率

memorandum 买卖备忘录，买卖通知单，便笺

merchant 商人，批发商，贸易商，零售商(美)

merchantable 有销路的，可买卖的

merchant bank 证券银行(英)

merchandise 商品

message form(blank)电报纸

Messrs. 实号(英)

methods Of production 生产方法

method of remittance 汇款方式

metric system 公制，十进制

metric ton 吨，法吨

mill 工厂，制造所

minimum charges 最低费用

minimum freight 最低额之运费

minimum premium 最低保费

minimum price 最低价

minimum profit 最低利润

minimum selling price 最低售价，廉价

Ministry of Economic Affairs 经济部

ministry of commerce 商业部

ministry of finance 财政部

ministry of industry and commerce 工商部

miscellaneous expense 杂项费用，杂费

miscellaneous goods 杂货，杂物

miscellaneous payment 杂项支出

model 衣服店的广告女人(标示衣裳所用)，时装模特儿

mode of producing 生产方式

moisture 水分，潮湿

monetary 货币的，财政(上)的，金融的

monetary system 货币制度

monetary unit 货币单位

money 金钱，货币，财产

money market 金融市场

monopoly 专利品(权)，公卖专利

monthly allowance 按月津贴

monthly balance 月计表

monthly fee 月费

monthly output 每月产量

monthly report 月报

monthly sales 每月销售情形

monthly statement 每月结单

most favoured nation clause 最惠国条款

multilateral agreement (contract)多边合

约(合同)

multilateral trades 多边贸易

mutual agreement 互相同意

N

name of article 货名

name of user 用户名称

name of vessel 船名

necessaries 必要条件

necessity for life 生活必需品

negligence 疏忽过失

negotiate 让渡，流通，押汇

negotiable bill 流通票据

negotiable bill of landing 可转让提单

negotiable letter of credit 流动信用状，可兑信用状

negotiable warehouse receipts 可转让仓单

negotiation 让与转付，流通交易，议价

negotiation of foreign bills 买卖外国汇票期票

negotiate 卖(让与)，使(证券票据等)流通，换成钱

negotiating bank 购票银行，洽款银行，让购汇票银行

negotiating date 汇票让购期限

net 获净利，纯净的，无虚价的

net amount 实数

net amount 净数，实数

net cost 净价

net income 净所得，纯收益

net loss 净损

net price 实价，净值

net proceeds 实得额，净收入

net profit 纯益

net profit on sales 销货利益

net sales 净销价，销货净额

net shipping weight 运出净量

net ton 美吨(2000 磅)，注册吨

net value 净值

net weight 净重

net worth 资本净值

New Taiwan Currency 新台币

No.1 quality 头等货

no entry 来宾(游客)止步

no entrance 禁止入内

no hook 不许用钩

no parking 禁止停车

no smoking 禁止吸烟

no thoroughfare 禁止通过

non-negotiable 不准抵押，不可转让

non-negotiable bill of lading 不可转让提单

non-payment 停止支付，不支付，无力支付，拒绝支付

non-profit 非谋利

non-revolving credit 不周转信用状

non-transferable 不可转让

normal cost 正常成本，平均成本

normal competition 正常经营

normal price 标准价格，正常价格

notarize 公证

notary public 公证人

not sufficient 基金不足

not otherwise provided for 无他种规定者，未列项目

notify 通知

notification 报告书，通知书，布告通知

notifying bank 通知银行

notice 招贴，传单，启事

notice board 布告栏(板)

nude cargo 裸装货

null and void 无效

numerical order 数目顺序

O

obligation 待付款，债务

obtain a high price 卖好价钱

obtain employment 就业

ocean bill of lading 海运提单

ocean freight 海运水脚，海运费

ocean liner 外洋轮船

ocean tramp 不定期货船

occupation 职业，工作

offer 出价，出售，出卖，作价，报价，发价

offeree 被发价人

offerer 发价人

office 营业处，办事处，行号，公司

office allowance 办公费

office clerk 职员，办事员

office copy 存根

office expenses 事务所费用

office supplies 事务用品，事务供应品

official exchange rate 官汇率

official invoice 正式发票

official rates 公定利率，官价，行巾

official rate of exchange 法定汇率,政府规定外汇率

official receipts 实收，正式收据

offset 抵消，补偿

oil paper 油纸

o.k. 核对无讹，无讹

old hand 熟练工人，熟练人才

old stock 陈货

on board B/L 装运提单

on demand 见票即付，即期

on hand 现存

open account 欠账交易，来往账目，贸易账户，开户

open an account 开立户头

open a shop 开铺子

open bid 公开投标，公开招标

open competition 公开竞争

open cover 预约承保契约

open credit 开发信用状

open market operation 公开市场买卖

open policy 预定保险单，未确定保单

open tender 公开招标

opening 就职门路，开盘(交易所用语)，交易开始时间

opening bank 开证银行

opening prices 开盘价，开价

opening quotation 开市行情，开市价，开盘

opening rate 开发汇率

operate 操纵市场，垄断买卖以扰乱市场

operating capacity 营业(生产)量

operating costs 营业费，经营成本

operating expenses 营业费，运输费，工作费

operator 接线生，掮客，经纪人，经营者

oral report 口头报告

order 订货(单)，汇兑(票)，订货通知

order bill of lading 指定人提单，装货人抬头提单，候命提单

order book 订货簿

order check 指定人支票(俗称抬头人

支票)

order for goods 订货单

order for sundries 订购杂货

order form 订货单，订货用纸

order sheet 订货单

ordinary 经常

ordinary quality 中等(指货品的)

organization 公会，协会，团体，编制

original 正单，正本

outlet 销路

outstanding 未付清的，未解决的

outstanding account 未消账款

outstanding claims 未决赔款

outturn sample 货物送达时所取之样本

out of business 歇业

out of employ 失业，赋闲

out of stock 卖完了，无存货

out of work 失业，无工可做

outward documentary bills 出口押汇

outward remittance 汇出汇款

overdraft 透支，汇款过额

overdraw 透支(存款)

overdue 过期

overdue bill 过期票据

overhead 管理费用，总支销，间接成本

overland common point 通常陆上运输可达之地区

over production 生产过剩

overseas buyer 海外买客

Oversea Chinese Commercial Bank 华侨商业银行

oversupply 供给过多

overture 加班，规定时间外的工作

overwork 加工，规定时间外的工作

owe 欠债，对……(义务，债务等)，应

支付(还债)的义务，该付的

P

pack 包捆，行李，包装，打包

pack a box 装箱

pack cloth 包装用布

pack thread 麻绳(包扎用的)

pack up 打包(美)

package 包装，包扎，包装费

packed cargo 包装货

packer 包装者，打包商

packet 包裹，小件行李

packing 包装，打包，填垫材料包装用品

packing and crating 打包，装框

packing box 货盒

packing case 货箱

packing charges 包装费用，打包费

packing credit 打包放款，包装信用状(装船前借款)

packing list 装箱单，花色码单，包装货物详单

packing machine 包装机

packing paper 包装纸

paid-up, capital 已缴资本，实收股本

pail 桶

paper 收据，债务，票据，证券，汇票，钞票

paper mill 造纸厂

paper money 钞票，纸币，不兑现纸币

par 同价，平价，票面金额

par avion(法文)航空邮递

par value 票面价值

parcel post 包裹邮递

parcel post insurance 邮包保险

parcel post receipt 邮包收据

parcel receipt 包裹收据

parent company 母公司

partial acceptance 局部认付

partial delivery 部分交付，局部交货

partial loss 部分损失

partial payment 部分支付

partial shipment 分批装船

particulars 摘要

particular average 单独海损

part time job 零星工作

partner 伙友，合伙人，合作者

partnership 合伙，合作

party concerned 有关人士

parties to a contract 签约人

patent 专利，专利品，专利制法

patent right 专利权，专利证书

pattern 样本，花样

pattern for reference 参考样本

patronage 光顾，顾客

pay 付，支付，发薪水

payable at sight 见票即付

payable to bearer 付持票人，认票不认人，凭票取款

payee 受账人，收银人

payer 付款人

pay in advance 预付

pay in cash 付现钱

pay in full 付清

paying agent 代付人，担当付款人

paying bank 付款银行

payment 支付，付方，缴纳，付款额

payment against draft credit 凭汇票付款信用状

payment agreement 支付协定

payments document 支出单据

payment by instalment 分期摊付(付款)

payment in advance 先付，预付，预付货款

payment in cash (for cash) 付现

payment in full 全付，全部付讫

payment in part 付一部分

payment on receipt credit 凭收据付款信用状

penalty 罚款，违约金

penny 便士

per annum 每年

per capita 每人，按人头

per capita income 每人收入

percent 百分比

percentage 百分率

per centum 每百

perfect competition 完全竞争

perfermance bond 履行保证

perils of the sea 航海危险

peril 危险事故

perils of the seas 海难

petty 小额

petty cash 零用钱，少数的现金支出

picul 担

piece 件，副，支，座，部，片，块

pier 码头，防波堤

pierage 码头税

pilferage 偷窃

piracy 海盗

place 贷(款)，发出(订单)，订(货)

place 地点，营业所

place of delivery 交货地点

place of loading 装货处

place of payment 付款地区

plain telegram 明电

planning of products 产品设计

please turn over 请阅后页

please pay 祈付

plus 加

plywood and artificial board industry 夹板工业

pocket money 零用钱，酒资

policy 保险书，保险单

policy of insurance 保险单，附加保险

poor workmanship 粗工

port 通商港口，港市，商埠

port duty 入港税

port of arrival 到达港

port of call 停靠港(沿途)，暂停港，寄航港

port of delivery 卸货港，交货港

port of departure 出发港

port of embarkation 起航港

port of sailing 起程港

port of shipment 装货港

port clearance 出口货单

porter 搬运工

porterage 搬运费，运费

position 职务

position vacant 征聘人才(事求人)

positions wanted 谋职(人求事)，待聘

possessor 持有人，所有人

post card 明信片

post office box 邮政信箱

postage 邮费，邮资

postal money order 邮政汇票

poster 广告，传单，标语，招贴

postscript 再者，又及，附笔

pound 镑(英重量名，等于 453.6 克，略 1b.)

pound 镑(英货币单位等于 20 先令略£)

pound sterling 英镑<货币单位>

power of attorney 委任状，代理委任权

practice 营业，生意，开业

premium 花红，贴水，奖金，保险费，佣金，升水

prepaid 先付的，付讫的(运费等)

prepaid expenses 预付费用

presentation 提示

president 董事长

prevailing price 当时价格

prevailing rate 市价

previous year 上年度

price 价格，价钱，市价

price list 价目单

pricing 标价，定价

prime quality 最上品，上等货

principal 资本，本钱，店主，基金

priority 优先权

prior period 上期

private company 私人公司

private enterprise 私营企业，民营事业

pro forma 估计的，假定的

proceeds 浮赚，收入，货价收入，实收款项

process 处理，过程

processed farm products 农业加工品

procurement 采购

procuration 代理权，介绍费

produce 提出(单据，证据等)，生产，生产量，物产

producer 生产者

product 产物，生产品

production 生产，生产量

productivity 生产力

profession 专门职业

profit 利益

profitable 有利益，合算的

profit and loss statement 营业损益表,损益计算表

pro forma invoice 估价单，备考货单，暂定的发票

program 说明书，节日表，程序表

prohibitive price 吓人的价钱

project 计划

promise 契约，约定

promissory note 本票，借据，期票，债务人所发期票

promotion 推广，推销，促进

promotion expenses 开办费，发起费用，推广费用

promotion policy 推销政策

promotional allowance 推广津贴

promotional literature 广告印刷品

prompt delivery 即时交货，即送，限时专送

prompt shipment 迅速装船，即期装船

proof 对证，证据

proposal form 要保书

proposer 要保人

proposition 企业计划

pro rata 比例分配，按照比例

prospect 有希望的客人

prosperity 繁荣，兴隆

protect 保护(国内产业)准备(汇票的)支付金

protectionist 保护(贸易)主义者

protective measure 保护办法

protective system 保护贸易制度

protective trade 保护贸易

provision 预付金，汇兑资金，条款，规定

proxy 代理人

publication 出版物

public agent 代办人

public auction 公开拍卖

public enterprise 公营企业

public market 公开市场

public relations 公共关系

public tender 公开投标

public weighter 公共重量检定人

publicity 宣传，广告

publicity agent 广告代理人，宣传员

publish 出版，发表，宣布，公布，颁布

published price 定价

purchase 买人，购买，采购

purchase confirmation 购货确认书

purchase contracts 购货合约

purchase contract 购物契约

purchase expenses 购货费用

purchase invoice 购货发票

purchase mission 驻外采购团

purchase order 购货订单

purchaser 买主，购买人

purchasing agent 代购人，购买代理商

purchasing cost 进货成本

purchasing department 采购部

purchasing power 购买力

purchasing power of money 货币购买力

Q

quadruplicate 第四副本，一式四份

quality 品质

quality certificate 品质证明书

quality control 品质管制

qualification 标准，资格

quantity 数量，定量，定额

quarantine 检疫，检疫停船，检疫期间

quarantine office 检疫所

quarter 四分之一，一码四分之一

questionnaire 询问表，调查表

quintuplicate 第五副本，一式五份

quota 限额(外国输入品，移民等)比额，配额

quota system 输入配额制

quota system 限额进出口制

quotations 行市，价目，估价单

quote 开价，报价，开估价单

R

raffle 彩签，抽彩义卖

rag 破布

railway bill of lading 铁路提单

railway freight 铁道运费

raise a price 涨价

rate 比例，比率，价格，行市，行情，估价

rate cutting 减低运费(保险费)

rate of discount 贴现率

rate of exchange 汇价，汇兑，兑换率

rate of interest 利率

rate per annum 利率

rating(保费)等级

ratification 批准(示)

rating 费率决定

ratio 比率

ration 限额，定额，定量，口量配给

raw 未加工的，粗坯

raw materials 原料

raw sugar 粗糖

rebate 回扣，折扣

reciprocity 交换(互惠)业务

receipt (documentary evidence)收方，收据

received 收讫

received for shipment 收货候装

received for shipment B/L 备运提单

recipient 受配人，收受人

recipient of goods 受货人

reciprocal buying 相互购买

reciprocal demand 相互需求

reciprocal purchase 互买

reciprocity 互惠业务

reciprocity clause 互惠条款

record 记录，档案，案卷

records 记录

recourse 追索(权)

recover 赔偿(损失等)，取得(损害赔偿等)

red bill of lading 赤色提货单

redemption 抵消(票据的)，偿还，购回(公债的)

redirect 改寄

reduce 减少，减价

reduce the price 减价

reduced price 减价，减低定价

re-export 再出口，再输出

refer 交付，委托

referee 公断人

reference 身份保证人，保人，证明书，介绍书，打听(关于人品能力等的)

refinancing 通融

refine 精炼，精制，提炼

refined salt 精盐，加工盐

refinery 精炼厂，加工厂，炼油厂

reflation 通货再膨胀，通货的复归

refund 付还，偿还，退回款项

registered 挂号的，登记过的

registered capital 注册资本

registered letters 挂号信件

registered mail 挂号邮件

registered post 挂号信

registered trade mark 登录商标

regular members 普通会员

regular price 正常价格

regular procedure 正规手续

regular service 定期航行，定期服务

regular subscriber 常年订阅者

regulations 规则，条例，管理，会章

reimburse 归垫，偿还，补偿

reimbursement 还款

reimport 再进口，再输入

reinsurance 再保险(公保)

reinsurance policy 再保险单

rejection 剔除数(货)

release 免除(债务等)让与(财产,债务等)重订契约出租

remarks 摘要，附注

remainder 剩余货，存货

reminder letter 催函

remit 汇寄，送出(金钱等)，减轻(捐税等)

remit money 划拨款项

remittance 汇款，汇寄，支付(金额)

remittance permit 汇款核准书

remittee 汇款领取人

remitter 汇款人

reminder 催单

remuneration 报酬，酬劳

renewal 续约，续保，续存

rent 租金，地租，房租，租借

renew 续订(契约等)

renewal 更换(票据等)重订(契约等)，期限延长

reorganization 改组，重整

repacking 改装

repair 修理，赔偿(伤害等)，维护

repairs and maintenance 修理及保养

repay 还钱，付还

repayment 偿还，付还，赔款

repeat offer 重复发价

report 报告，报告书，报告单

report form 报告格式

reporter 呈报者，新闻记者

reproduction 复制，再生产

reproduction cost 复制成本

repurchase 买问

request notes 中清单

requirement 必需品，需要

resale 再卖，专卖，贬价出售

resell 转卖

reserve 准备金，公积金，限价最低价格

reserve bank 准备银行，储备银行(美)

reservation 预定，预约，租定(房间等)，权益保留

reship 再装上船，改装其他船

resignation 辞职

resources 资源，财产，物资，资力

responsibility(偿付)责任

restraint 扣禁

restraint of trade 贸易约束

restriction of import 输入限制

resume 小传，摘要

resume business 复业

retail 零售

retail business 小买卖，小生意
retail dealer 零售商
retail price 零售价目
retail store 零售店
retail trader 零售商
retailer 零售商
retirement 退休，退股
return 报告书，回报，缴还
returnable 可退
returns 统计表，赢利，利润，赚头
return cargo 回头货
returned goods 退货
revaluation 重估价值，再估价
revenue 税捐，收入(国家的，财产的)，所得总额财源，税务署(美俚)
review 评议，研究
revision of treaty 修正条约
revocable letter of credit 可取消信用状
revocable unconfirmed banker's 可取消银行未确认信用状
revolving 循环，周转
revolving credit 回复信用证书，重复周转信用状
revolving letter of credit 循环信用状
right 权利
right of priority 优先权
riot & civil commotion insurance 暴动及民众骚乱保险
risk 风险，被保险人(物)
risk plan basis 实际危险制
risk of breakage 破损险
risk of hook damage 钩损险
risk of leakage 漏损险
risk of non-delivery 遗失险
risk of oil damage 油渍险

risk of sling damage 吊索损险
risk of sweat damage 潮腐险
risk of theft and/or pilferage 盗窃险
risk of warehouse to warehouse 仓库至仓库险
rise in price 涨价
rival commodities 竞争商品
rival firms 竞争公司
rock bottom price 最低价
rotten 腐烂
rough estimate 概算
round voyage 全航程
royalty 上演捐，权利金，版税，采掘权

S

sabotage 怠工，怠业
sack 袋，包，囊
sacrifice 折本出卖，大牺牲，大贱卖
salable 销路好的，畅销的
salary 薪金
salability 销路，畅销，易卖
sale 出售，销路，贱卖
sales allowance 销货折让
sale book 销货簿
sale by brand and/or description 凭厂牌和说明售货
sale by bulk 批发，估堆卖
sale by description and/or brand 货物分类出售
sale by inspection 看货买卖
sale by sample 凭样本买卖，照样本出售
sale by specification 凭规格交易，凭说明书买卖

sale by standard 凭标准买卖

sale confirmation 售货确认书

sale contract 售货合约

sales invoice 销货发票

sales letters 销货信件

salesman 销货员，店员，推销员

sales manager 营业主任

sales potential 推销潜力

sales promotion 促进销售

sales quotas 销货限额

sales system 销售制度

sales tax 销货税

sales territory 销售区域

sales woman 女店员，女推销员

salvage 抢救费，抢救起之货物

sample 样品

sample card 货样片(卡)

samples of goods 货样

sample room 货样室，样品间

savings bank 储蓄银行

sea damage 海损，海水渍

sea risk 海险

seals 印章，封印

secondhand goods 陈货，旧货

secondhand wooden case 旧木箱

second party 乙方

secretary 秘书

security 保证，保证书，保证金

securities 证券，债券

seizure 夺取，扣留

selected quality 上选品质

selection 选择，精选品

sell goods 销货，贩卖

sell on credit 赊售

sell out 卖完

sell well 好卖，行销

seller 卖主，卖方，售货人

sellers' market 卖主市场(求过于供)

selling agent 销售代理商，代销人

selling cost 推销成本

selling at half price 半价出售

selling at less than cost 蚀本出售

selling expenses 销货费用

selling price 售价，时价

selling profit 销货利润

selling rate 卖价，卖出比率

semi-annual 半年度

semi-annual report 半年度报告

semi-finished goods 半成品

semi-manufactured goods 半制成品

serial number 物品编号

service 服务

service business 服务事业

service department 服务部

set 套，具

settle a claim (bill) 解决赔偿

settle account 结账，清算，决算

settlement 结账，清算，支付，汇款方式

settlement of exchange 结汇

share holder 股东

shares of stock 入股份

ship 船舶，用船运，装货

ship broker 船舶掮客

ship cargo 落货，装货

shipowner 船主

ship (discharge) the cargo 装(卸)货

shipped on board B/L 装运提单

shipper 货主，运货者，装货人

shipping advice 落货纸(通知)

shipping agent 装船代理处，运货代理人，运货经纪人

shipping business 航业，航运业

shipping company 航运公司

shipping documents 寄货文件，装运单据

shipping expenses 装货费用

shipping note 装运通知单

shipping order 发运单

shipping receipt 装货收条

shipping sample 装船货样

shipping space 舱位，船位，吨位

shipping ton 装载吨，总吨数(船的)

shipping weight (intake weight) 装船货物重量，按运入重量，运出重量

shipment 运送，运送货物，装载，装船

shipment as soon as possible 尽速装船

shipment by first opportunity 有机会即装运

shipment sample 装运货物货样

shop 工厂，商店

shop girl 女店员

shop keeper 零售商人，店主，老板

shopping center 市场，购物中心

short 空头(卖方)

short bill 短期汇票

short contract 空头

short credit 短期信用

short form bill of lading 简式提单

shorthand 速记

short term 短期

short tons 短吨(2000磅)

shortage 短少，缺量

shortage in weight 重量不足

showroom 样品间

shrinkage 短缩

shut out 退关，轧出

shut the book 停止交易(来往)

signature 签名，署名

signing of contract 签约

sight bill 即期汇票，见票即付的汇票

sight draft 即期汇票

sight letter of credit 即期信用状

silver coin 银币

simple contract 单纯契约

skyrocketing price 飞涨价目

slack season (off season) 淡季

slip 传票，承保条

slip system 传票制度

slogan 标语，口号

slump 狂跌

sluggish 萧条的(市场)，缓滞的

small change 零钱

small quantity 小量

smuggle 走私，漏税，偷税

smuggled goods 漏税货，私货

smuggler 私枭

soaring 飞涨

soft goods 毛织品

sole agents 包销人，独家经理人

sold 卖完了

sorting 拣选费

special clause 特别条款

special column 专栏

special discount 特别折扣

special expenses 特别开支

special order 特别订货

special price 特价

special tax 特种营业税

special value 特别价值

specialization 专业化

specification 规格

specimen 样本，参考品

speculation 投机交易

speculative business 投机事业

speculator 投机买卖者

sponsor 用无线电或电视做商品广告的人，保人

spot 现货，当场交货价

spot delivery 当场交付

spot goods 现货

spot market 现货交易

spot sales 路货，当场买卖，现货销售

stale bill of lading 失效提单

stamp 邮票，印花税

stamp duty 印花税

stamp tax 印花税

standard 准则，标准，定额

standard of living 生活水准

standard sample 标准货样

standardization 标准化，合标准

stand-by letter of credit 备用信用状

staple 主要产物，大宗出产，名产，重要商品

state enterprise 政府企业

state monopoly 国有专卖

statement 表，报表，贷借对照表，报告书，清单

statement of assets and liabilities 贷借对照表

statement of loss and profit 损益表

statistics 统计，统计学

steamship (or steamer) 轮船

stencil 空印花板，蜡纸

stenograph 速记机

stenographer 速记员

stenography 速记术

sterling 英镑的

sterling area 英镑区域

sterling bloc 英镑集团

stevedore 装卸作业人，装货卸货的工头，码头工人

stock 股份，存货，存量

stock in hand 现有货

stock keeper 存货管理人

stock market 股票市场

stock on hand 存货，盘存，财产目录

stop payment 止付

stop work 收工，停工

storage (godown rent) 仓租，保管费

storage charges 存货费

storekeeper 材料管理员

storage charges 栈租，存货费

straight bill of lading 不转让提单，收货人抬头提单

straight credit 直接信用状

straight letter of credit 简明信用状

stranding 搁浅

straw 稻草，不值钱之货

strike 决定(市价)，订(买卖合同等)，结算，罢工，罢课

strong (firm) 有起色

strong market 市面旺盛

sub-contract 副合同

sub-company (subsidiary company) 附属公司

sub-manager 襄理，副理

subscribe 订阅，预定，预约，书押签名，认购股本

subsidiary 附属

subsidiary company 附属公司

subsidies 津贴

sub-total 小计

subtract 扣除

successful bidder 拍卖成交，得标商

sum 总数，全额

sundries (or all sorts of goods) 杂货

superintendent 监督者

superior quality 优等品

supervision 监督

superfine quality 极上品

supermarket 超级市场

superior 高级的，上等的

supply 供应，供给，存货，供应品

supply and demand 供应与需要

supply department 供应部

supporting document 原始单据(文件)，证明文件

surplus 溢额，盈余，公债(金)

survey method 调查法

surveyor 验货官，鉴定人，检验公证行

surveyor's certificate 鉴定证书

surveyor's report 验货报告书，鉴定人报告，公证人报告

suspend 暂时停止(作废)

suspend payment 停止支付

suspension of business 停业

suspension of publication 停刊

syndicate 工业公司，企业组合

synthetic industry 人工合成工业

T

table of freight charges 运费表

table of rates 税率表

tabulated quotation 行情表

tabulation 造册，制表

tabulator 制表人

tag 标价牌，标签，贴纸

Taiwan Handicraft Promotion Center 台湾手工业推广中心

Taiwan Supply Bureau 台湾物资局

Taiwan Tobacco and Wine Monopoly Bureau 台湾省烟酒公卖局

tale quale(tel quel)现状条件

tally 点计(上货卸货时)，点数

tally man 上货卸货的计数人，卖赊人，暂赊店主

tally sheet 计数纸

tanker 油轮

tannery 制革厂

tare 皮重(货物的)，包装重量

tariff 关税表，关税率，关税，税则，关费表

tax 税，租税，抽税，征税

taxation 征税，抽税，关税

tax bearer 纳税人

tax collection office 税捐稽征处

tax exemption 免税

tax exemption certification 免税证

tax evasion 逃税，偷税

tax free 免税的

tax free imports 免税进口货

telegram charge 电报费

telegraphic address 电报挂号

telegraphic transfer 电汇

telephone directory 电话号码簿

telex 电报交换机(打字电报)

temporary employment 短工

temporary payments 暂付款项

temporary receipt 临时收据

tender 投标

tenor 汇票期限

term 结账期，季节(支付)价钱，费用，条件

term bill 期票

terms of credit 信用状条款

term of payment 付款条件

termination of contract 合约终止

termination of employment 雇用终止，解雇

terms of sale 推销条件

territory(推销员等的)推销区域

textile factory 纺织厂

thanks for patronage 鸣谢惠顾

theft 偷窃

this side up 此端向上

through bill of lading 联运提货单

tight 紧迫的，银根紧

tight money market 银根紧的金融市场

time bill 期票

time charter 定期租船契约，论时计

time deposit 定期存款

time draft 远期汇票

time letter of credit 远期信用状

time limits 期限，索赔期限

time of delivery 交货时日

tin 锡，洋铁柜

tin-lined cases 铅皮胎木箱

tissue paper 棉纸，薄纸

to collect 收账

tolerance 可准许偏差

tonnage 吨位(数)

to open an account 开立账户

total 总数，总计的(金额等)，合计

total amount 总计，总额

total cost 总成本

total loss 全损(保险)，亏损总额，全部损失

total price 总价

total value 总值

tour 观光旅行

trade acceptance 商业承兑汇票

transit clause 运输条款

type 类型，型，样本

typewriter 打字机

tramp 不定期货船

transaction 买卖，交易

transfer 让与，过户凭单，股票过户交割，汇兑

transferable 可转让的

transferee 承买人，承让人

transferor 让股人，让与人，卖者

tranship goods 驳货，转口货

transhipment 转运

transhipment B/L 转运提单

transit 运输中，过境

travel allowance 旅行津贴

traveller's cheek 旅行支票

traveller's letter of credit 旅行信用证书

treasury bill 财政郡证券

treaty obligation 条约义务

trend 倾向，趋势

trial 试算

trial balance 试算表(簿记的)

trial order 试订(购)货单

trial sale 试销(卖)

triplicate 第三副本，一式三份

truckage 货车运货费，货车租费

trucking expenses 卡车运费

trust 委托，委托物，保管，赊账，赊卖

trust fund 信托基金

trust receipt 信托收据

turnover 营业额，周转，周转率

type sample 标准样品

U

ultimate consumer 最后消费者

ultimo 前月

unassignable letter of credit 不可转让信用状

unclean B/L 有债务提单

unconditional delivery 无条件交货

unconfirmed credit 未确认信用状

unconfirmed letter of credit 未确认信用状

uncommercial 非商业(性质)的，不是买卖的，违反商业道德

uncontrollable costs 不能控制成本

under-developed countries 工业落后国家，低度开发国家

underestimate 估低，把……的价值估计过低

undertake 包办，承包

underwriter 立约保险者，经营(海上)保险业

unearned 不劳而获的，自然得到的 (收入等)，分外的

unearned income 未获利润

unemployed 没有利用的，赋闲的

unemployment 失业

unfavourable balance of trade 贸易逆差，入超

unfavorable trade balance 入超

unfilled orders 未发货订单

unfinished work 未完成工作，未成品

uniform customs and practice for documentary credits 押汇信用状统一惯例实务

uniform prices 不二价

unilateral trade 单边贸易

unindorsed check 未经背书支票

union 工会，公会

unit cost 单位成本

unit price 单价

unload 卸货，起货，抛出

unload cargo 卸货

unloading (discharge) 卸货

unprecedented rise 空前涨价

unprecedented sales 空前销售

unreasonable prices 不合理价格

unsaleable 卖不掉，不能卖的，非卖品

unskilled labor 不熟练工人

unsold 未卖出

unsuccessful bidder 未得标商

unused balance of letter of credit 信用状未用余额

upset price 最低售价，开拍价格

upward 上涨的

urgent telegram 急电

usance 支付期票的期限，先付汇票的习惯期限

usance bill 远期汇票

usance letter of credit 远期信用状

use no hooks 不可用钩

user 用户

usual discount 普通折扣

V

vacation (工作的)假日

valid period 有效期限

validity 有效期

valuable merchandise 贵重品

value 价值

value of import 输入价值

variable cost 可变费用(成本)

variable expenses 可变动费用

variance 差异

vend 叫卖(小商品)出售

vendee 买主，受买人

vendor 卖主，出卖人，叫卖商，小贩

ventilated compartment 通风舱

venture 商业冒险

verbal (oral) contract 口头契约

verify 校对，查验

via 经由(路线)

vice-general manager 副总经理

victim 苦主，受害人

visible trade 有形贸易

vocation 职业，买卖

void 无效(=null and void)

volume 体积

volume(space)tons 容积吨

voyage charter 论次计租轮

voyage policy 航程保单

W

wages 工资，薪水

walkout 罢工

wanted 招请(广告用语)，征求，征聘

warehouse (godown)仓库，货栈

warehouse certificate 栈单，仓库凭单

warehouse to warehouse clause 由仓库运到另一仓库保险条款

warehouse receipt 仓单，存货单，仓库收据

warehouse warrant 栈单

warrants 认股权证，支付命令，仓单

war risks 战争险

wares 商品，货品，制品

waste 耗费，废料(货)

waterproof 不透水

water stain 水渍

waybill 运送单

wealth 财富，财产

wear 擦损，磨破

wear and tear 日久耗损

weekly reports 周报

weigher 过磅员，掌秤官，衡器

weight 重量，斤两

weight list 重量单，磅码单

weight note 码单，重量单

weight tons 重量吨

weights and measures 度量衡

welfare 福利

well-assorted goods 各色俱全的货物

wharf (pier，qua)码头

wharfage 埠头税，码头费，系船设备

wholesale business 批发业

wholesale dealers 批发商人

wholesale goods 批发货

wholesale merchant 批发商

wholesale price 批发(趸售)价格

wholesaler 批发商

with average 全损之外担保分损，特别分损担保

with recourse 有追索权

without recourse 无追索权，无偿还义务

without return 不可退货，无利的

withdraw 收回(通货等)，取消(申请)提款，退股

withhold 扣留，不给，扣款，扣除

witness 证人

wooden case 木箱

work 工艺品，制造品

workman 职工，工人，劳动者，熟练工人

workmanship 手艺，技巧(职工等)

workwoman 女工，女裁缝

worker 工人，劳工，劳动者，职工

working capital 流动资本，运用资本，资本周转金

working day 工作日

working expenses 经营费用，工作费用

working hour 工作时间

World Bank 世界银行

world market 世界市场

world's fair 万国博览会(美)

worth 值

wrapping paper 包装纸

written agreements (contract)书面契约

written contract 正式合约

written document 书面证明

written evidence 字据

written permission 书面许可证，签单

Y

yard 工厂，制造厂，工作场，堆置场

year 年度

yearly installments 按年摊付

yield 出产，产品，产量，收益

yielding 获利

Z

Zone improvement Program (ZIP code) 邮政区号

Appendix 4

Useful Abbreviations

A

@	at，to，from	单价，至(航)，从(航)
A.A.R.	against all risk	担保全险，一切险
acc.	acceptance，accepted	承兑，承诺(已)
a/c，A/C	account	账，账户
ackmt	acknowledgement	承认，收条
a/d	after date	出票后限期付款(票据)
ad.，advt.	advertisement	广告
adv.	advice	通知(书)
ad val.	ad valorem (according to value)	从价税
A1	first class	一级
AID	Agency for International Development	美国国际开发总署
A.M.，a.m.	ante meridiem(before noon)	上午
A. M. T.	Air Mail Transfer	信汇
amt.	amount	额，金额
A. N.	arrival notice	到货通知
A. P.	account payable	应付账款
A/P	Authority to Purchase	委托购买证
a. p.	additional premium	附加保费
A. R.	all risks	全险，一切险
Art.	article	条款，项
A/S	account sales	销货清单
a/s	after sight	见票后限期付款
assn.	association	协会
asst.	assistant	助理，助手
asstd.	assorted	各色俱备的
att.，attn.	attention	注意

av., a/v	average	平均，海损
a/v	a vista (at sight)	见票即付
Ave., Av.	Avenue	街道

B

B/—, b/—	bale, bag	包，装
bal., balce.	balance	余额
B/C	bill for collection	托收票据
B/D	bank draft	银行汇票
b/d	brought down	承前页
b'dle, bdl.	bundle	束，把
B/E	bill of exchange	汇票
B/F	brought forward	承前页
bg	bag	袋
BIS	Bank for International Settlement	国际清算银行
B/L	Bill of Lading	提单
BMF	bound measurement feet	板尺
B/N	bank note	银行纸币
b. o.	buyer's option branch office	买方有权选择分公司
b/o	brought over	承前
bot.	bottle	瓶
B/P	bill purchased	买入票据，出口押汇
B/P	bills payable	应付票据
B/R	bills receivable	应收票据
B/S	balance sheet	资产负债表
bsh., b/s	bushel	英斗
BTN	Brussels Tariff Nomenclature	布鲁塞尔税则分类
bx	box	箱，盒

C

C/—	case, currency, coupon	箱，通货，息票
c.	cent, centimes, centigrade	分(美)分(法)，百分度(寒暑表)
c.a.d.	cash against documents	凭单证付现金
c.a.f.	cost and freight	运费在内价
cat.	catalogue	货品目录

C.B.	clean bill　光票
c.c.	carbon copy，cubic centimeter　副本，立方厘米
C/C,C.C	Chamber of Commerce　商会
CCC	The Commodity Credit Corporation 美国商品金融公司
C/D	cash against document　凭单据付款
c/f	carried forward　过次页
C&f	cost and freight　运费在内价
C.F.S.	container freight station　货柜集散场
c.f.& i	cost freight and insurance　运费保险费在内价
c.i.a.	cash in advance　预付现金
cif,c.i.f.	cost，insurance and freight　运费保险费在内价
c.i.f.&c.	cost，insurance.freight and commission　运费，保险费，佣金在内价
ck.	cask　樽
C/N，C.N.	credit note，covering note，consignment note　贷方通知,保险承保单,发货通知书
C.O.	certificate of origin　产地证明书
c/o	care of，carried over　烦转，过次页
Co.	company　公司
c.o.d.	cash on delivery　货到付款
Con.Inv.	Consular Invoice　领事发票
corp.	corporation　法人，公司
C/P	charter party　用船契约
cr.	credit　贷方，债权人
cs	case　箱
csk.，ck	cask　樽
C.W.O	cash with order　现金订货,下定付款
cwt.	hundred weight　衡量名
C.Y.	container yard　货柜集散场

D

D/A	documents against acceptance　承兑后交付单据，备承
	documents for acceptance　兑单据，附有单据
	deposit account　存款账户
d/a	days after acceptance　承兑后……日付款
D/D.，D.D.	demand draft，documentary draft　期汇票、跟单汇票

d/d	day's date (days after date) 出票后……日付款
d.f.，d.fet.	dead freight 空载运费(船)
D/N	debit note 借方通知
D/O	delivery order 卸货通知书
do.	ditto (the same) 同上
D/p	documents against payment 付款后交付单据
Dr.	debit debter 借方，债务人
d/s.d.s.	days'sight (days after sight) 见票后……日付款

E

ea,	each 每、各
e.e.E.E.	error excepted 错误除外
EEC	The European Economic Community 欧洲经济组合(共同市场)
e.g,	exempli gratia (for example) 例如
EIB	Export-Import Bank 进出门银行(美国)
Enc. ,encl.	enclosure 附件
E.&O.E.	errors and omissions excepted 错误或遗漏不在此限
Esq.	Esquire 先生(信内尊称)
ETA	estimated time of arrival 预定到达日期
etc. &c.	et cetera(and so forth) 等等
ex	out of, without 自，无，交货
ex	example，executive，exchange，extract 例子，执行官，外汇交换，摘要

F

f	foot，franc 尺，法郎
f.a.a.	free of all average 全损才赔
f.a.q.	fair average quality 良好平均品质
f.a.s.	free alongside ship 船边交货价
F.B.E.	foreign bill of exchange 国外汇票
f.c.l.	full container load 整货柜装满
f.d.	free discharge 卸货船方不负责
f.i.	free in 装货船方不负责
f.i.o.	free in and out 装卸货船方均不负责
f.i.o.s.t.	free in，out，stowed and trimmed 装卸堆储平仓船方均不负责

f.o.	free out 卸货船方不负责
f.o. ，f/o	firm offer 规定时限的报价
f.o.b.	free on board 船亡交货价
f.o.c.	free of charge 免费
f.o.r.	free on rail，free on road 火车上交货价
f.o.s.	free on steamer 轮船上交货价
f.o.t.	free on truck 卡车上交货价
f.p.a.	free of particular average 单独海损不保
fr.f	franc，from，free 法郎，从，自由
F/P	floating policy 流动保单
FX	foreign exchange 外汇
FY	fiscal year 会计年度

G

g.	good，goods，gramme 佳，货物，克
G/A	general average 共同海损
GATT	General Agreement on Tariffs and Trade 关税贸易总协定
gm.	gramme 克
g.m.b	good merchantable brand 品质良好适合买卖之货品
G.m.b.H.	Gesellschaft mit beschrankter Haftung (company with limited liability) 责任有限公司(德文)
g.m.q.	good merchantable quality 良好可售品质
G.P.O	General Post Office 邮政总局
g.s.w.	gross shipping weight 装输总重量
gr.wt.	gross weight 毛重

H

h.	hour，harbour，height 寸，港，高度
H.O.	Head Office 总公司
h.p.	horse power 马力
hr.	hour 时

I

IATA	International Air Transport Association 国际航空运输协会
ICC	International Chamber of Commerce 国际商会
id.	idem (the same) 同上

277

i.e.　　　　id est (that is)　　即是

IMF　　　　International Monetary Fund　　国际货币基金

inc.　　　　incorporated　　有限责任公司(组织)

Incoterms　International Commercial Terms　国际商业用语

inst.　　　　instant (this month)　　本月

int.　　　　Interest　　利息

Inv.　　　　invoice　　发票

IOP　　　　irrespective of percentage　　不论损害大小

IOU　　　　I owe you　　借据

ISIC　　　　International Standard Industrial Classification　国际行业标准分类

it　　　　　item　　项目

J

j.jour.　　　journal　　日记账

Jr.　　　　　Junior　　年少者

K

k.　　　　　carat　　卡拉(纯金含有度)

kg.　　　　　keg kilogramme　　小，千克

K.W.　　　　Kilo Watt　　千瓦

L

£　　　　　pound or pounds sterling　　英镑

lb.　　　　　libra (pound or pounds in weight)　　磅

lbs.　　　　　pounds　　磅

I/C　　　　　letter of credit　　信用状

L/C/L　　　　less than carload lot　　不足一辆货车载量

L/I　　　　　letter of indemnity　　赔偿保证书

L/G　　　　　letter of guarantee　　保证函

I.t.　　　　　long ton　　长吨

L/T　　　　　Letter Telegram　　书信电报

Ltd.　　　　　Limited　　有限责任

M

m.　　　　　mile，metre，mark，month minute，mille (thousand)，哩，米，记号，月，分
　　　　　　meridiem (noon)　　千，中午

M.	Monsieur	先生
m/d	month after date	出票后……月付款
Mdme	Madame (Madam)	太太，夫人
memo.	memorandum	备忘录，便条纸
Messrs	messieurs	先生(多数)
M.I.P.	marine insurance policy	海上保险单
misc.	miscellaneous	杂项
M/L	more or less	增或减
MM.	Messieurs	先生(多数)
Mme	Madame	夫人
MO	Money Order	拨款单，汇款单
Mr.	Mister	先生
MR	Mate's Receipt	大副收据
Mrs.	Mistress	太太，夫人
m/s	months after sight	见票后……月付款
m.s.	mail steamer，motor ship	邮船，轮船
M.T.	metric ton，mail transfer	吨，信汇
m.v.	motor vessel	轮船

N

N.B.	Nota bene (take notice)	注意
NL	night letter	夜间拍发电报
NO.	number	号码
n.o.p.	not otherwise provided for	无其他规定者，未列名者
n.o.s.	not otherwise specified for	其他说明(规定)者
n/p	non-payment	拒付
Nt.Wt.	Net Weight	净重

O

o.	Order	订单，订货
O/	to the order of	凭……人之指示
O.B/L	order bill of lading	指示式提单
O.C.P.	Overland Common Point	通常陆上运输可到达地点
O/d	overdraft，on demand	透支，要求即付款(票据)
OECO	Organization for Economic Cooperation and Development	经济合作开发

组织

OEEC	Organization for European Economic Cooperation	欧洲经济合作组织
O.K.	all correct，approved	无误，同意
O/No.	order number	订单编号
o.p.	open policy	预约保单
ORD	ordinary telegram	寻常电报
o/s	on sale，out of stock outstanding	廉售，无存货，未决账款
O/S	old style	老式
o.t.	old term	旧条件
oz	ounce	盎司

P

P/A，p/a	particular average	单独海损，委任状，私人账户
pa	power of attorney private account	
p.a.	per annum (by the year)	每年
P.c.	per cent，petty cash	百分比，零用金
per pro，pp.，p.p.		
	per procurationem (by proxy，on behalf of)	代理
p.l.	partial loss	分损
P.&L.	profit and loss	损益
p.m.	post meridiem (afternoon)	下午
P.M.O.	postal money order	邮政汇票
P/N	promissory note	本票
P.O.B.	postal office box	邮政信箱
p.o.d.	payment on delivery	交货时付款
P/R	parcel receipt	邮包收据
pro forma	for form's sake	估计的，形式的
prox.	proximo (next month)	下月
PS.	postscript	再启
pt.	pint	品脱
P.T.O.	please turn over	请看里面
PTL	private tieline service	电报专线业务

Q

qlty	quality	品质

qr	quarter	分之一
qty	quantity	数量
quotn	quotation	报价单
qy	quay	码头

R

reed	received	收讫
recpt	receipt	收据
ref.	reference	参考，关于
RFWD	rain，fresh water damage	雨水及淡水险
remit.	remittance	汇款
rm	ream	令
r.m.	ready money，ready-made	备用金，现成的
R.P.	reply paid.return of post	邮费或电费预付，清即回示
R.S.D.	receiving，storage and delivery	港务局装卸费用
R.S.V.P.	reply if you please	请回答
R.T.	rye term	裸唛条件
rt.	rate	率

S

S.A.	Statement of Account	账单
s.a.	subject to approval	以承认(赞成，批准)为条件
S/D,	sight draft	即期汇票
S/D	sea damage	海水损害
secy	secretary	秘书
Sir.	Signor (mr.)	先生
sig.	signature	签名
S/N	shipping note	装运通知
S.O.s.o.	shipping order，seller's option	装船通知书，卖方有权选择
Sr.	Senior	年长者
SRCC	strike，riot.civil commotions	罢工，暴动，内乱条款
S/S，s/s，ss，s.s.	steamship	轮船
s.t.	short ton	短吨
st.	street	街
ste.ayme	societe annonyme (limited company)	有限责任公司组织

s.v.	sailing vessel	帆船

T

T/A	telegraphic address	电报挂号
TC	collated telegram	校对电报
tgm	telegram	电报
T.L.O.	total loss only	只担保全损(分损不赔)
TM	multiple telegram	分送电报
T.M.O.	telegraphic money order	电报汇款
T.R.	trust receipt	信托收据
T.T.	telegraphic transfer	电汇
T.Q.	tale quale	现状条件(运输途中损害买方负担)
TPND	theft，pilferage and nondelivery	盗窃遗失条款

U

ult.	ultimo (last month)	上月
uos	unless otherwise specified	除非另有规定
u/w	underwriter	保险业者

V

v.，vs	versus	对于
viz	videlicet (namely)	即是
voy.	voyage	航次
V.P.	Vice-President	副首长
V.V.	Vice Versa	反之亦然

W

w.a.	with average	水渍险(单独海损赔偿)
war	with all risk	担保一切险
W/B	way bill，warehouse book	货运单，仓库簿
wgt	weight	重量
whf	wharf	码头
W/M	weight or measurement	重量或尺寸量
w.p. a.	with particular average	单独海损赔偿
W.R.	War Risk，warehouse receipt	战争险，仓单
wt	weight	重量

| w.w. | warehouse warrant | 仓单 |
| w.w.d. | weather working day | 良好天气工作天 |

X

x	ex(out of without)exclusive	除外，无
x.d.	ex dividend	除息
XX	good quality	良好品质
XXX	very good quality	甚佳品质
XXXX	best quality	最佳品质

Y

Y.A.R.	York-Antwerp Rules	约克安特卫普规则
yd.	yard	码
yr.	your，year	你的，年
Yr.B.	year book	年鉴

 # Appendix 5

Key to Exercises

Unit 1

1.

(1)   On the recommendation of China Council for the Promotion of International Trade, we learn the name and address of your company.

(2)   We are very glad to introduce ourselves to you with a view to establishing trading relations with you.

(3)   We enclose a copy of our catalogue for your reference.

(4)   I would like to recommend you some new products which are suitable for EU market.

(5)   We have been specializing in the export of chemical products for more than 20 years.

(6)   If you have any further questions, please feel free to ask us.

2.

(1)   我公司拥有二十多年的制造经验，并已出口各类产品至欧美市场。

(2)   我会另写一封邮件给您，附上详细的报价单。

(3)   我们对贵公司最近在广交会上展出的皮革产品感兴趣。

(4)   我们不仅能提供最好的价格和品质，还能帮助客户解决问题。

(5)   欢迎访问我公司网站 www.AAA.com.cn，看是否有您感兴趣的产品。

(6)   我们期盼早日收到贵公司的意见或咨询。

3.

Dear Sirs,

Through the courtesy of China Light Industrial Products I/E corp., we got your name and address. We are glad to learn that you are seeking for Chinese bicycles.

Our Company was founded in 1990 and has grown to be one of the leading companies in China, specializing in producing and exporting bicycles. As the commodities we supply are of good quality and reasonable price, we have won a very good reputation from our clients.

We take the liberty of writing to you with a view to establishing business relations with you and are enclosing our illustrated catalog for your reference. If any of our products is of your interest, please let us know.

We look forward to your early reply.

Sincerely,

…

4.

敬启者：

我们从伦敦商会得知贵公司名称和联系方式。

我们希望购买高品质的全自动咖啡机。如贵公司能提供上述产品，请邮寄给我们你方报价单和有详细说明的产品目录。

期待您早日回复。

…… 谨上

Unit 2

1.

(1) We are interested in the product A1009 in the catalogue. Please quote us the price on CIF Shanghai basis.

(2) We shall be appreciated if you can quote us your best price on FOB Los Angeles basis.

(3) Please provide us the full details of the goods and the earliest delivery date.

(4) Thank you for your inquiry dated May 6 for our silk products.

(5) We have received your inquiry dated April 20 about our leather products and are glad that you like our products.

2.

(1) 请向我们提供随信所附询价单上所列货物的报价。

(2) 兹复你方 3 月 4 日询价，现寄送一份我方最新价目表供你方参考。

(3) 若你方报价有竞争力且交货期合适，我们会下大订单。

(4) 如能寄送样品，将不胜感激。

(5) 如能供应 50 吨花生，请告知每吨价格和付款方式。

3.

Dear Mr. …,

Thank you for your letter together with your catalogs.

Having thoroughly studied the catalogs, we find that Art. No. 15 is quite suitable for our market. We may need 50,000 pieces for August, 2014 delivery. Please kindly inform us if you are able to supply and quote us your most favorable price for the above goods on the basis of CIFC3 NEWYORK with details, including packing, shipment, insurance and payment.

We look forward to your early reply.

Yours faithfully,

4.

×××先生：

感谢您 6 月 3 日对我公司电子产品的询价函。

应贵方要求，现寄送我方价目表和一些样品。关于支付方式，我方惯例是以不可撤销的及其信用证方式支付。

如能在本月内下订单，我方会尽快安排装运。

期待您早日回复。

······ 谨上

Unit 3

1.

(1) As your request, we are pleased to make you an offer as follows, subject to your acceptance reaching here before May 30.

(2) The price above is the lowest we can offer.

(3) Unless otherwise stated or agreed upon, all prices are net without commission.

(4) In reply to your letter of June 10, we regret to state that your price has been found too high to be accepted.

(5) This is out of out target price.

(6) We can offer you a better price if you increase your order.

(7) Thank you for your reply of March 29, but we are sorry to know you felt our price too high.

(8) Considering the excellent quality of our products, it is impossible for us to make any further reduction.

2.

(1) 现报价如下，以我方确认为准。

(2) 如果数量达到 1 个 40 米集装箱，我们可以给您 5%的特别折扣。

(3) 您可以放心，我们的价格绝对有竞争力。

(4) 你的最终报价比同行高了 10%。

(5) 除非你方报价降低 2%，否则恐怕交易无法达成。

(6) 鉴于我们与其他客户均按此价成交，我们不能再降价。

(7)　我们做此让步是希望与贵公司达成第一笔交易，但必须强调这是我们所能做的最大努力。

(8)　如果能降价 10%，我们会考虑再追加一个 40 米集装箱订单。

4.

Dear Mr. Smith,

Thank you for your inquiry dated May 10. As request, we are making the offer as follows:

Commodity: Ladies Denim Skirt

Unit price: USD10.00 per piece FOB Shanghai

Shipment: Not later than August 30th, 2014

Payment: 50 % deposit by T/T in advance, the balance against copy of B/L

Since the market demand is rising and prices are bound to go up, we hope you can make your decision as soon as possible.

We await your reply.

Yours faithfully,

5.

×××先生：

感谢您 6 月 4 日的报价。

尽管我们对贵公司产品感兴趣，但仍然很遗憾地发现你们价格太高，我方几乎没有利润。如你所知，中国其他厂家生产的台灯质量优良，价格却比你们的低了约 10%。所以希望贵公司能降价 5%以适应竞争。

请仔细考虑以上建议，若能早日回复，不胜感激。

…… 谨上

Unit 4

1.

(1)　At present, we have only a limited stock. If you order before May 30, we could supply 1000 cases.

(2)　Owing to heavy commitments, if you order today, the earliest time of delivery is in November this year.

(3)　We are pleased to place the following orders with you if you can guarantee shipment from Shenzhen to Singapore before August 30.

(4)　In reply to your letter of March 9 quoting us the prices of peanuts, we are satisfied with the price and quality, so we are pleased to place an order as mentioned in the enclosed sheet.

(5)　We are pleased to inform you that we have accepted your order No. 123. We are sending you our Sales Confirmation No. 456 in duplicate, please countersign and return one copy for our file.

2.

(1)　已收到贵方产品目录和价格表。现按所示价格订购下列货物。

(2)　贵方 443 号订单已收到，谢谢。我们接受此订单并将于 6 月初交货。

(3)　你方能按我方第 656 号订单再次供货吗？

(4)　贵方 5 月 5 日订购 500 箱罐头牛肉的订单已收到，谢谢。对此订单我方乐意确认予以接受，如所附销售合同所示。

(5)　很抱歉，贵方所订购 101 型号产品目前已无存货，故推荐 102 型号产品，此产品与贵方指定的产品在质量上非常相近，而且价格更便宜。

(6)　由于工资和原料价格大幅上涨，很抱歉我方无法按半年前的报价接受订单。

3.

Dear Sirs,

Thanks for your quotation and samples sent on August 15. Both the price and quality are satisfactory, so we now place an order for 2,000 pieces as shown in the enclosed order sheet.

We are in urgent need of the goods, so please arrange shipment as soon as possible. If the order can't be shipped from stock, please let us know immediately.

As the amount of this order is not big, we recommend payment by T/T.

We look forward to your early confirmation.

Yours　faithfully,

…

4.

×××先生：

感谢贵方的 223 号订单。很高兴和贵方开始第一次合作。

我方将尽最大努力执行该订单，并保证会高度重视产品质量，装运时间以及你方要求的其他事项。

此外，今天下午迟些时候我方会传真 89990 号合同给贵方，请及时会签并回传。

感谢贵方注意上述事项，并期待收到相关信用证。

…… 谨上

Unit 5

1.

(1)   Thanks to our mutual efforts, we succeeded in putting the deal through finally.

(2)   We are enclosing our sales confirmation No. 990 in duplicate. Please return to us one of them by airmail, complete with your signature.

(3)   Could you advance the date of delivery since we are in urgent need of the goods?

(4)   We assure you that we shall try our best to execute the contract to your satisfaction.

(5)   As stipulated in the contract, the relevant L/C should reach us 20 days before the shipment month.

2.

(1)   我方已收到 990 号售货确认书，现我方已会签并回寄一份给你方。

(2)   感谢你方合作，相信所交货物会令你方完全满意。

(3)   如贵方商品质量上乘、工艺精湛、价格合理，我们今后会大量向贵方订购。

(4)   为避免以后修改麻烦，相关信用证条款必须严格与合同一致。

(5)   你方上次订购的货物我们尚有一些库存，你方若愿意重复上次订单我们能满足你方的要求。

3.

Dear Mr. …,

We have received the Sales Confirmation No.567. Enclosed please find the duplicate with our countersignature. This is our first cooperation. I believe with our joint efforts of both sides, the transaction will go smoothly.

The relative L/C has been established with Bank of China in your favor. It will reach you soon.

If the consignment is of good quality, and popular on our market, we will continue to order.

Yours faithfully,

…

4.

本合同由买卖双方共同订立，根据下述条款，买方同意购买，卖方同意出售下述商品：

品名及规格	数 量	单 价	金 额
儿童被 (100% 棉)	600 件	CIFC5 迪拜 20 美元/条	72000.00 美元
Total	600 件		72000.00 美元

总金额: 柒万贰仟元整

装运日期:

根据合同条款, 收到信用证后 60 天内装运。

装货港和目的港:

从中国大连, 运至阿联酋迪拜。

禁止分批装运和转运。

保险:

由卖方按照发票金额的 110%, 向中国人民保险公司依照其 1981 年 1 月 1 日颁布的《海洋运输货物保险条款》, 投保一切险和战争险。

检验:

以上海 SGS 机构出具的品质证明作为交货依据。

Unit 6

1.

(1) The Buyer shall pay 100% of the sales amount in advance by T/T to reach the Sellers not later than Oct. 10, 1998.

(2) The Buyer shall open through a bank acceptable to the Seller an Irrevocable Letter of Credit at 30 days after sight to reach the seller by the end of Aug. 1998, valid for negotiation in China until the 15th day after the date of shipment.

(3) We have received your confirmed and irrevocable L/C No. 3299 in our favor issued by Bank of China.

(4) The amount of this L/C shall be restored automatically twice after negotiation.

(5) In order to ensure the requested prompt shipment, please open the covering L/C which should reach us 20 days before the date of shipment。

(6) We can only accept L/C at 60 days after sight as payment term.

2.

(1) 你方由中国银行开来的第 7766 号保兑的, 不可撤销信用证已收到。

(2) 为了避免以后修改信用证, 请务必注意下列事项。

(3) 买方凭卖方开具的跟单汇票于见票时立即付款，付款后方可获取运输单据。

(4) 买方对于卖方开具的见票后 30 天付款的跟单汇票，于提示时应立即承兑，并应于汇票到期日即予付款，付款后方可获取运输单据。

(5) 我们可以接受即期付款交单，但是以后不得引以为例。

(6) 如果您坚持信用证方式，恐怕我们只能额外收取 3%的操作费用。

3.

Dear Mr. …,

Our past purchase of agricultural products from you has been paid by L/C, which has cost us a great deal. Form the moment we open an L/C till the time our buyers pay us, the tie-up of our funds lasts for at least 3 months.

If you could kindly make easier payment terms, we are sure that such an accommodation would be conductive to our further cooperation. We propose payment by Cash against Documents on arrival of goods.

Your careful consideration of the above request and an early favorable reply will be highly appreciated.

Sincerely,

…

4.

×××先生：

关于我方在 3 月 15 日的传真中要求贵方开立所述订单的相关信用证，很遗憾直到目前我方仍未收到相关信用证。

由于货物已经备妥待运，所以贵方应立即采取措施。请尽快开立有关信用证。

期盼早日收到贵方回复。

…… 谨上

Unit 7

1.

(1) We wish to call you attention to the fact that up to the present moment no news has come from you about the shipment under the contract No. 228.

(2) The goods ordered have been forwarded to you in three lots.

(3) We shall be very sorry if this delay has put you to any inconvenience and hope this matter will not effect our good relations.

(4) We will fax you shipping advice as soon as the goods are shipped.

(5) As there is no direct steamer from here to your port, we suggest that you accept transshipment at Hong Kong.

(6) The shipping mark will apply to all shipments unless otherwise instructed.

2.

(1) 收到你方信用证修改书后，我方会将剩下的 3000 件在第一时间装运。

(2) 如你方能尽快安排装运，我们将不胜感激，这样的话我们的客户就可以赶上销售旺季开始时出售。

(3) 很高兴地通知您，货物已经装上"东风"号货轮，并将于明天运出，希望能货物能完好地到达。

(4) 根据合同要求，货物装运后，我方会立即向你方寄出全套不可转让副本单据。

(5) 由于下个月月底前的舱位都已经被预订一空，我们建议贵方允许一半货物的运输在香港中转。

3.

Dear Mr. Green,

We are pleased to inform you that the following goods have been shipped:

Order No.:	CW-8899
Commodity:	socks
Quantity:	2,000 dozens
Packing:	20 dozens in a carton, 100 cartons in total.
B/L No.:	CN300900
Name of Vessel:	S.S. DONGFENG
Voyage No.:	9889W
ETD:	May 30, 2014
ETA:	June 15, 2014
Port of Shipment:	Shanghai
Ports of Destination:	Los Angeles

We hope that the above-mentioned goods will reach you on time and in good condition. Meanwhile, we look forward to the pleasure of enjoying the further cooperation with you in the near future.

Yours sincerely,

…

4.

×××先生：

关于 356 号订单项下的 10 吨蔬菜，虽然装运期已经临近，而且我方早已与 4 月开立相关信用证，但至今仍未收到你方关于装运日期的具体信息。

由于该批货物是季节性商品，我们的客户急需整批货物以备销售旺季之需，所以你方的延迟将给我们带来很大麻烦。我方必须要求你方尽最大努力在规定时间装运，否则我方有权取消合同并就我们的损失提出索赔。

请 3 天之内给我们确切答复。

…… 谨上

Unit 8

1.

(1)　Please insure the goods against all risks and war risk.

(2)　If you want to cover War Risk, additional premium will be for your account.

(3)　We have insured/covered the goods against W.P.A. and War Risk at the rate of 0.8% for the sum of US $50,000

(4)　We will arrange/effect insurance on your behalf.

(5)　Generally we cover WPA and War Risks in absence of definite instructions on insurance from our clients.　If you desire to cover All Risks, please let us know in advance.

(6)　If any damage to the goods occurs, a claim may be filed with the insurance agent at your end, who will undertake to compensate for the loss sustained.

(7)　We enclose an inspection certificate by the Shanghai Commodity Inspection Bureau and the shipping agent's statement, as well as the original Insurance Policy.

(8)　W.P.A. coverage is too narrow for this shipment, please extend the coverage to include T.P.N.D.

2.

(1)　根据你方要求，我们已按发票金额的 110%向中国人民保险公司投保一切险。

(2)　由卖方按照发票金额的 110%，向中国人民保险公司依照其 1981 年 1 月 1 日颁布的《海洋运输货物保险条款》，投保一切险和战争险。

(3)　我们注意到你方要求投保战争险，但是我方 CIF 报价中只包括水渍险。

(4)　我们知道按你方惯例，你们只为货物按发票金额加成 10%投保，因此额外费用由我方承担。

(5)　请告知贵方保险商承保渗漏险的保险费率。

(6) 在未收到贵方明确保险要求的情况下，我们按惯例对你方所订购货物按发票金额110%投保了一切险。

(7) 保险索赔应在该批货物到达目的港后30天以内提交保险公司或其代理。

(8) 保险公司拒付此项索赔，不是因为没有投保破碎险，而是因为该险别是按10%免赔率承保的。

3.

Dear Mr. …,

We wish to refer you to our Order No. 998 for 500 TV sets, from which you will see that this order is on CFR basis.

As we discussed in our telephone conversation, we now desire to have the consignment insured at your end. So it shall be appreciated if you could kindly arrange to insure the goods on our behalf against All Risks for 110% of invoice value, i.e. US$2,200,000.

We shall of course refund the premium to you upon receipt of the debit note for it or, if you like, you may draw on us at sight for the amount required.

We sincerely hope that our above request will meet with your approval.

Yours faithfully,

…

4.

×××先生：

兹回复您5月4日请我方代办998订单项下货物保险的信函。很高兴地告知您，我方已经向中国人民保险公司投保一切险，保险金额为2200000美元，保险费率为0.3%。

保险单正在准备中，保险费的索款通知将在一个星期内送达你方。

······ 谨上

Unit 9

1.

(1) We can meet you special requirements for packing but extra expenses should be borne by you.

(2) The dimensions of the carton are 40cm long, 20cm wide and 30cm high with a volume of about 0.024 cubic meter. The gross weight is 25kg while the net weight is 24kg.

(3) Each piece packed in a polybag, 12 pieces packed into an export carton with assorted sizes and colors. Exported carton must be strong.

(4)   Main marks should be printed in black ink on the front side of the carton, including AAA, P/C No., port of destination, and carton No.

(5)   A detailed survey report will be dispatched to you subsequent to the further study of individual cases.

(6)   These cartons and goods inside have all been inspected. Inspectors from insurance company confirmed that the damage to the goods is because of improper packing.

(7)   Although the inspection has been made before shipment, the buyer shall have the right to reinspect after the arrival of the goods.

2.

(1)   20 条毯子装一个出口标准纸箱，每个纸箱内同色同码。

(2)   回收标志必须用黑色油墨印刷在所有塑料袋及纸箱外部。

(3)   纸板箱内有塑料布衬里，有很好的防潮效果。

(4)   如有必要，我们会请贵方另外寄送一套样品到香港的实验室作前期检验。请等候我们的通知。

(5)   货物应通过中国商品检验局进行检验，该局所签发的品质检验证书应作为最后依据。

(6)   现随函寄去上海商品检验局出具的检验报告一份。请尽快解决此案。

3.

Dear Mr. Brown,

We thank you for your letter dated May18, enclosing the sales contract No. 998 in duplicate. But we note that the packing clause in the contract is not clear enough.

In order to avoid possible future trouble, we would like to make clear beforehand our packing requirements as follows:

The furniture under the captioned contract should be packed in wooden case. One set in a case, and each case is lined with foam plastic in order to protect the goods against press.

On the outer packing please mark our initials: AF, under which the port of destination and our order number should be stenciled. In addition, directive marks like KEEP DRY, and AWAY FROM PRESSURE should also be indicated.

We have made a footnote on the contract to that effect and are returning herein one copy of the contract, duly countersigned by us. We hope you will pay special attention to the packing.

Yours faithfully,

…

4.

×××先生：

您 4 月 20 日询问商品检验的信函我方已收到。

按照惯例，所有的出口商品都需经过该国的商检机构检验，并于检验后出示检验报告。

为利于买卖双方，买方有权在合同规定的时限内对商品进行复检。即买方有权向验货代理申请在目的港进行检验。

复检证明书可作为最后依据，如复检时发现与合同不符，该证明书可作为索赔的依据。

希望以上信息能对您有所帮助。

…… 谨上

Unit 10

1.

(1)　I'm writing to complain the inaccurate logo printing on the boxes.

(2)　Please be assured that we will look into the matter immediately. We will notify you as soon as there are possible results.

(3)　We shall not be liable for any discrepancy of the goods shipped due to causes for which the Insurance Company, Shipping Company or other transportation organizations are liable.

(4)　We can compromise but the compensation should not exceed US$ 500, otherwise we have to submit the case to arbitration.

(5)　Considering our good business relationship for a long time, we agree to remit you US$500 as compensation for your loss.

(6)　We have to withdraw our order No.109 owing to your repeated delays in delivery.

(7)　In all cases, claims must be accompanied by Survey Reports of Recognized Public Surveyors agreed to by the Sellers.

2.

(1)　品质异议须于货到目的口岸之日起 30 天内提出，数量异议须于货到目的口岸之日起 15 天内提出。

(2)　如属我公司责任，我们会在收到你方索赔 20 天内答复并提出处理意见。

(3)　若因自然灾害，战争或其他不可抗力原因造成部分或全部货物不能交付或延迟交付，我方不承担责任。

(4)　虽然该批货物质量不如样品质量，若你方降价 15%，我方仍可接受。

(5)　因为纸箱的状况良好，而且看起来在运输过程中没有被打开，所以我们推测你们一定是漏装了。

(6) 由于你方质量问题，我们遭受了重大损失，索赔额至少要 2000 美元。

(7) 由于你方费用清单不够清楚，所以我方不会付这笔钱。

3.

(1)

Dear Mr. Smith,

We have received the 300 cartons of bed sheets under Order No.286. However, we regret to inform you that we found that the quality was not satisfactory. The Survey Report issued by Shanghai Commodity Inspection Bureau proved that the goods delivered are not up to the standard of samples. The quality is too inferior to be suitable for the requirements of this market.

As the whole lot is useless to us, we have to return the goods to you and lodge a claim against you for US$ 5000.

We await your early settlement.

Yours faithfully,

…

(2)

All disputes arising out of the performance of contract, or relating to this contract, shall be settled through negotiation. In case no settlement can be reached through negotiation, the case shall then be submitted to the China International Economic and Trade Arbitration Commission for arbitration in accordance with its arbitral rules. The arbitration shall take place in Shanghai. The arbitral award is final and binding upon both parties.

4.

(1)

×××先生：

你方延迟交货的索赔函已收到。不过我们必须解释，延迟交货主要有以下原因：

首先，签完合同后 30 天我们才收到你方信用证，这段时间我们什么也不能做，只能等着你方开证。

其次，应你方要求改进质量约 1 周后才得到你方确认，在你放确认之前我们都不能安排大货生产。

某些方面我们应负部分责任。我们应该在装运之前再多提前几天通知您。

相信我们会继续加强交流，避免业务上潜在的问题。

…… 谨上

(2)

延迟交货及惩罚：

如果延迟交货，买方有权取消合同、拒收货物，并对卖方提出索赔。除不可抗力原因外，如果发生延迟交货，卖方须支付罚金。罚金率为每延迟 7 天收取 0.5%，不足 7 天视为 7 天，罚金将由付款行或买方从货款中扣除。

Unit 11

1.

(1)　CONTRACT 889 DESKLAMPS READY PLSOPENLC ASAP

(2)　TKS YR INQUIRY 20/JUN BLANKETS AVAILABLE

(3)　YC4/MAY REGRET D/A UNACCEPTABLE SUGGEST D/P SIGHT PLSCABLE ACCEPTANCE

(4)　YR OFFER 8/MAR TVSET PRICE ACCEPTABLE PROVIDED SHIPMENT ENDOFAPR PLSREPLY BYCABLE

(5)　S/C998 DELIVERY OVERDUE PLSRUSH SHIPMENT BEFORE1/AUG OTHERWISE CANCEL ORDER RESERVING CLAIM RIGHTS

(6)　FIRMOFFER 5000PCS SKIRT USD40 PERPC CIFNY VALID BEFORE31/JAN

2.

(1)　无直达船只请修改 656 号信用证为允许转运。

(2)　钢材价格看涨建议立即接受。

(3)　第 109 号合同项下永久自行车已装 "东风" 号 4 月 15 日发运预计四月底抵达。

(4)　请发实盘告知 1000 吨绿豆 CIF 纽约价格支付方式及最早装运日期。

(5)　你方 4 月 15 日电传 5000 台计算机报价接受信用证开立中。

(6)　兹复你方 7 月 5 日电传因同样产品售价低约 10 美元请降价 20%如同意将订购 5000 吨。

3.

YRL/C577 RCVD TKS REGRET AMOUNT USD60, 000 BUT CONTRACTED US$65,000 PLSAMEND ASAP ENABLING CATCH SSDONGFENG SAILING JUN. 8TH.

4.

RE ARTNO.909 S/C356 5000PCS BEDSHEETS SHPT ARRIVED BUT NOT ACDG TO SPECIFIED SAMPLE IN SIZE COLOR AS STATED IN S/C CANNOT BE ACPTD BY CUSTOMERS W REQ A COMPENSATION USD20, 000 PLS TLX REPLY.

Bibliography

[1] 博斌，袁晓娜. 国际贸易实务与案例[M]. 北京：清华大学出版社，2007.

[2] 易露霞，方玲玲，陈原. 国际贸易实务双语教程[M]. 北京：清华大学出版社，2010.

[3] 邓迪，陈晶莹. 国际贸易术语解释与国际货物买卖合同[M]. 北京：经济管理出版社，2012.

[4] 廖英，张春敏. 实用外贸英语函电教程[M]. 北京：对外经济贸易大学出版社，2011.

[5] 仲鑫，外贸函电[M]. 北京：机械工业大学出版社，2006.

[6] 檀文茹，徐静珍. 外贸函电[M]. 北京：中国人民大学出版社，2004.

[7] 腾美荣，徐楠. 外贸英语函电[M]. 北京：首都经济贸易大学出版社，2006.

[8] Grahame T Bilbow. 朗文商务致胜英文书信[M]. 北京：外语教学与研究出版社，2001.

[9] 戚云方. 新编外经贸英语写作与套语[M]. 杭州：浙江大学出版社，2003.

[10] 戚云方. 新编外经贸英语函电与谈判[M]. 杭州：浙江大学出版社，2007.

[11] 祝卫，程洁. 国际贸易操作能力使用教程[M]. 上海：上海人民出版社，2006.

[12] 梁晓玲. 国际商务英语函电[M]. 北京：对外经济贸易大学出版社，2010.

[13] 祝卫，程洁，谭英. 国际贸易操作能力使用教程[M]. 上海：上海人民出版社，2006.

[14] 毅冰. 十天搞定外贸函电[M]. 北京：中国海关出版社，2012.

[15] 许群航等. 经贸英语口语[M]. 北京：对外经济贸易大学出版社，2011.

[16] 田翠欣，张付先. 外贸英语口语[M]. 天津：天津科技翻译出版社，天津外语音像出版社，2008.